The Patent Duffer

101 Incredible Inventions From The Wacky World Of Golf

Jordan Kaiser

Automatic Press Publishing
Dallas, Texas

Copyright © 1991 by **Automatic Press Publishing**. All rights reserved. No part of this book may be reproduced or transmitted in any form or by any means, electronic or mechanical, including photocopying, recording or by any informational storage or retrieval system – except by a reviewer who may quote brief passages in a review to be printed in a magazine or newspaper – without permission in writing from the publisher. For information contact:

Automatic Press Publishing
P.O. Box 140966
Dallas, Texas 75214
1-800-369-6135

Manufactured in the United States of America

10 9 8 7 6 5 4 3 2 1

Library of Congress Catalog Card Number 91-77455

Publisher's Cataloging In Publication

Kaiser, Jordan.
 The patent duffer : 101 incredible inventions from the wacky world of golf / Jordan Kaiser
  p. cm.
  ISBN 0-9629318-8-8

  1. Golf. 2. Inventions. 3. Golf equipment industry - Patents.
I. Title.

GV963.K3 1992   796.352
                       QB191-1663

Hear Ye, Hear Ye,

It is a well known fact that Goffers are a tribe apart.

Through playing Goff unceasingly their very natures change, and they become tacurne, sullen, peevish and irritable!

They speake, eat, drink, sleepe and jabber Goff, forgetting their chattels and infants and spend monies only on balls, clubbs, or a majic drink called wiski.

The clubb makers and wiski-sellers make enormous fortunes, while the Goffers families are in greate famine.

These Goffers have been knowne to rise with the lark to play Goff, and continue throughout the daylite hours only stopping for short tymes and wiski.

Such are the very odd ways of Goffers.

Banned by decree of James IV in 1491:
It is again the common good of the realme and defence thereof;

Contents

Notes on the Text and Drawings — viii
Acknowledgments — ix
Introduction — x

One. *Now Why Didn't I Think Of That?* — 2

Golf Clubs With Interchangeble Reminder Buttons *4*, Golf Clubs *6*, Golf Club *8*, Golf Club Carrier *10*, Simulated Golf Club Beverage And Cup Container *12*, Breakable Golf Club *14*, Scoring Device For Golf-Players *16*, Means For Indicating Proper Stroke In Golf *18*, Combined Golf Club And Ball Retriever *20*, Golfing Aid *22*, Golf Club *24*, Golf Practice Device *26*, Golfing Accessory For Positioning Golf Tee *28*, Golf Club Attachment *30*, Combination Container, Practice Golf Ball And Tee *32*, Golfer's Aid *34*, Golf Club Carrier *36*, Golf Club Head Attachable Rake *38*, Golf Tee Marker *40*

Two. *Well, That's Really Using Your Head* — 42

Indicating Device *44*, Golf Cap With Means For Indicating Raising Of Head *46*, Head Down Persuader *48*, Golfer's Head Movement Indicator *50*, Appliance For Teaching Or Practicing The Game Of Golf *52*, Golf Stance Steadying Device *54*, Golfer's Head Restrainer *56*, Golfer's Aid *58*, Golfing Aid *60*

Three. *Golfers In Bondage – Not A Pretty Sight* — 62

Golf Instructing Apparatus *64*, Golf Form Apparatus *66*, Golf Instructor *68*, Golf Teaching And Playing Device *70*, Golf Practicing Apparatus *72*, Training Device *74*

Four. *Save Your Strength – Don't Bend Over* — 76

Ball Projecting Golf Cup *78*, Device For Setting Golf Balls And Tees *80*, Golf Flagpole Retriever *82*, Golf Club *84*, Golf Ball Retriever *86*, Golf Tee Holder and Carrier *88*

Five. *Grips & Gloves* — 90

Interlocking Glove and Handle *92*, Golf Grip Guide *94*, Grip Attachments For Golf Clubs *96*, Grip Guide For Golf Clubs *98*, Wristband Grip For Golf Clubs *100*, Nonslip Golf Glove *102*, Adjustable Golf Glove *104*, Dry Grip Sleeve *106*

Six.	*Feets Don't Fail Me Now*	108

Golfer's Foot Holding Device *110*, Golf Training Device *112*, Magnetically Liftable Foot Positioning Block For Golfers *114*, Game And Apparatus For Playing The Same *116*, Golf Practicing Apparatus *118*, Shoes For Golfers *120*

Seven.	*The Law of the Straight Left Arm*	122

Golfer's Arm Bend Indicator *124*, Golfer's Arm Positioning Device Comprising Elbow Bend Restraining Means *126*, Golfer's Arm Bend Restraining Device *128*, Arm Stiffening Device *130*

Eight.	*The Drive For Distance*	132

Golf Club *134*, Golf Club *136*, Golf-Club And Other Sporting Implement *138*, Golf Club *140*, Golf Club *142*, Golf Club *144*

Nine.	*Golf Balls*	146

Method OF Toughening Golf Ball Covers *148*, Practice Golf Tee Including Mirror Means *150*, Golf Ball *152*, Electroluminescent Game Ball *154*, Parachute Golf Ball *156*, Golf Ball *158*, Practice Ball *160*, Golf Practice Device *162*, Walking Golf Ball *164*, Golf Practice Projectile *166*, Practice Golf Ball *168*

Ten.	*The Art Of Putting*	170

Golf Club *172*, Golf Club With Slope Indicating Means Thereon *174*, Golf Putter With Aligning Device *176*, Golf Putter *178*, Golf Putter *180*, Golf Putter With Wheel-Supported Head *182*, Billiard Cue Shaped Golf Putter *184*, Golf Putter *186*, Golf Putter Hand Grip *188*, Golf Putter Grip *190*, Putting Stroke Analyzer *192*, Golf Putting Practice Device *194*, Golf Club Head *196*, Optical Device For Reading Golf Greens *198*, Mechanical Putter *200*

Eleven.	*Tees*	202

Golfing Tee *204*, Golf Tee *206*, Golf Tee *208*, Rubber Shield Tee *210*, Golf Tee *212*, Golf Tee *214*, Disappearing Golf Tee *216*, Golf Tee *218*, Golf Tee *220*, Writing Implement *222*, Golf Tee Match Book *224*

Appendix	229

Notes on the Text and Drawings

For an inventor to receive a patent from the patent office, a drawing illustrating the invention, along with descriptive text explaining what is new and useful about the invention, must be submitted. Some illustrations are professionally done, and some are obviously done by the inventors themselves. The illustrations contained in this book are the best available copies from original patents contained in the Patent Library. In most cases, one can discern from the illustrations how the inventions work. When an invention is obvious from the illustration, only the inventor's rationale as to what is new and useful have been excerpted. When an invention is complicated or intricate, portions from the inventor's description accompany the illustration.

Acknowledgements

The author would like to thank Jim Schutze and Patty Smith for their invaluable assistance in editing the introductions. Valerie Velten has also been a patient wife during the writing and more importantly, the research of this book which was done at golf courses all over the country. In my initial research at the Patent Repository section of the Dallas Public Library, numerous librarians lugged countless volumes of Patent Gazettes for my inspection. The muscles they acquired doing this bears witness to my appreciation for their patient efforts. Special thanks is also extended to all the kind people at the Patent Library in Washington, D.C. for their assistance in the research of these patents. Finally, a word of thanks to my golfing buddies; Steve, Jack, Derek, and Tom for putting up with my incessant chatter about the book – usually while they were trying to sink a crucial putt.

Introduction

What is it about the ancient game of golf that inspires such mindless dedication – and agony? What possible fascination is there about a game so difficult to master that men spend untold fortunes in acquiring equipment and instruction, pay outrageous green fees, and bet upon their limited ability with the verve of a blind burglar. Why do otherwise God-fearing men imperil their mortal souls with blasphemous language, and abandon their families on the most beautiful weekends of the year? Lives there a golfer who has never stared down at that motionless, mocking sphere and wondered what could be so difficult about efficiently dispatching it toward the flag-stick? After all, the ball is just sitting there. Surely, hitting a moving target such as a baseball should take greater hand/eye coordination. Yet who among us can't hit a baseball with a far greater measure of success?

Even after the most miserable shank, what golfer has not bravely stepped up to the ball somehow hoping to fade a career 2 iron around a tree. What human emotion is the basis for this behavior; Hope? Redemption? Ignorance? Stupidity?

And so it goes, stroke after stroke, knees slightly bent, shoulders parallel to target line, feet about shoulder width apart, keep the head down, slow take-away, weight shift to the right, head is still down, straight left arm, hips rotate, let the wrists cock naturally, slight pause at the top, head is still down, hips start to unwind first, knees drive toward target, upper body follows, head is still down, hips clear for the hands to come through, head is still down, wrists release, left arm is still straight, head is still down, and on and on and on. Surely, in the two and a half seconds it takes to swing the club, this should not be too much to attain.

Naturally, practice and more practice in backyards and driving ranges and putting greens is a prime requisite for any measurable improvement. In the never-ending pursuit of this goal, all the creative forces of the human mind have been employed – all aiming at the perfection of the golf swing.

Toward this end, a wide variety of devices, appliances, and other bizarre paraphernalia have been invented to help the flailing duffer. Harnesses, straps, gloves, oddly-shaped clubs, exercise devices, a miscellany of sure-fire inventions to cure some real or imagined fault.

Even though the patent office wasn't established until the game of golf had been played for hundreds of years, it should not be assumed that inventive golfers were not hard at work in ages past. Anthropological digs in Scotland have unearthed flat pieces of ivory with scored markings that were first thought to be some type of amulet. Further examination and wear pattern analysis have proven conclusively that these were some of the earliest driver inserts. Other ivory relics, first identified as combs, were recently identified as groove cleaners.

From this and other evidence, anthropologists have identified a subspecies of Homo Sapiens which they have named Homo Golfus, or golfing man. This book will examine the work of a subspecies of Homo Golfus, namely, Homo Golfus Inventus – the inventive golfer.

The game of golf did not escape the industrial revolution. A new mindset was born in which any activity that could be mechanized was mechanized. Men with dreams of automating every human endeavor, tinkered and toiled in dingy basements and drafty garages, with bits of pipe, leather belts, lengths of rubber tubing, old clubs, and other cast-off scrap. Cursed with a bad case of lifting the head, or flying elbows, or an uncontrollable slice, a few stalwarts of the game have invented unique devices to cure their particular fault. Some of these contraptions look like medieval torture devices, and were probably as comfortable.

Other inventors sought to gain prodigious advantage through revolutionary putters, drivers, balls, tees, etc. Unfortunately for their creators, the most successful of these devices stray so far from the spirit of the game, they are not legal under USGA rules.

In the great tradition of gadgeteers, other inventors have come up with an array of devices to take the drudgery out of the game. Ball picker-uppers, cleaning tools, tee holders, and multi-purpose club combinations of all kind have been thoroughly invented, and reinvented.

Naturally, if these devices work so well for the individual inventor, why not patent the device for the relief of their fellow golfers and hopefully make a few extra bucks to help with the bill at the 19th hole? So patent they did, thousands of patents relating to the game of golf – or some form of it.

Herewith, we are pleased to exhibit some of the more ingenious devices the golfing world has ever seen, created by men who are truly a tribe apart.

THE PATENT DUFFER

OR

*101 INCREDIBLE INVENTIONS FROM
THE WACKY WORLD OF GOLF*

ONE
Now Why Didn't I Think Of That?

We start out with a selection of inspired devices chosen because they immediately elicit the same response, *"Now why didn't I think of that?"* The answer to this question is probably, *"Because you didn't see the problem."* If you don't know you have a problem, you naturally don't have a need to come up with a solution. The following inventions are the solutions to problems that perplexed these individual golfers. At some point, when you see the answer to someone else's problem, all of a sudden you realize you have that problem also. On a global scale, this behavior is known as progress.

Take frustration, or temper, for instance. Are there any golfers among us who have not, at one time or another, been tempted to wrap a club around a tree, or some other immobile object? Imagine the relief one could obtain by immediately snapping a traitorous putter across the knee when a putt fails to drop. This behavior is not all that unusual, even if it does prove to be expensive.

George McLoughlin of Scranton, Pennsylvania either must have been spending a lot of money on clubs or living with an awful lot of frustration. The way George spells relief is with his **Breakable Golf Club** (page 12). The difference between this invention and the putter you usually carry is the fact that it has a replaceable dowel for a shaft so it can be broken, and quickly repaired, time and time again. See, you're probably saying to yourself right now, *"Why didn't I think of that?"*

Tired of putting a smile on those expensive balata balls when your driver is a little off? Maybe if there were some rubber bumpers on the top and bottom edge of the club, this wouldn't be such a problem. That's exactly what Jackson Walton of Toronto, Canada has done with his special **Golf Clubs**, (page 6).

> Inventing is a combination of brains and materials.
> The more brains you use, the less material you need.
>
> *Charles F. Kettering*

Golfers must be a thirsty lot. Maybe it's the strenuous physical exertion of getting in and out of golf carts in warm climates. Whatever the reason, golfers seem to have some favorite beverages that might be out of place in their original containers. John Fernicola of Centerville, Maryland has certainly thought about this problem. His **Combination Container, Practice Golf Ball And Tee** (page 32) looks like a ball, you can hit it once it's empty, and who would look twice at a golfer drinking out of a ball?

Remember the last time you sliced a drive so far into the woods you needed a compass to find your way out? Naturally, your partners were out of sight, so you figured you would just throw the ball out. When you met up again, as they stare incredulously at the ball in the middle of the fairway, did you tell them you used your hand-mashie, or did you lie about it? Well, thanks to Albert Hutchison of Cleveland, Ohio, and his **Combined Golf Club And Ball Retriever** (page 40), you can tell them it was your hand-mashie, point to the club and not say another word. Only you and the squirrels will really know. It's also useful for retrieving balls from watery locales when the hand-mashie that's attached to your shoulder is too short.

Suppose the pool your wife made you put in the backyard has taken up all the space you formerly used for chipping practice. If you were as clever as Max Simon of Canoga Park, California, you would have invented an inflatable green which can be anchored in the pool. His **Golf Practice Device** (page 36) predates Pete Dye's island greens by quite a few years, but without the railroad ties. Besides, when else will you ever wear those thongs with the spikes on the bottom?

Now aren't you just saying to yourself, *"Why didn't I think of that?"* Well, read on to find out what else you could have come up with.

Golf Club With Interchangeable Reminder Buttons

Patent No. 3,410,562 (1968)

Alvin Lefleur of Miramar, Florida

A plurality of interchangeable reminder buttons are provided for attachment one at a time to the shaft of a golf club. Each button carries different indicia on its face which will act as a reminder to the golfer of a particular deficiency of his golf swing.

To play golf well, an accurate and repetitive swing is required. Over the years certain basic fundamentals have been developed as a means for achieving an accurate and repetitive swing. These fundamentals include, but are not limited to, such things as keeping the head down, knees bent, left arm straight, a correct grip, and a slow backswing. Deviations from these fundamentals usually result in a poor score.

Although most golfers are aware of the necessity for perfecting the golf swing in accordance with the fundamentals outlined above, there is difficulty in remembering to perform all of them simultaneously. Thus, a golfer may remember to do all but one of the fundamentals, such as slowing down the back swing, with a resultant inaccuracy in his shots and therefore poorer score. The present invention provides a means whereby the golfer may constantly remind himself of those things which he tends to forget.

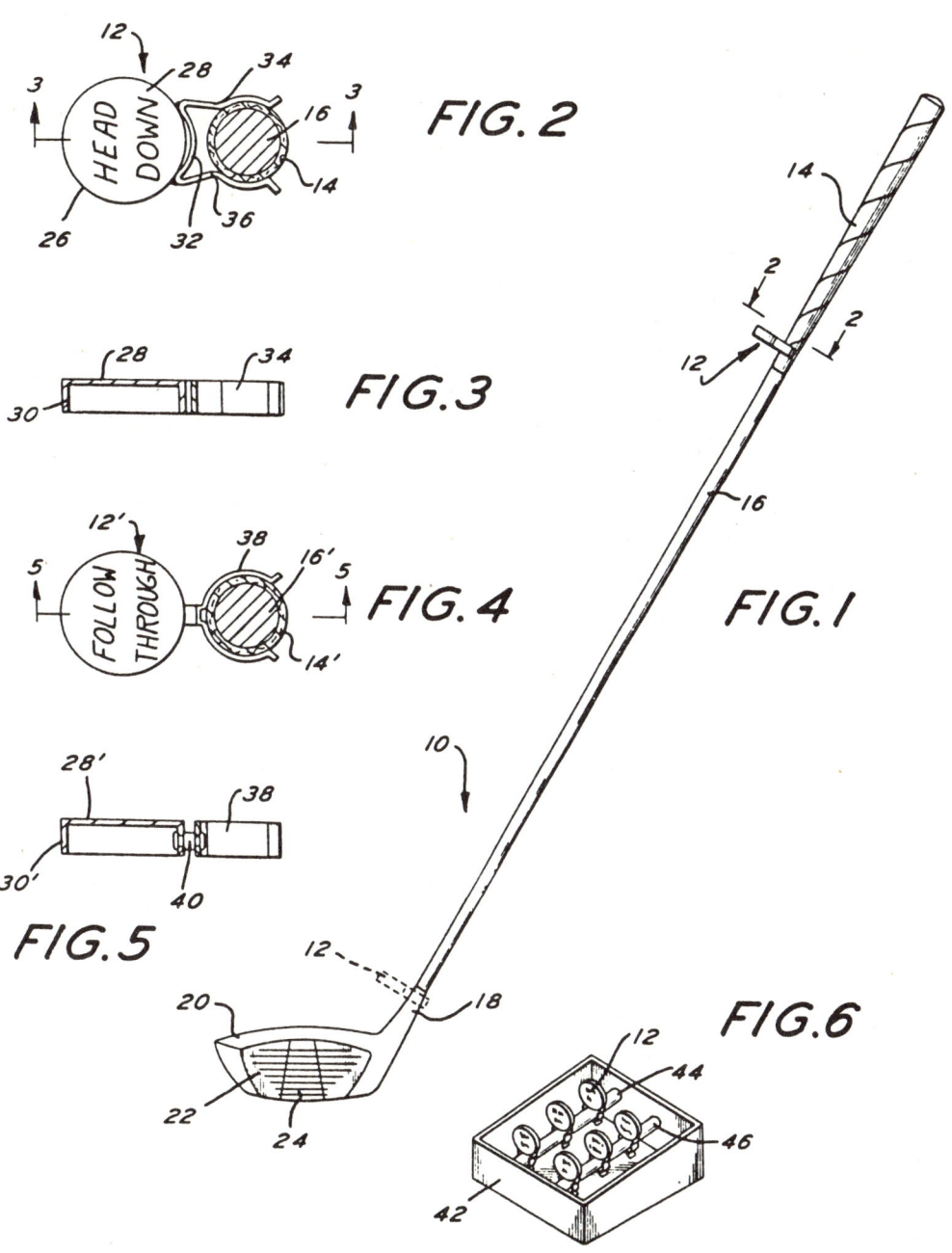

The Patent Duffer 5

Golf Clubs

Patent No. 2,968,486 (1961)

Jackson Walton of Toronto, Ontario

In driving a golf ball from a tee or from the fairway with a wood, the cover of the ball may be cut by the top or the bottom edge of the club head as a result of hitting the ball too low or too high. Damaged or deformed golf balls are usually unplayable and constitute a source of added expense in participating in the game in addition, of course, to adding strokes to the player's game.

The present invention is particularly directed to providing improvements in the club head which are designed to overcome the damaging effects of the ball when it is struck improperly. These improvements are in the form of slightly resilient, slightly rounded strips or inserts **7** which are secured along the top and bottom edges of the exposed face of the club head.

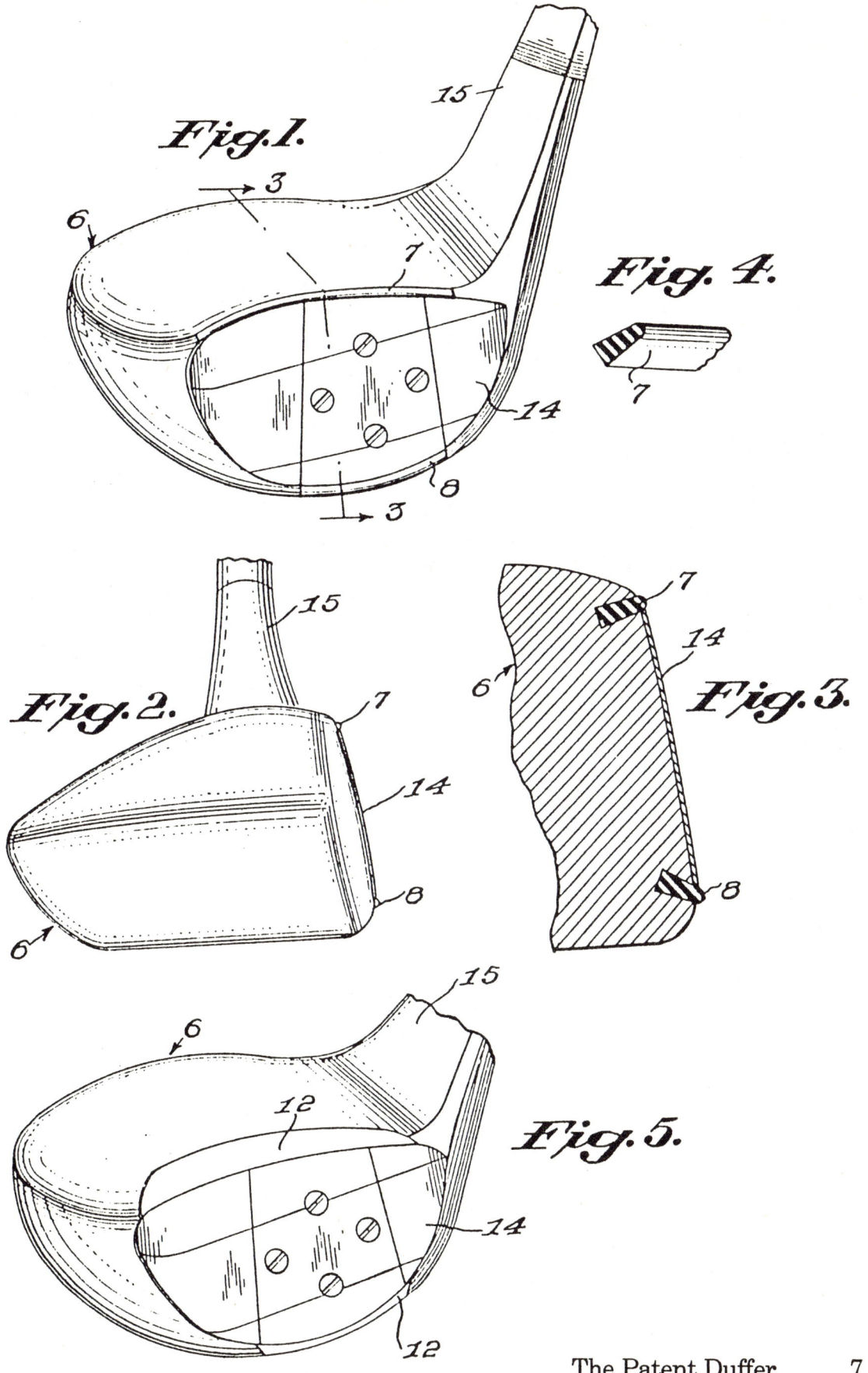

The Patent Duffer

Golf Club

Patent No. 1,618,638 (1927)

Howard Coles of Tarrytown, New York

In the preferred form of the improved club the shaft or handle has adjustably mounted upon it a suitable casing in which is mounted a two-part or double acting spring device acting through a movable part of the casing on which is mounted a club. The movable part of the casing is adapted to be drawn back by hand to place under tension the spring device, which when released imparts a striking movement to the club. Part of the spring device is arranged to act as a buffer to limit the follow-through of the club. The spring device is preferably arranged in the form of two springs which oppositely engage the club carrying casing member, and means are provided for independently adjusting the tension of the springs to regulate the striking force of the club and of the cushioning effect of the buffer. It is intended to provide the club with interchangeable heads to simulate the different kinds of clubs usually employed in playing the game of golf. This interchangeability may be effected by having a series of clubs which are detachably mounted upon the movable casing member or a single club shaft upon this movable casing member may be arranged to receive interchangeable club heads.

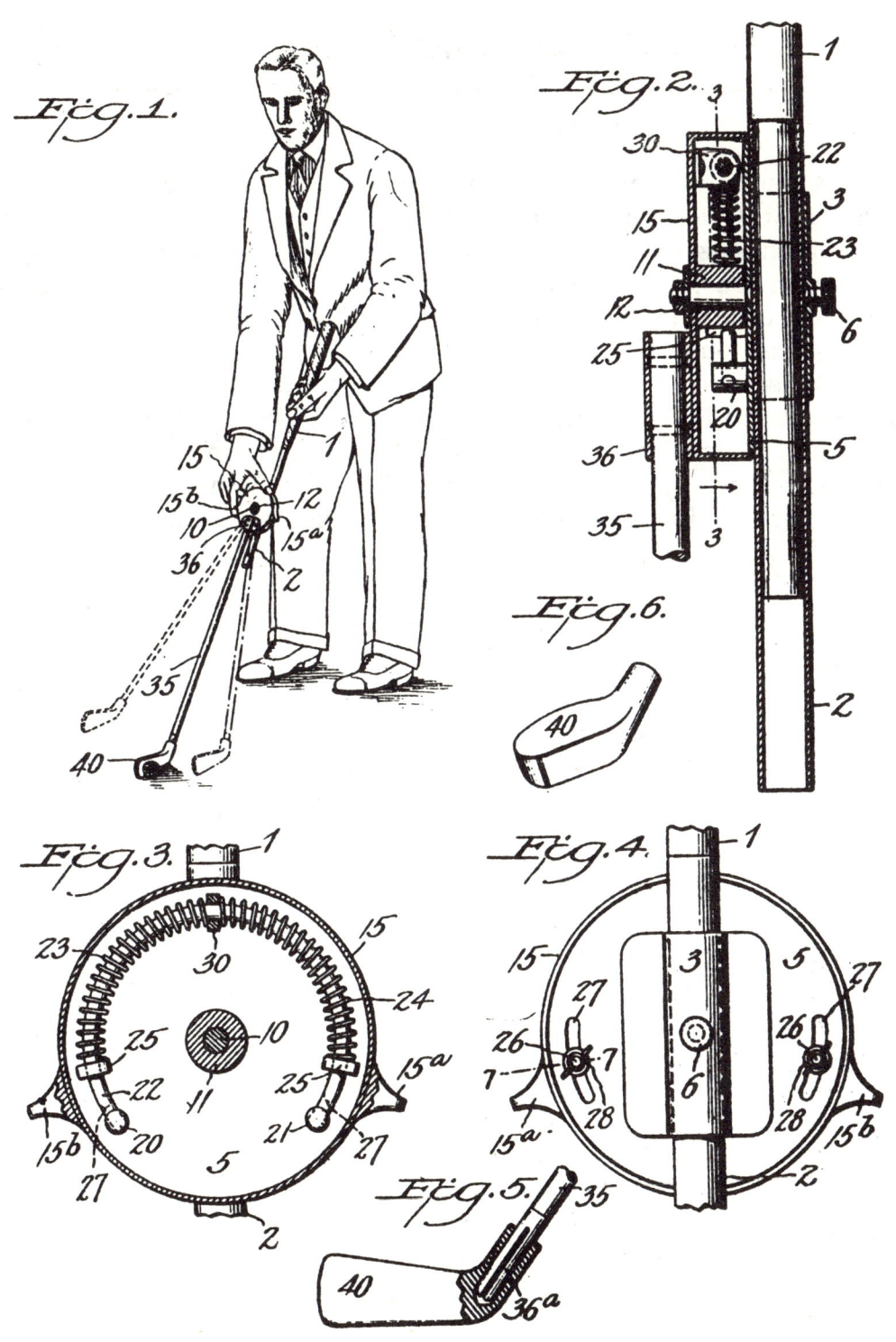

Golf Club Carrier
Patent No. 4,136,724 (1979)
Ammon Leitzel of Portland Oregon

An improved carrier includes a cart **12** a container **14** and a pillow pocket unit **16** for carrying accessories. The cart includes a tubular frame or chassis, carried by wheels through a folding resilient torsion bar suspension system held by a handle actuated linkage in either a stand fold condition as shown in broken lines in FIG. **5** or an open or running position as shown in full lines in FIG. **5**. The cart also includes a seat **26** selectively movable between an operative position shown in full lines and a folded position shown in broken lines. The container **14** is adapted to grip irons **28** with their heads down and grip woods **30** with their heads up. The container is releasably held on the cart by a latching arm and a wire loop carries the pocket unit and is carried by the container.

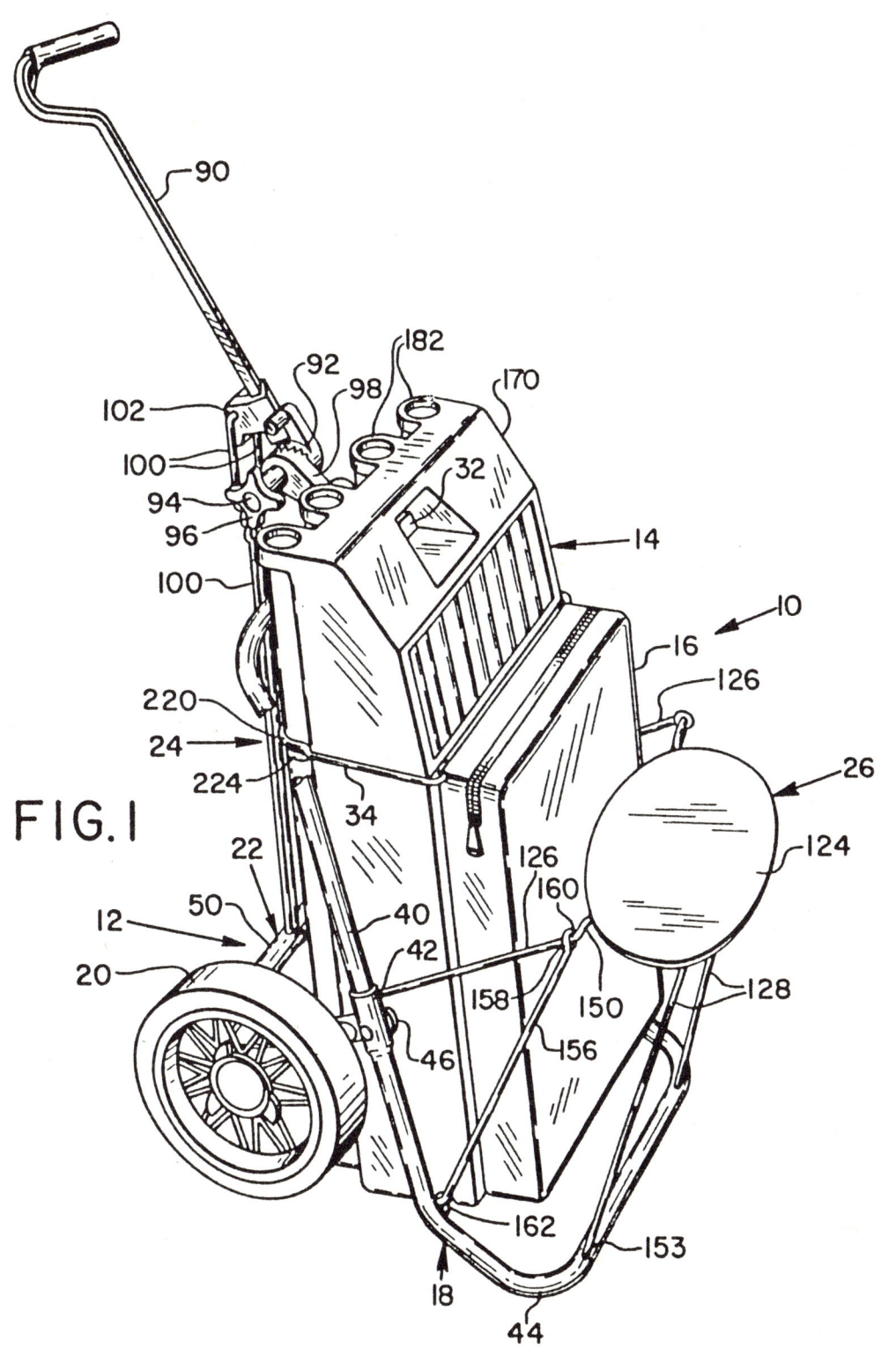

FIG.1

The Patent Duffer 11

Simulated Golf Club Beverage And Cup Container

Patent No. 2,639,804 (1953)

Emanuel Merahn of Brooklyn, New York

When playing golf, the player usually must carry his heavy golf bag and its assortment of clubs and golf balls, tees and the like, over rolling terrain, often remaining out in the weather for several hours. Even when a caddie is employed for this work, the exertion and exercise in the open air has its effect upon the golf player, as he walks about on the golf course, up hills and over rough terrain, in the course of the game. A source of liquid refreshment is thus necessary.

An object of the invention is to provide a novel form of article which has the outward appearance of a genuine golf club, and in addition is provided with means for receiving beverages and also cups or glasses for use therewith.

A further object of the invention is to provide novel means whereby a golf player may unobtrusively carry with him a source of liquid refreshment, which being styled just like a golf club in size and appearance, will fit right into his golf bag so as to be protected thereby against the elements, and can be carried right along onto the playing golf course for use when needed.

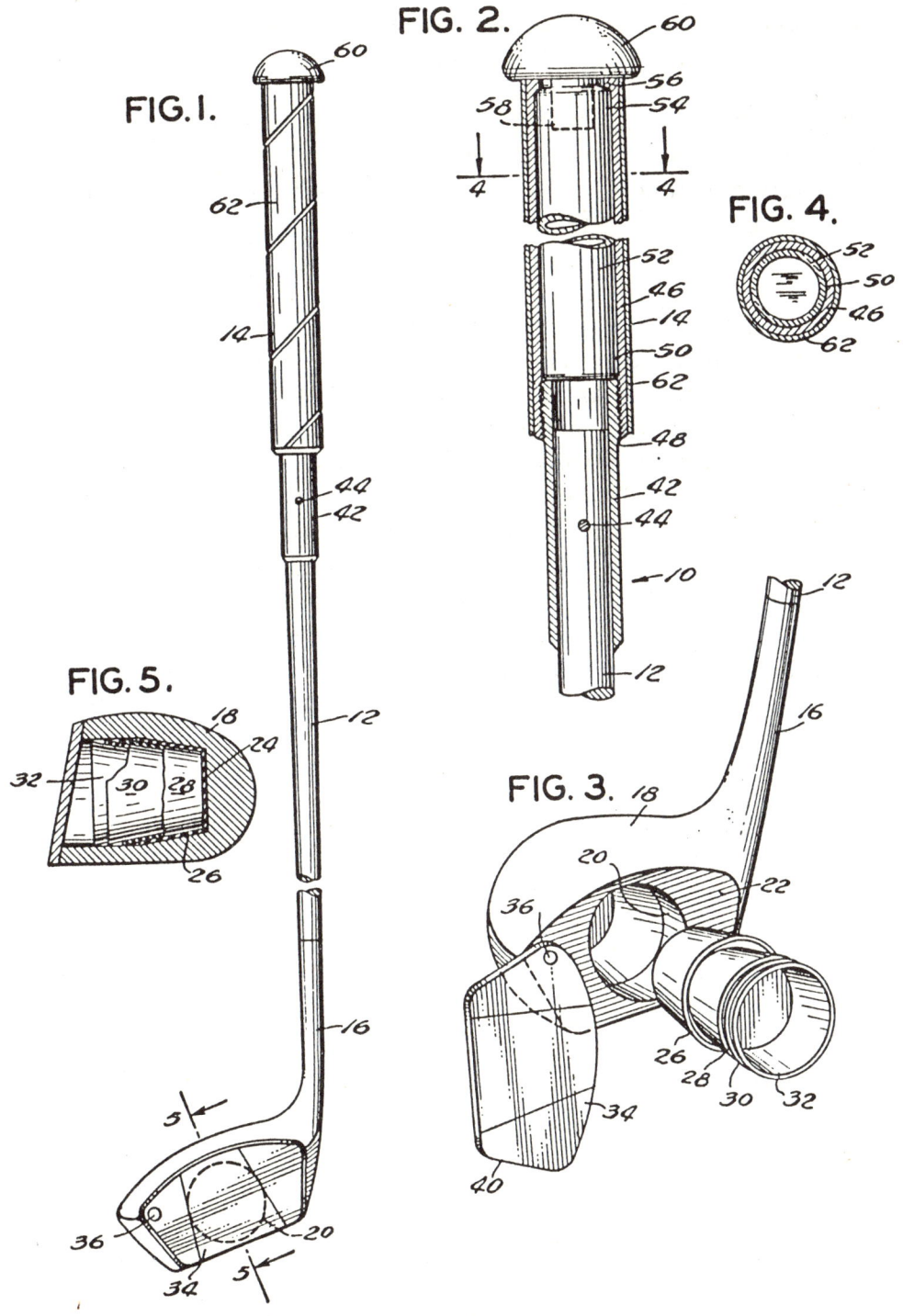

The Patent Duffer 13

Breakable Golf Club
Patent No. 3,206,205 (1965)
George McLoughlin of Scranton Pennsylvania

A golfer would find the use of this club a cheap way to express his pent up feelings after missing the hole, thereby helping him to regain his composure and increase his chances of making a better score.

The objects of this invention are as follows:

(1) The club can be broken any number of times without destroying it.

(2) After breaking, the club can be restored to useful condition in a few minutes, ready for another play and another break when desired.

(3) The rod feed method eliminates the need to carry spare parts.

(4) The cost of replacing the wood rod is very small since standard wood dowels can be used and purchased in any lumber yard.

To break the club, the head section **8** is grasped in one hand and the handle section **2** is grasped by the other hand. The middle of the club is then struck sharply against the golfer's leg. When sufficient force is used, the threads **5** and **6** will pull apart, separating the club into two parts.

FIG. 3
FIG. 2
FIG. 1
1
2
3
4
5
6
7
8
9
10
11
12
13
14
15
16
17
18
19
20
21
22
23
24

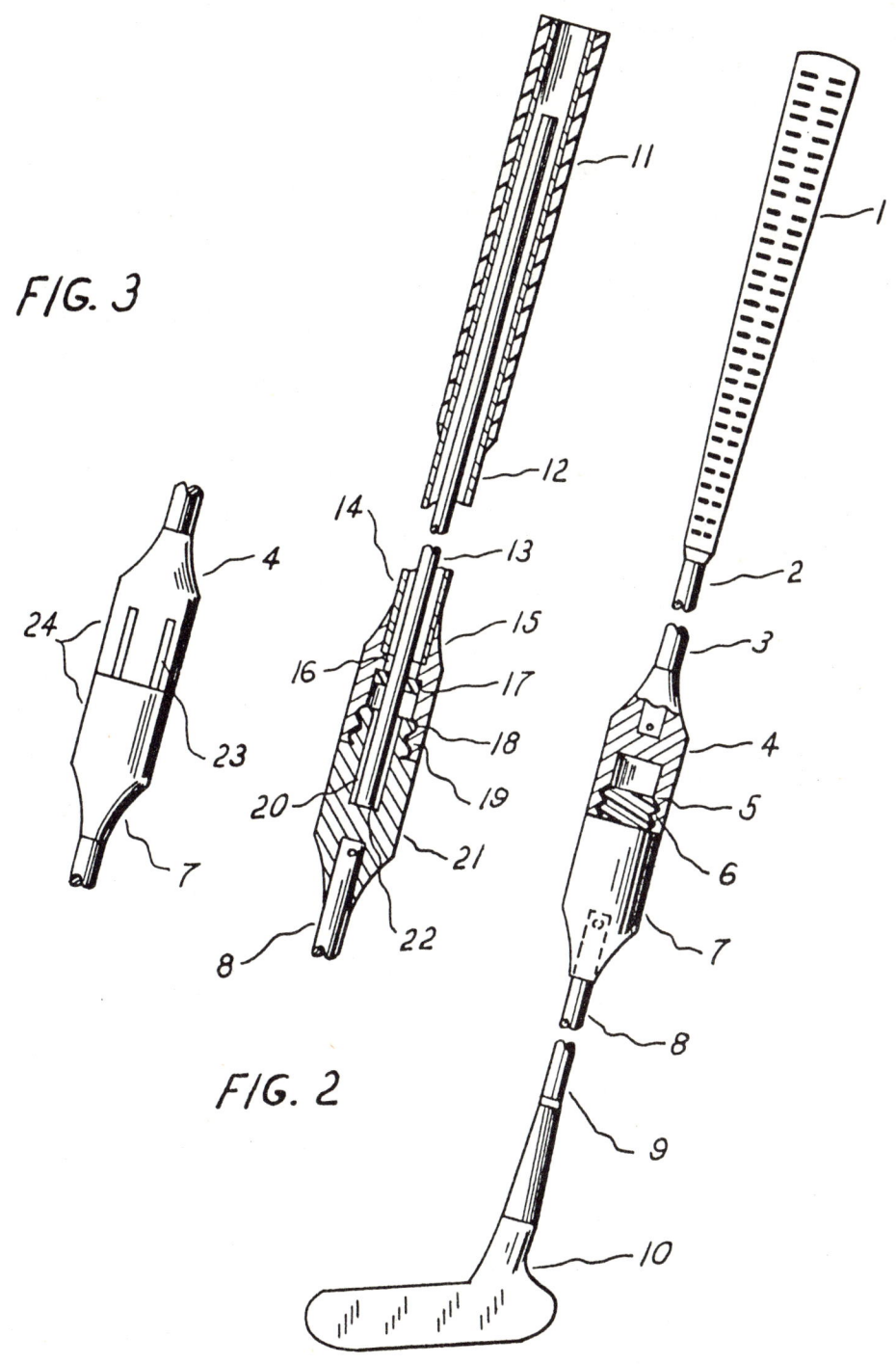

Scoring Device For Golf-Players
Patent No. 753,457 (1904)
Willis Weissbrod of Greenfield, Massachusetts

This invention relates to a device which is adapted to be worn upon the wrist for players of golf or other games in which a score or entries of the play are to be made during the progress of the game, the object of the invention being to provide a scoring device which may be conveniently engaged about the wrist, which may enable readily and quickly the scoring entries to be made, which will retain the score-sheet clean during the play, and which will permit the removal of a complete score, leaving other blank score-sheets for further utilization.

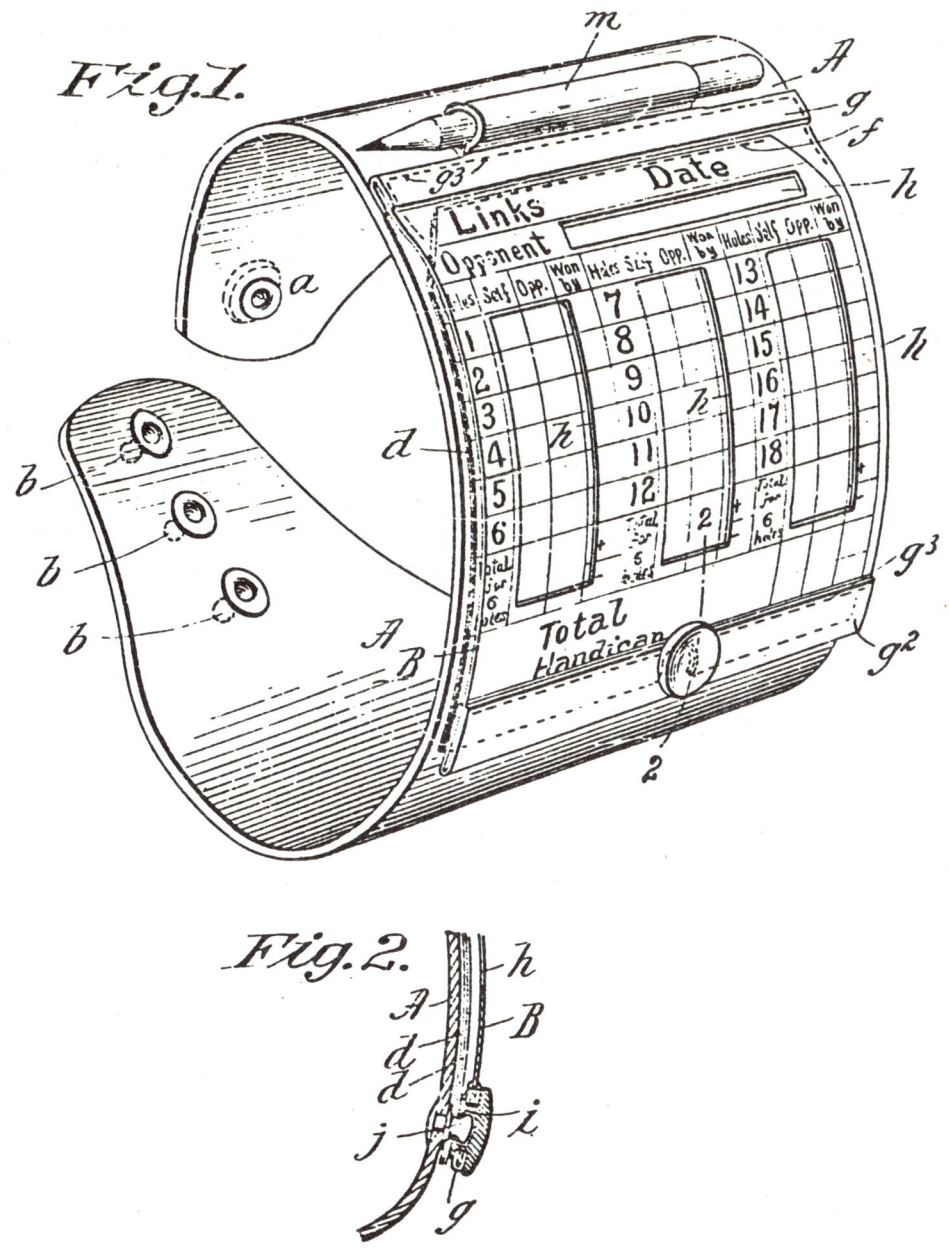

Means For Indicating Proper Stroke In Golf

Patent No. 2,910,297 (1959)

Michael Bonetate of Naugatuck, Connecticut

In operation, both sets of spinners will operate on both the back and forward strokes, but their effect is greater on the forward stroke than on the back stroke as the movement of the club is muck slower on the back stroke and much more rapid on the forward stroke and the follow-through part of the forward stroke. Deviation from the desired direction in either stroke will be indicated to the golfer by reduced rapidity of the rotation of the spinners, and will usually be readily discernible both to the eye of the player and any onlooker. It is, of course, the passage of the spinners through the air by the stroke of the club which causes them to rotate, and by watching the action of these spinners the golfer can tell whether his stroke is in the proper line, and by the feel of the resistance created by these spinners in both the back and forward strokes, he can judge whether he is getting proper speed, and also the proper amount of back stroke and the follow-through

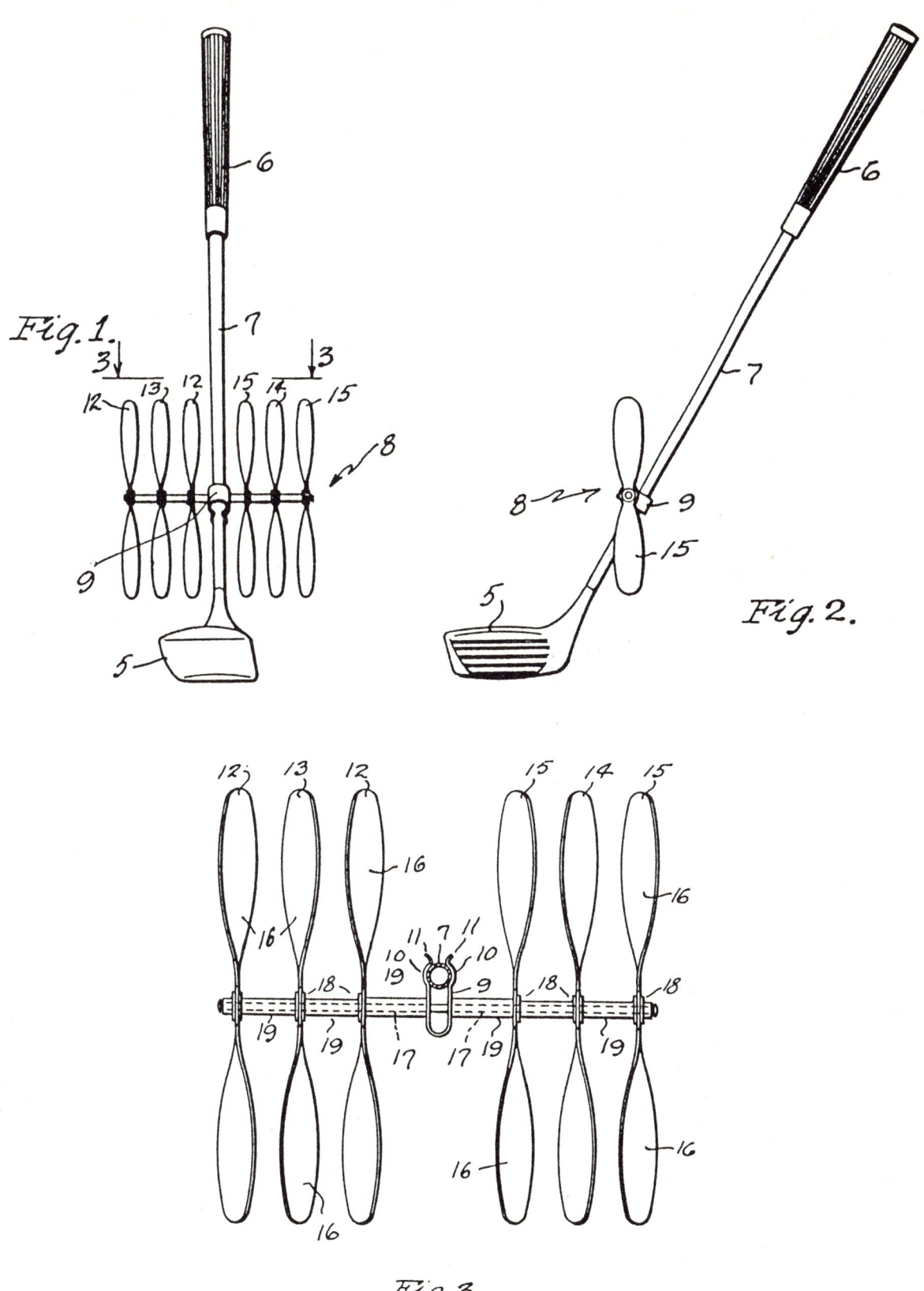

The Patent Duffer

Combined Golf Club And Ball Retriever

Patent No. 3,224,781 (1965)

Albert Hutchison of Cleveland, Ohio

In golfing, the hand mashie is facetiously termed that club which is employed when a ball is picked up and thrown to obtain a better lie. Few players will admit to having used a hand mashie. Accordingly, a visible hand mashie in a golfer's bag will leave no question as to his veracity and such is apt to be a major subject of conversation at the 19th hole.

A hand mashie is often employed when the shot of a right-handed player lands in an impossible lie for a shot using a right-handed club. Most players do not carry an extra club of opposite hand and accordingly the more conventional hand mashie is employed in such situations. The hand mashie is also sometimes employed when the ball obtains a difficult to reach location such as a pond, beyond a barrier such as a fence, or other unplayable hazard. Golf balls have been known to land up in trees, for example. The conventional hand mashie is often too short to retrieve the ball and in such situations, the golfing novelty of the present invention may be employed.

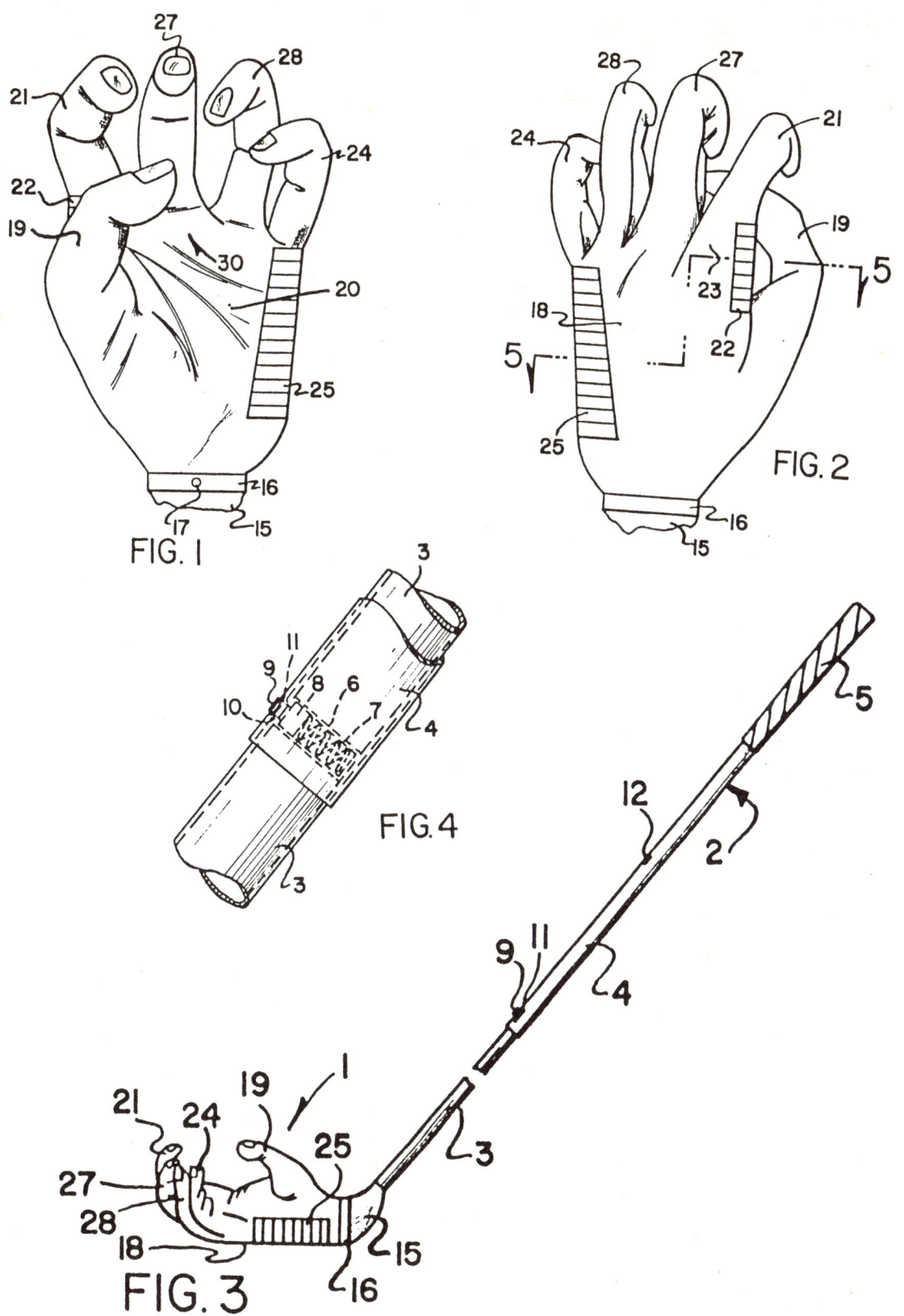

The Patent Duffer 21

Golfing Aid
Patent No. 3,679,206 (1972)
Howard Shambaugh of Forest River, Illinois

It is a common but mistaken belief of those not thoroughly familiar with the game that when the ball is on a sidehill lie on an upslope relative to a right-handed golfer and the ball is hit directly toward the hole or a selected intermediate point, the ball "hooks", i.e., the ball acquires a counterclockwise spin which causes it to curve toward the golfer's side of the hole, and that when the ball is on a downslope, the ball "slices" because it acquires a clockwise spin.

Expert golfers are aware that when the ball lies on a sidehill, the club should not be lined up directly toward the hole or an intermediate selected point. They employ experience and intuition to use a stance, club alignment and line of swing which compensates for the sloping surface and the loft of the particular club used.

Very generally, and with reference to FIG. 1 of the drawings, a golf aid means or device in accordance with the present invention is designated by the reference numeral **10** and is illustrated in the position in which it is employed on a sidehill lie when a shot is to be made approaching the green. The device permits the golfer to determine the proper line of swing to direct a golf ball **12** toward the hole **14**. By using the device **10**, the golfer can determine the required quantitative compensation for his swing for the degree of slope of the surface and for the loft of the particular club which is to be used to reach the hole. In this manner, the guess work heretofore used by golfers to compensate for these factors is eliminated.

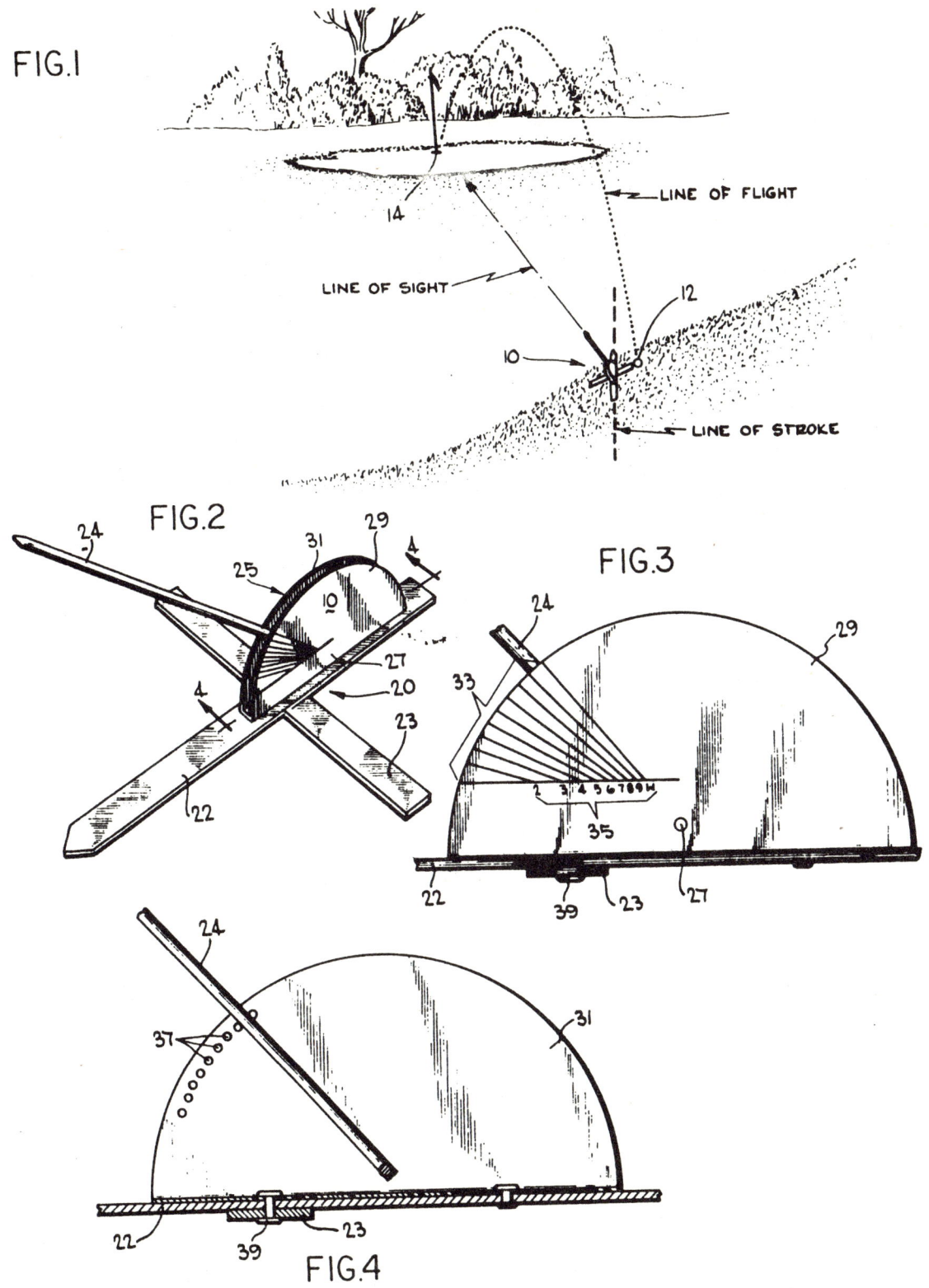

The Patent Duffer 23

Golf Club
Patent No. 1,686,323 (1928)
George von der Heyde of Montclair, New Jersey

In playing the game of golf, it is not deemed in good form or sportsmanlike to carry a regular umbrella, in the caddy bag, or along with the player; and as the game is often played in uncertain weather, a sudden shower or hard rain is sometimes encountered when the player is some considerable distance from any form of shelter, so that the player is liable to great danger to health, by being drenched before a shelter or protection from the storm can be reached, that not infrequently results in the player contracting a severe cold, or influenza or even pneumonia may result.

The purpose of the present invention is to provide an umbrella that as carried has all the appearances of a regular golf club, and can be carried in the customary caddy bag with the other clubs, and which when a rain comes up, can be quickly and easily brought into use to protect the player.

The Patent Duffer 25

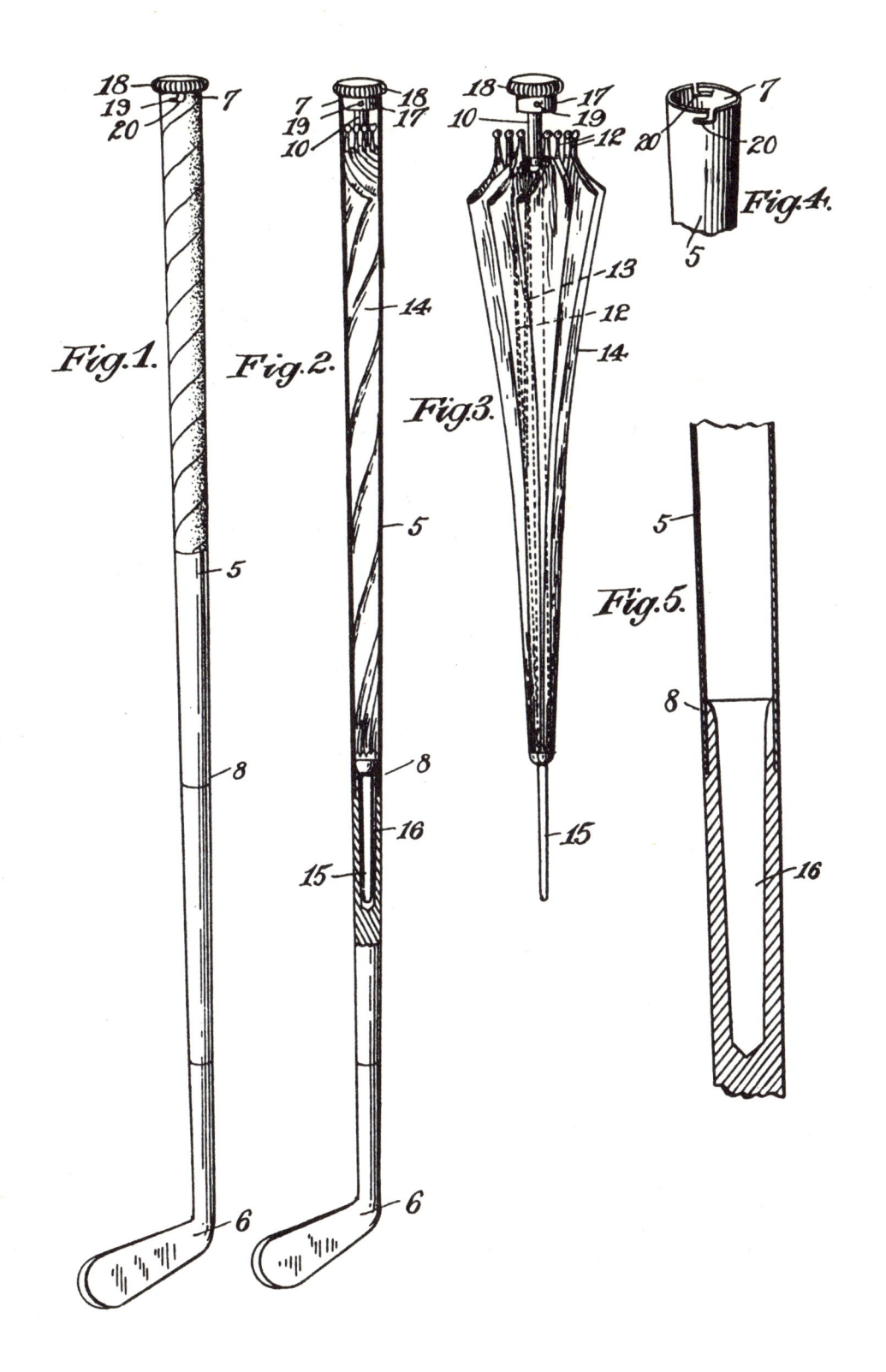

Golf Practice Device

Patent No. 3,814,439 (1974)

Max Simon of Canoga Park, California

Many devices are on the market to allow golfers to practice various shots at home These include many devices to practice putting and some to practice driving.

There are also devices such as plastic golf balls and balls made of other soft materials used for golfers to practice at home.

It is an object of the present invention to provide a device for a golfer to practice chip shots while he is at home around his or her pool.

It is a further object of this invention to provide a floatable device resembling a golf green with a cup and flag that a golfer can use to float in his swimming pool and practice chip shots or other shots.

Referring now to the drawings there is shown the device **10** of the present invention, shown floating in a swimming pool, depicted by the edge **12**. A golfer **14** is poised ready to hit a ball **16** with a golf club **18**.

While the golfer is shown near the edge of the pool **12**, in practice generally he would be at a further distance from the pool with the ball located on some grassy surface near the pool or at any distance chosen by the golfer depending upon the amount of room available to the golfer and the type of shot he wishes to practice. This device is particularly adaptable to practice chip shots or short irons but any shot may be practiced depending upon the room available.

FIG. −1

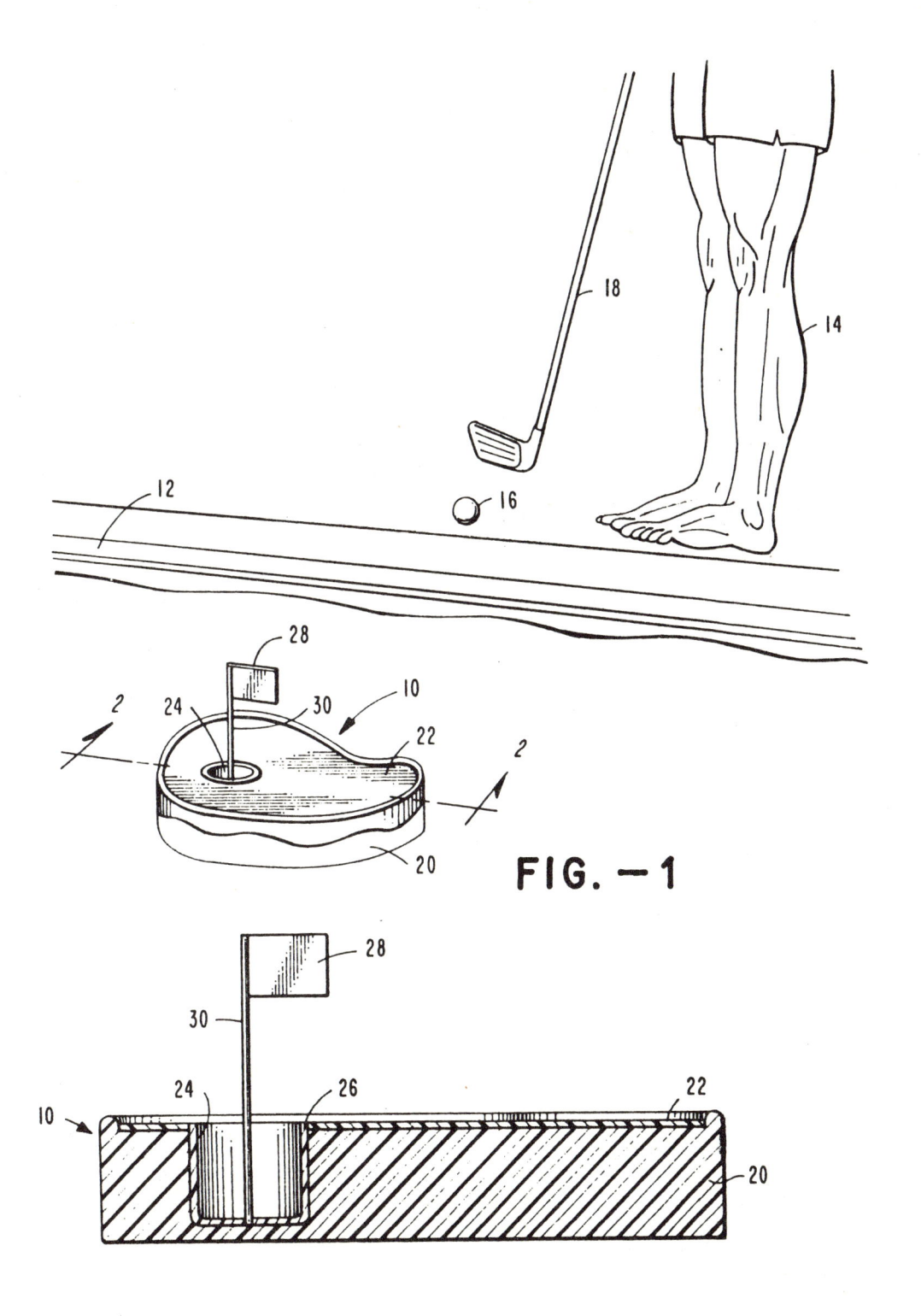

FIG. −2

The Patent Duffer 27

Golfing Accessory For Positioning Golf Tee

Patent No. 2,801,852 (1957)

Dwight Hottle of Akron, Ohio

Under normal conditions, the user of a golf tee merely pushes the pointed end of the tee into the ground by manual force to effectuate positioning of the golf tee. However, during a dry spell, when the ground becomes hard, it is oftentimes difficult to effectuate such positioning, because sufficient downward pressure cannot be applied centrally of the cup area to cause the golf tee to pierce the hard ground. Accordingly, tees will be oftentimes broken or improperly positioned during such periods when the ground is hard.

As a further disadvantage of such manual forms of positioning golf tees as are above described, it will be noted that no means are provided for positioning the cup head at a uniform distance above the ground on repeated occasions of use, with the result that the golf ball will invariably be located at different elevations above the ground upon teeing up on successive holes.

Accordingly, it is one object of this invention to provide a tee positioning device that enables the user thereof to accurately position the head of a golf tee at a uniform elevation at each period of use.

It is a further object of this invention to provide a tee positioning device that enables the user thereof to position a golf tee in hard, dry ground without damage to the golf tee.

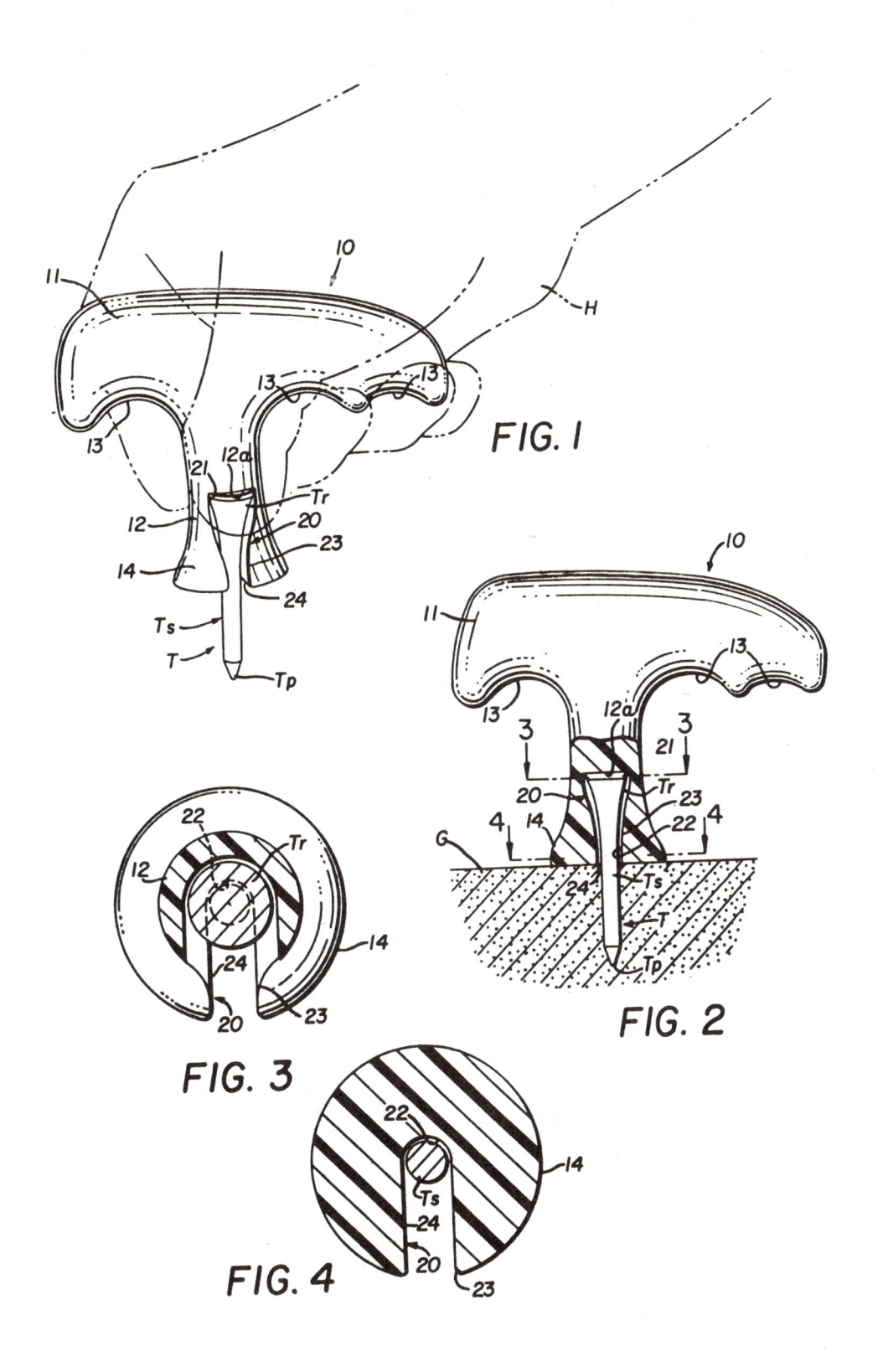

FIG. 1

FIG. 2

FIG. 3

FIG. 4

The Patent Duffer   29

Golf Club Attachment
Patent No. 2,938,728 (1960)
Barney Green of San Carlos, California

The present invention generally relates to an attachment for a conventional golf club and more particularly to an attachment in the form of an auxiliary handle or shaft which is spaced from and rigidly attached to the conventional handle or shaft so that the right hand of a golfer may engage the auxiliary handle so that the golfer employing the device while practicing will keep his right hand from overpowering the left hand and imparting the proper feeling necessary when the left hand is actually stroking through the ball into a perfect finish which is highly desirable and which will aid in the golfer arriving at a desired swing and aiding him in finding the proper feeling for such a swing.

By spacing the right hand in the manner shown, the right hand will tend to tag along behind the left hand thus it would be almost impossible for the right hand to overcome and dominate the swing. Thus, with the right hand weakened, the left hand is forced to do the job it was meant to do, that is, swing through the ball and after the left hand has been accustomed to doing this by using the present device, the conventional golf club may be employed and, by habit the left hand will continue to swing through the ball and the right hand will continue to move in its proper relationship to the left hand and will not overpower the left hand during the swing.

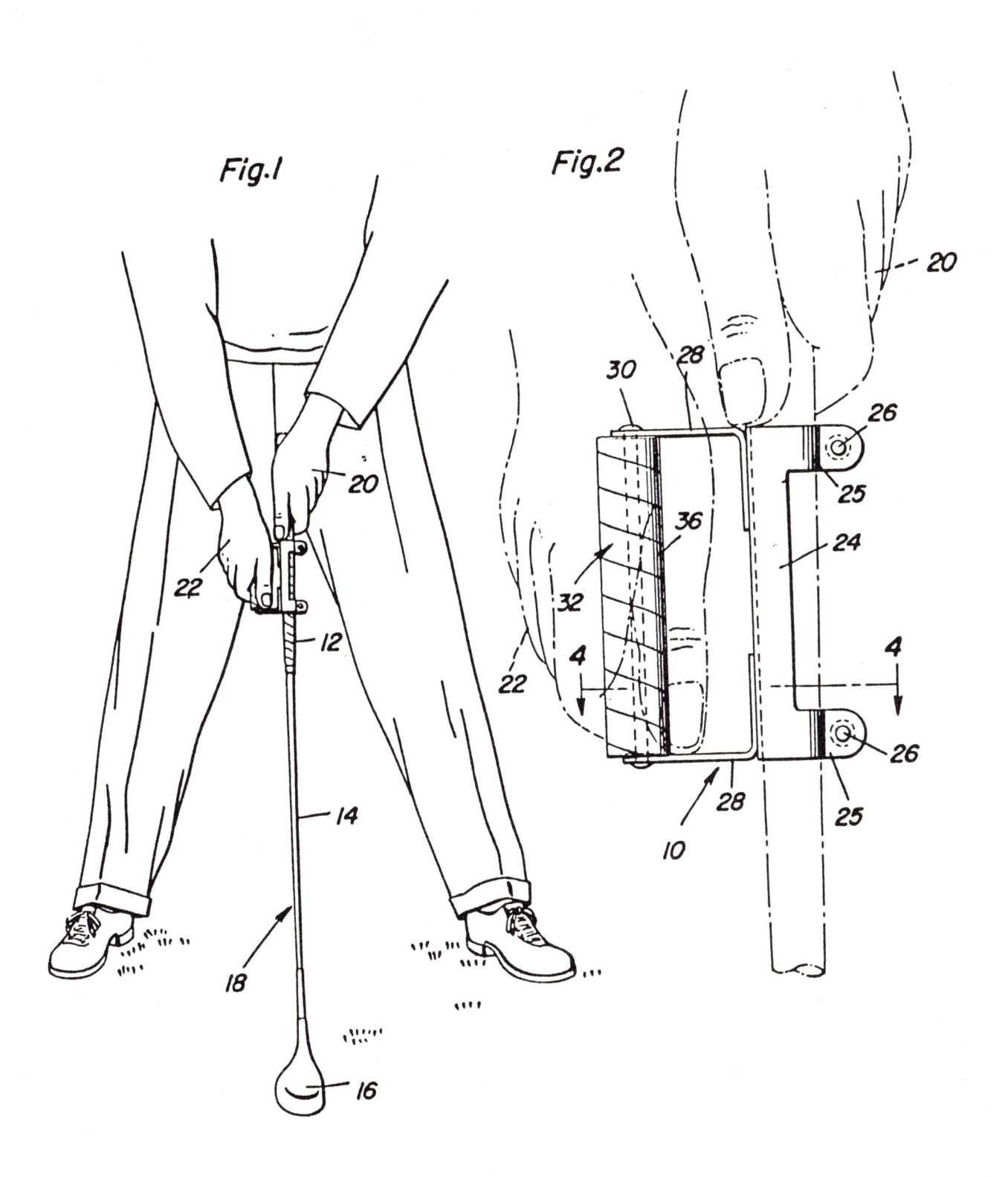

Fig.1

Fig.2

The Patent Duffer 31

Combination Container, Practice Golf Ball And Tee

Patent No. 3,099,452 (1963)

John Fernicola of Centreville, Maryland

The article may be used as a container for refreshments and/or medical composition, one of its advantages being that, it may be carried along in the same place reserved for the regular golf balls. It may also be used as a decoration or novelty about the home, clubs, taverns or for a desk ornament.

When used as a container, the stopper **S** may be removed and the ball filled with any desired contents such as stimulants, medication etc. as shown at **15** in FIGURES **1** and **2**, which may be for the pleasures or necessity of the party. When the desired amount of ingredients have been placed in the hollow ball the stopper **S** is inserted and tightened down. The stopper is so designed as to tightly seal the contents within the ball. The ball may then be set upon the broad outer edge **16** of the stopper similar to the pedestal of a lamp or vase as shown in FIG. **1**.

When the ball is to be used as a practice ball of course it is empty. When empty the ball may be used by sitting it on its neck **12** as shown in FIGURE **3**, the neck being about the average height of a standard golf tee. Should the player desire his ball higher, he removes the stopper and tees up his ball by placing the spherical surface of the ball of the portion **16**, as shown in FIGURE **4**.

The Patent Duffer 33

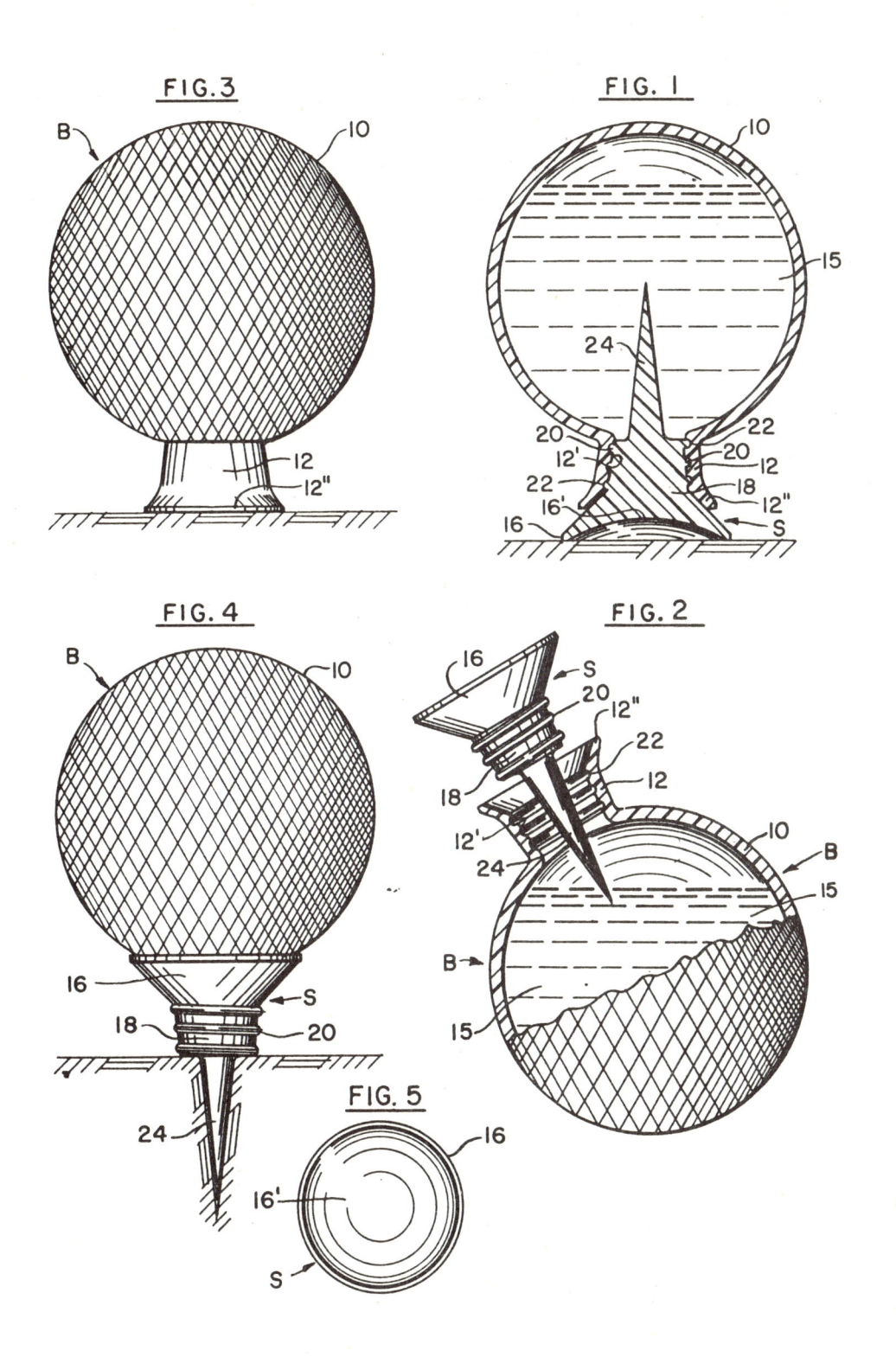

Golfer's Aid
Patent No. 3,415,518 (1968)
Bailey Root of Newport, Kentucky

A golfer's aid including detachably connected first and second portions. The second portion is cylindrical and has a cavity therein. The first portion has rigidly embedded therein a pair of spaced elongated rigid tool members having sharp pointed ends which normally extend into the cavity of the second portion. The second portion also has a recess formed in its outer end surface with a metal disc ball marker positioned therein and held in said position by a magnet carried be the second portion. The free end of the first portion may include a mechanical pencil which is accessible from the exterior of the body means.

The Patent Duffer 35

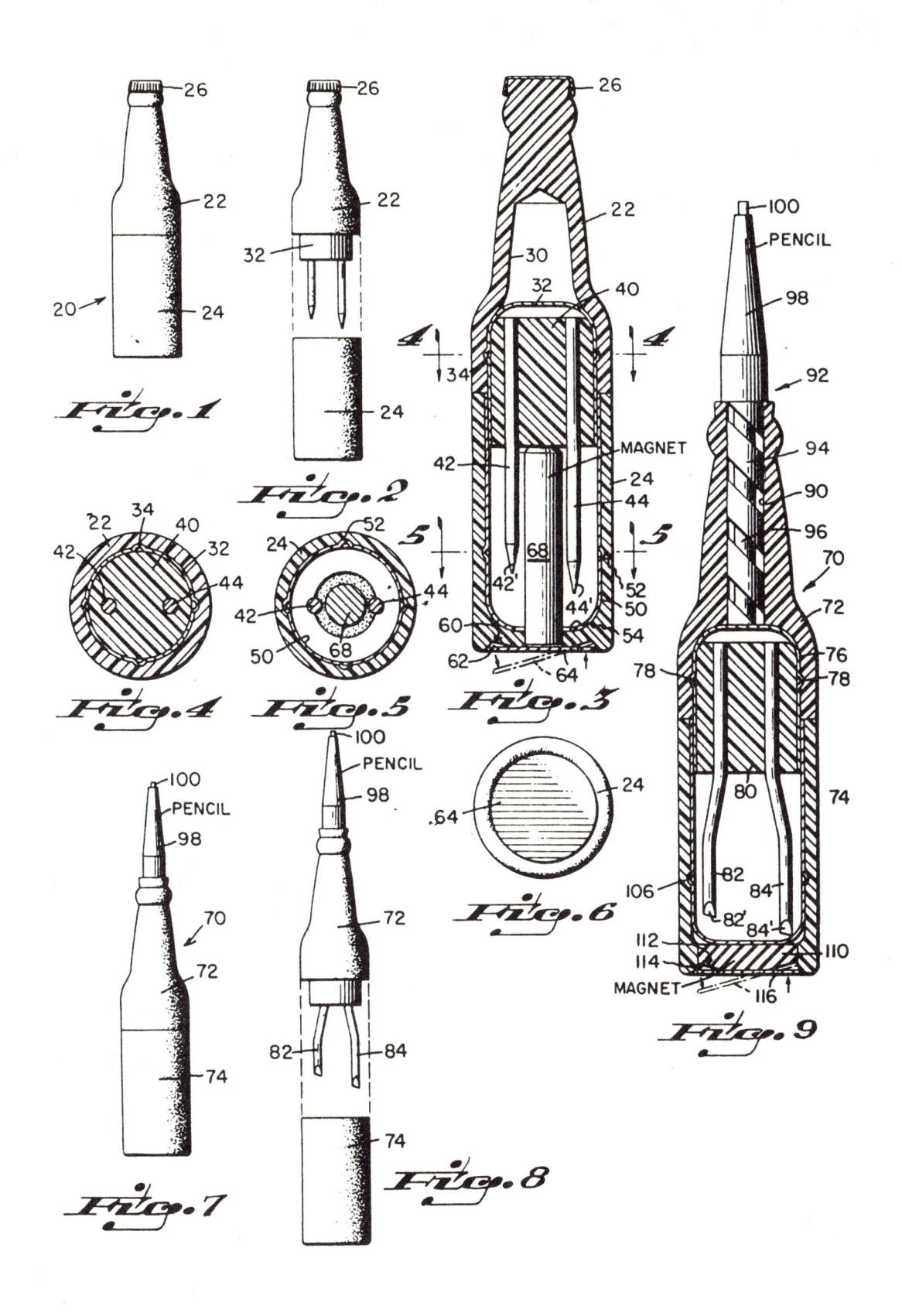

Golf Club Carrier
Patent No. 2,858,868 (1958)
Alexander Wallace of Salt Lake City, Utah

Golf bags are particularly inconvenient to handle during the many times that a club must be taken out and the bag put down for the actual playing of the game. The bag is normally laid on the course while a club is being used, and must be picked up again following the play. This means that the player is constantly called upon to stoop down or bend over, which adds much strenuous and largely unrewarding activity to the game.

A feature of my invention resides in the provision of a shaft, tapered and pointed at one end for pressing into the turf, and at least two golf club receiving rings secured to the shaft in mutually spaced relationship along its length. Both rings are offset relative to the shaft, so as to leave their openings free to receive the handles of golf clubs. The upper ring is rigidly fixed in position, but the lower ring is free to swing about the shaft as an axis.

Accordingly, when the golf clubs are positioned in the rings with their relatively heavy heads at the pointed end of the carrier shaft, and such shaft is pressed into the ground in upright position, the clubs fan out and largely support themselves in the upright position established by the carrier.

FIG.1. FIG.2.

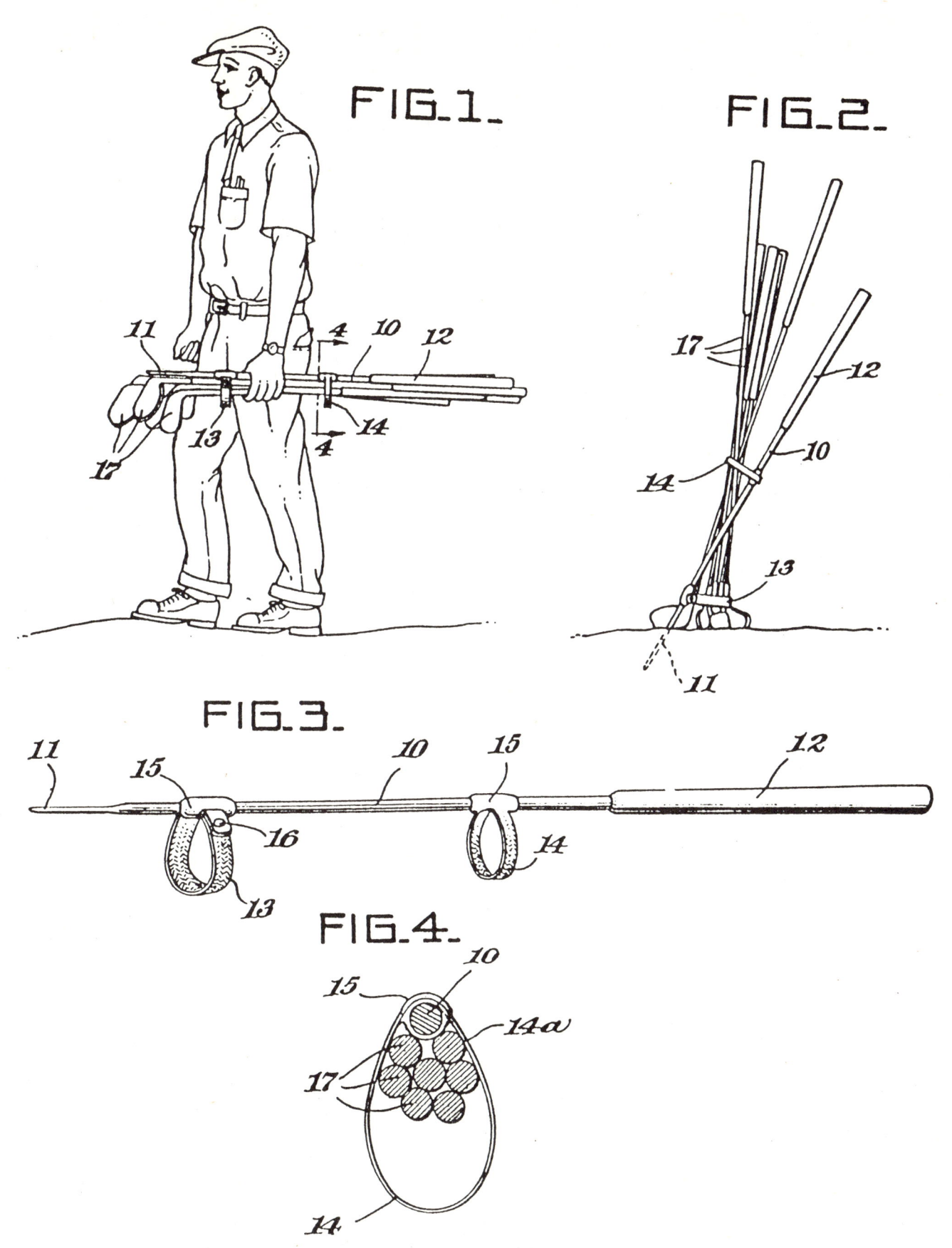

FIG.3.

FIG.4.

The Patent Duffer   37

Golf Club Head Attachable Rake
Patent No. 3,210,111 (1965)
William Gallon, of Westboro Massachusetts

One of the hazards of the sport of golfing is that, despite extreme care on the part of the golfer, the ball often leaves the main fairway where the grass is cut fairly short and enters an area of weeds, tall grass, vegetation and the like. Trying to find the ball in the "rough" is difficult, since the use of one's foot is tiring and the use of a golf club is not effective because the golf club head is so small. While a rake makes an excellent tool for searching for a ball in tall grass, it is a rather awkward implement to carry around the golf course.

The golf accessory **10** would normally be carried in the pocket of the golf bag. When a ball is lost in tall grass, weeds, or the like, the golfer holds the accessory in his left hand and inserts the golf club shank in the gap **24** between the edge **22** and the bead **15** at the upper edge of the main body. The golfer then uses the golf club in a normal manner grasping it by the handle and swinging it through the grass. The teeth **16**, **17**, **18**, and **19** pass through the grass, and if the ball is present in a certain area, will indicate that fact to the golfer visually or by the feel. By swing the golf club and the attached accessory through the deep grass or weeds, the finding of the ball is facilitated.

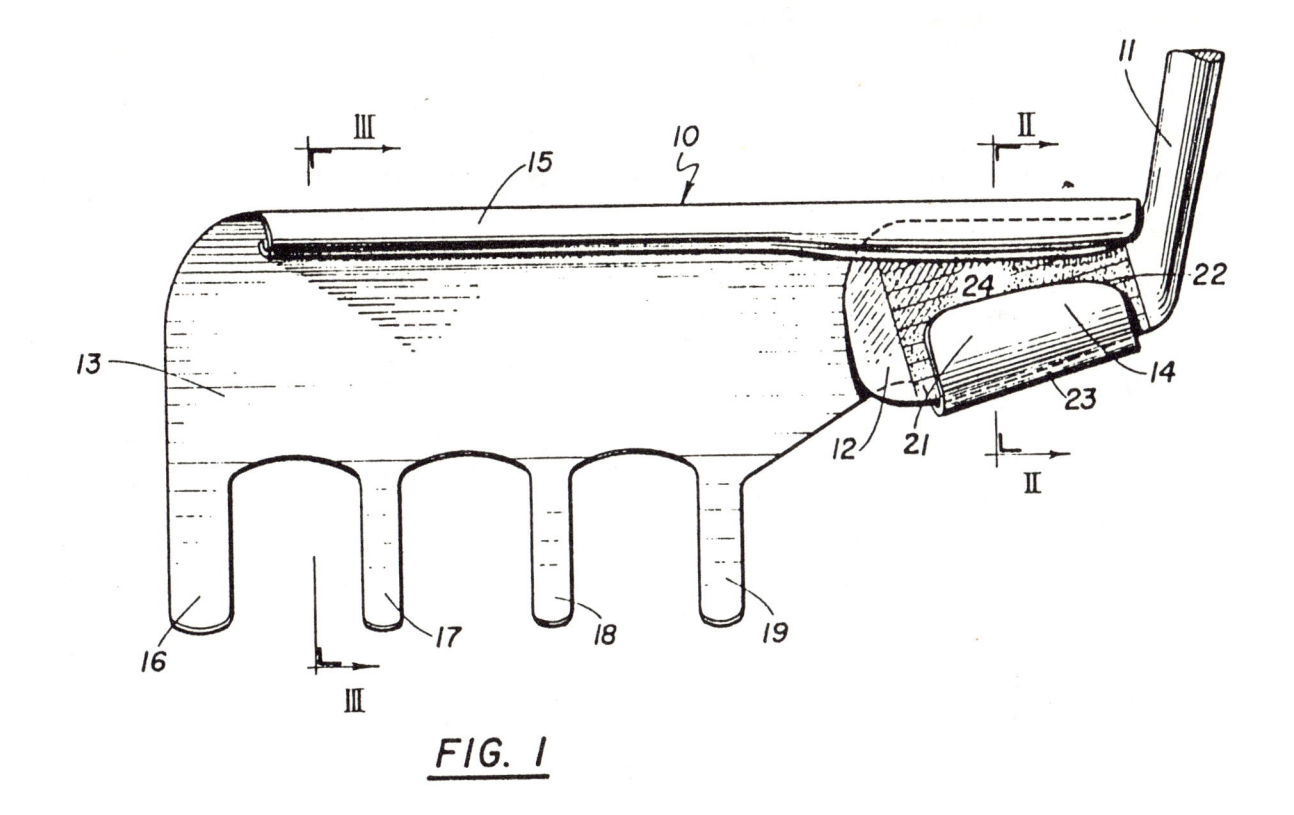

FIG. 1

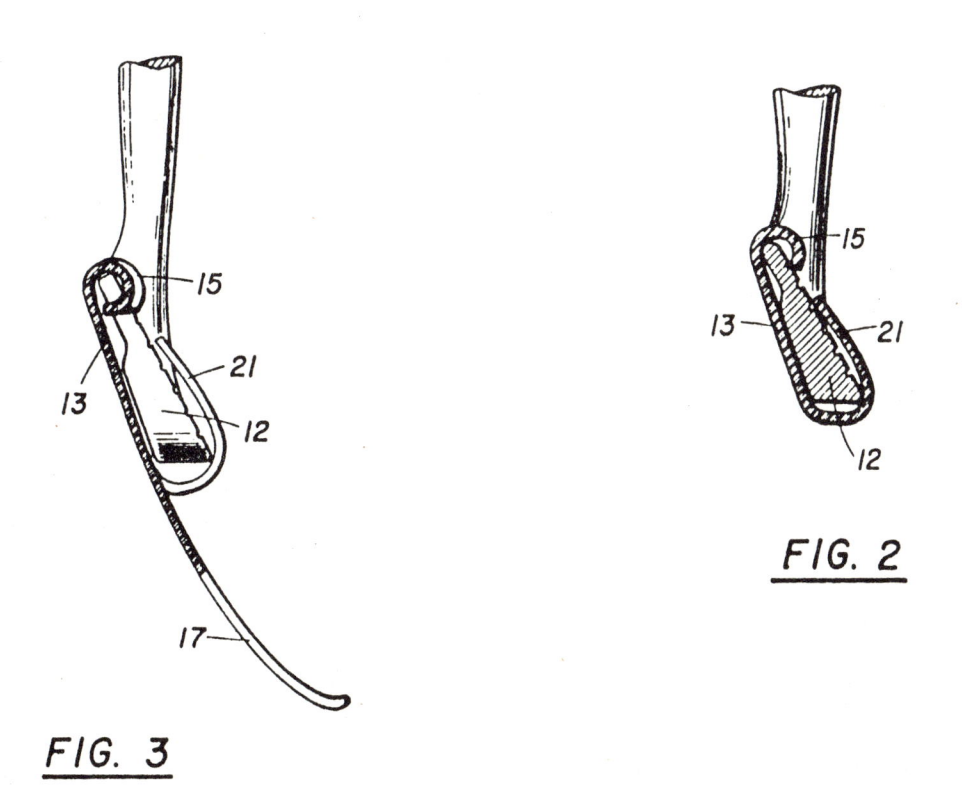

FIG. 2

FIG. 3

The Patent Duffer 39

Golf Tee Marker
Design Patent No. 155,576 (1949)
Julius Burch of Borger, Texas

Editors Note: This is a design patent so there is no description other than *"The drawing as substantially illustrated"*.

We may guess that Borger, Texas must be a place of some variable and gusty wind to necessitate the inclusion of a aeronautical wind sock on his tee marker. Being in Texas, the distance from tee to green must also be excessive to the extent that the arrow is necessary to guide the direction of one's drive.

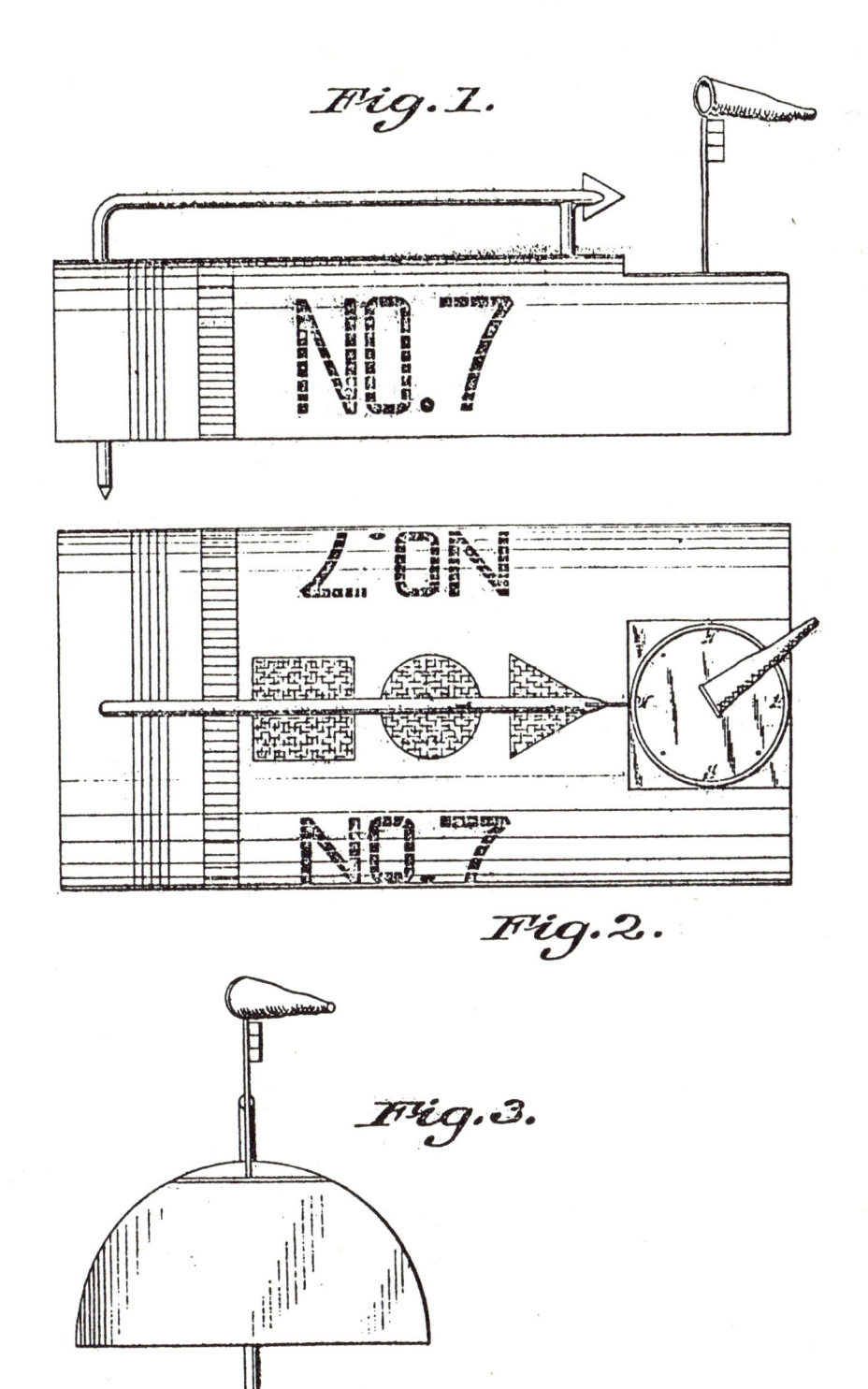

Fig. 1.

Fig. 2.

Fig. 3.

The Patent Duffer 41

TWO
Well, That's Really Using Your Head

Then there's the story about the Scottish clergyman out for his daily round. The reverend was an enthusiastic, if somewhat erratic, golfer. His faithful caddie was more aware of the abilities of his employer than the minister himself. One day, while approaching the green, the caddie proffered a 6 iron. "I think I can make it with a 7," the minister answered. Sure enough, the ball was short and ended up in a trap.

"Well, I guess the good Lord didn't hear me," the minister said.

"Could be," snapped the caddie, *"but in my church, when we pray, we keep our heads down."*

Keep you head down! Is there any more apocryphal advice in all of golf? Surely anyone who has ever attempted to play the game has been so admonished. It is an axiom, a law, an unbreakable tenet for those wishing to make solid contact with the ball.

American ingenuity has not neglected this aspect of the game. The granddaddy of all the inventions that have been used to remind golfers to keep their head down has come right out of the tackle box. A dangerously sharp fishhook is attached to a three-foot length of line, which is then tied around the head. This hook is then attached lightly to the pants, below the zipper. Should the hapless duffer raise his head during the swing, he is immediately made aware of the situation. This device usually didn't need to be used more than a few times to get the point across.

> It would be hoped one's head might be put to greater use than a convenient place to hang one's hat.
>
> *Steven Corie*

Thankfully, there are more humane appliances that were designed to accomplish the same lesson. The tackle box provided Ed Comitz of Tucson, Arizona with the materials for his own contribution to his fellow head-raisers. With Ed's **Golf Cap With Means For Indicating Raising Of Head** (page 46), the forgetful golfer is lightly struck in the face with a fishing weight which hangs from the bill on his cap. Notice Ed's Mona Lisa-like expression in his illustration. This is obviously a golfer at peace with his game.

Gabriel Presta of Racine, Wisconsin has come up with the **Golfer's Head Restrainer** (page 56). This is a stiff collar worn around the neck, putting pressure on the back of the head to keep it tilted forward. How one is supposed to follow through and watch the ball in flight without ending up at the chiropractors isn't explained.

If golf makes you cross-eyed now, wait until you try the **Golfing Aid** (page 62) that Charles Hull of Greencastle, Pennsylvania has put together. What we have here is basically a pair of sunglasses with two small clear areas through which the ball must be sighted. If there is any movement of the head, it is immediately apparent, as the ball will disappear from view. Any similarity to the x-ray glasses you used to see in the back of comic books is purely coincidental.

So remember, when you play and the pressure is really on, keep your wits about you and use your head, but by all means keep it down.

Indicating Device
Patent No. 3,156,211 (1964)
Paul Mallory Jr. of Houston, Texas

This invention is an aid which indicates to a golfer that his golfing form is improper. Many golfers allow bad habits to destroy proper form with the habits becoming more rigidly adhered to as time passes. In the past, the advice of an expert has often been needed to tell the puzzled golfer exactly what he is doing improperly.

This invention makes it possible for the golfer himself to correct his own difficulties by providing an indication or signal if the golfer improperly moves his head. Thus, this invention is a particular aid in reminding the golfer to "keep his eye on the ball," and although especially valuable to the casual golfer, it may also be a significant aid to more experienced golfers and even professionals.

The ball **B** is held in the central portion of the indicating device **C** by the biasing magnet **21**. When the golfer's head is moved abruptly during the back-swing, the ball **B** will be released by the magnet **21** and strike the end of the device at **20'**. The impact of the ball **B** upon the end of the device at **20'** will announce to the golfer that his head movement has been excessive. This impact may be felt vibrationally through the hat or heard as a result of the impact.

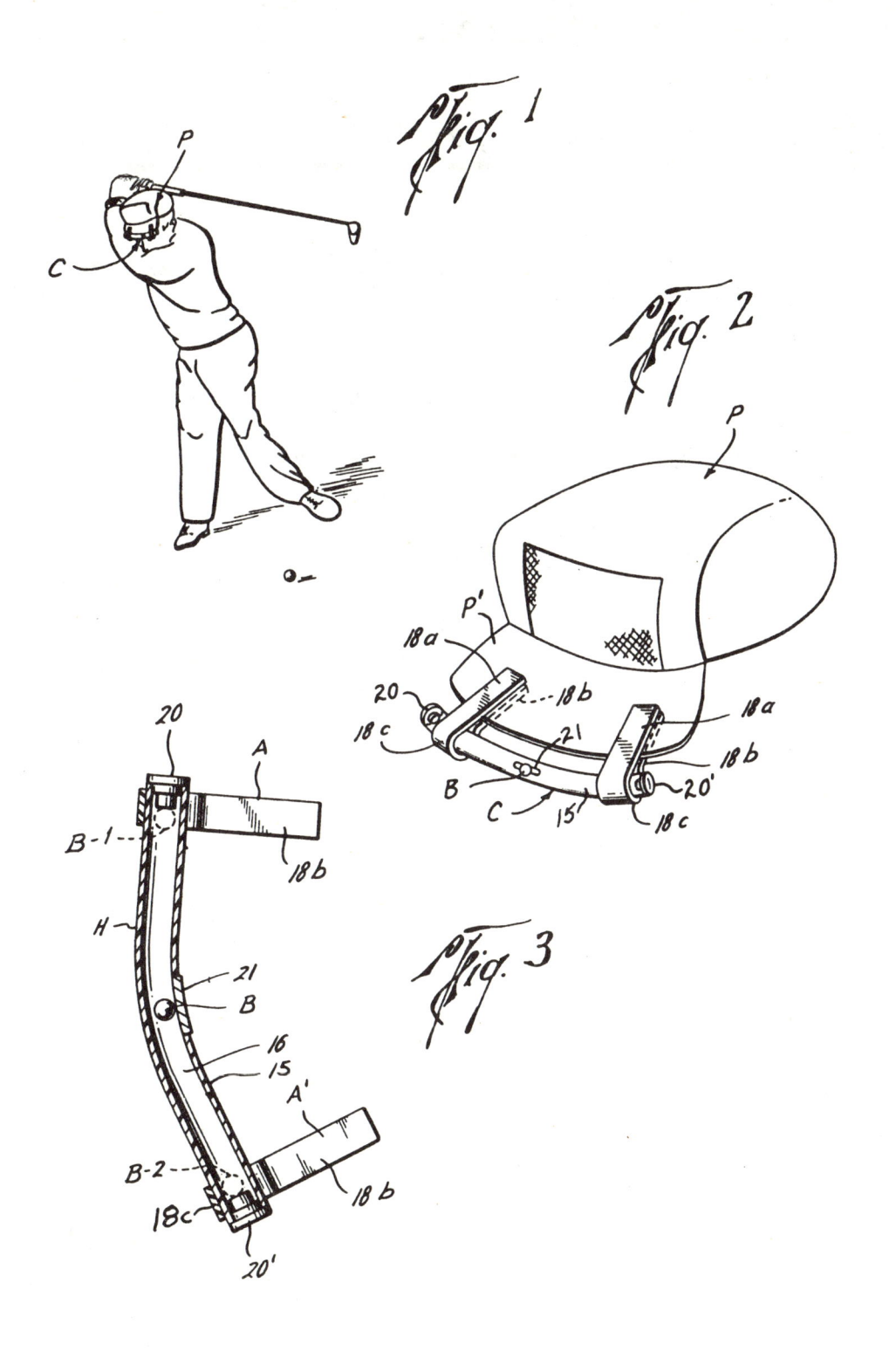

Fig. 1

Fig. 2

Fig. 3

The Patent Duffer 45

Golf Cap With Means For Indicating Raising Of Head

Patent No. 3,109,654 (1963)

Ed Comitz of Tucson, Arizona

This invention relates to a golf cap, and has as its primary object the provision of an attachment for golf caps which will enable a golfer to improve his game of golf by keeping his head down as he addresses the ball.

A further object of the invention is the provision of a freely suspended, relatively light weight pendulum which is attached to the visor of a golf cap, and which, when the golfer raises his head while addressing the ball or putting, will swing toward his face and strike the same, indicating to him the error of his swing.

A further object of the invention is the provision of a device of this character which will induce the golfer to keep his head down during putting or similar strokes, since each time he raises his head the movable member will lightly impact against his face, thus indicating to him the fact he has raised his head during the putt.

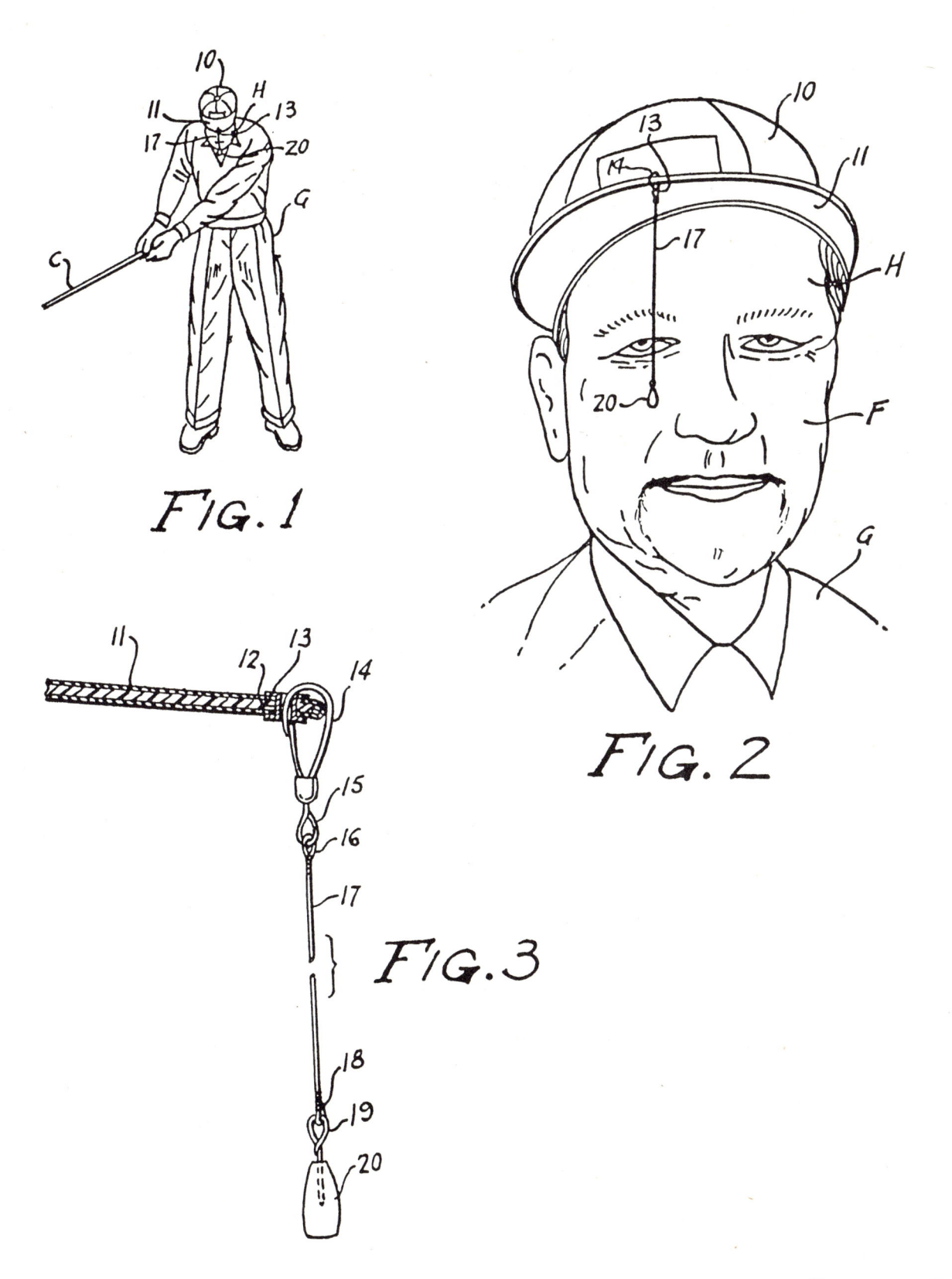

Fig. 1

Fig. 2

Fig. 3

The Patent Duffer   47

Head Down Persuader

Patent No. 1,980,101 (1934)

Adolph Schneider of Allentown, Pennsylvania

This invention relates to eye screens and particularly to an eye screen adapted to be worn upon the head normally beyond the field of vision of the wearer but operable by a sharp movement of the head to bring the screen into vision-intercepting position.

More especially the object of the invention is to provide a device, which I term a head-down persuader, useful to golf players in guarding against, or breaking themselves of, the very common and disastrous habit of jerking the head in the intended direction of a golf shot, before completing the full follow-through motion of the stroke, to watch the ball as it leaves its position. This habit, which tends to spoil the accuracy of golf shots, is easily acquired, and once acquired is very difficult to break. By means of my invention a player is repeatedly reminded of his weakness – and thereby assisted in overcoming it – through the operation of a screen or shutter which is automatically flashed before his eyes when a golf stroke is improperly executed.

Preferably the screen assumes the form of a visor or sun shade which, besides serving a useful purpose of itself, also acts to disguise the nature of the device as a prompter or persuader and relieve the wearer from any feeling of conspicuousness. The device may me worn upon the head of a player in any suitable manner, the screen being normally latched in raised position out of his range of vision and so designed that upon a jerk of the head in a side-wise direction a control member is actuated to release the latch and permit the screen to snap downward, under the influence of a spring, into vision - intercepting position. The spring is advantageously provided with mechanism for regulating its tension so as to vary the sensitivity of the device.

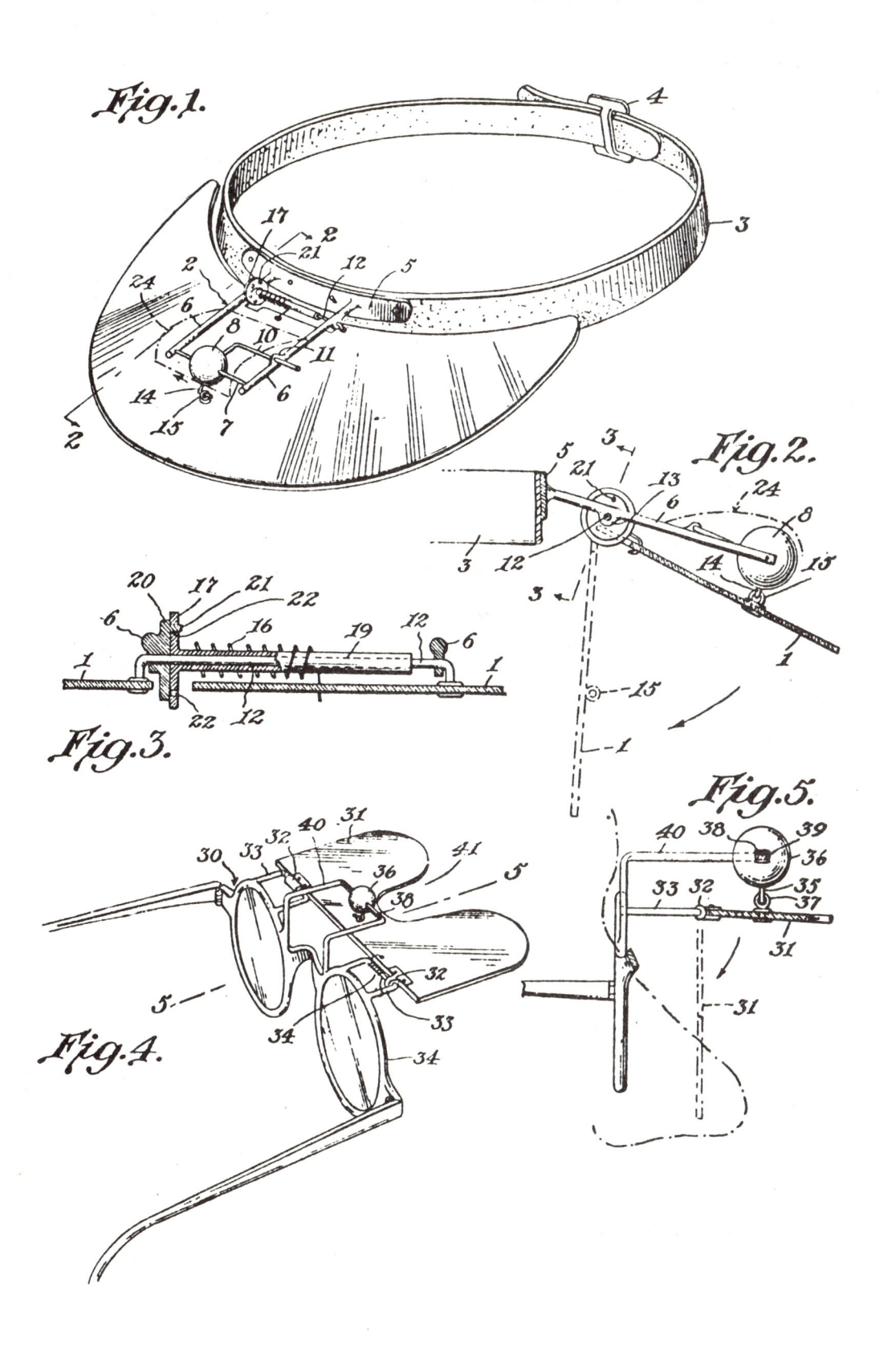

Fig.1.

Fig.2.

Fig.3.

Fig.4.

Fig.5.

The Patent Duffer   49

Golfer's Head Movement Indicator

Patent No. 3,178,187 (1965)
Lloyd Cardwell of Barrington, Illinois

The average golfer does not appreciably improve his game in spite of years of practice and play. One reason for this is that he cannot see himself swinging a golf club and thus cannot observe mistakes of form. Moreover, in many instances rather minor departures from proper stance may cause serious defects in the ultimate swing. In particular, the position of the head of a golfer is a very important factor to proper stance and execution and it is also a reliable indicator of numerous errors in stance and execution. Improper head position is also probably the most common defect, and all, except professional golfers, are guilty at one time or another. If the head is moved either up or down or sideways or fore and aft, the execution of the golf swing is spoiled because the golf ball is not in the same relative position to the body of the golfer at the time of address. Limited rotation of the head, about an axis of turning movement projecting centrally through the head and shoulders, is desirable and necessary and should not be indicated.

The Patent Duffer   51

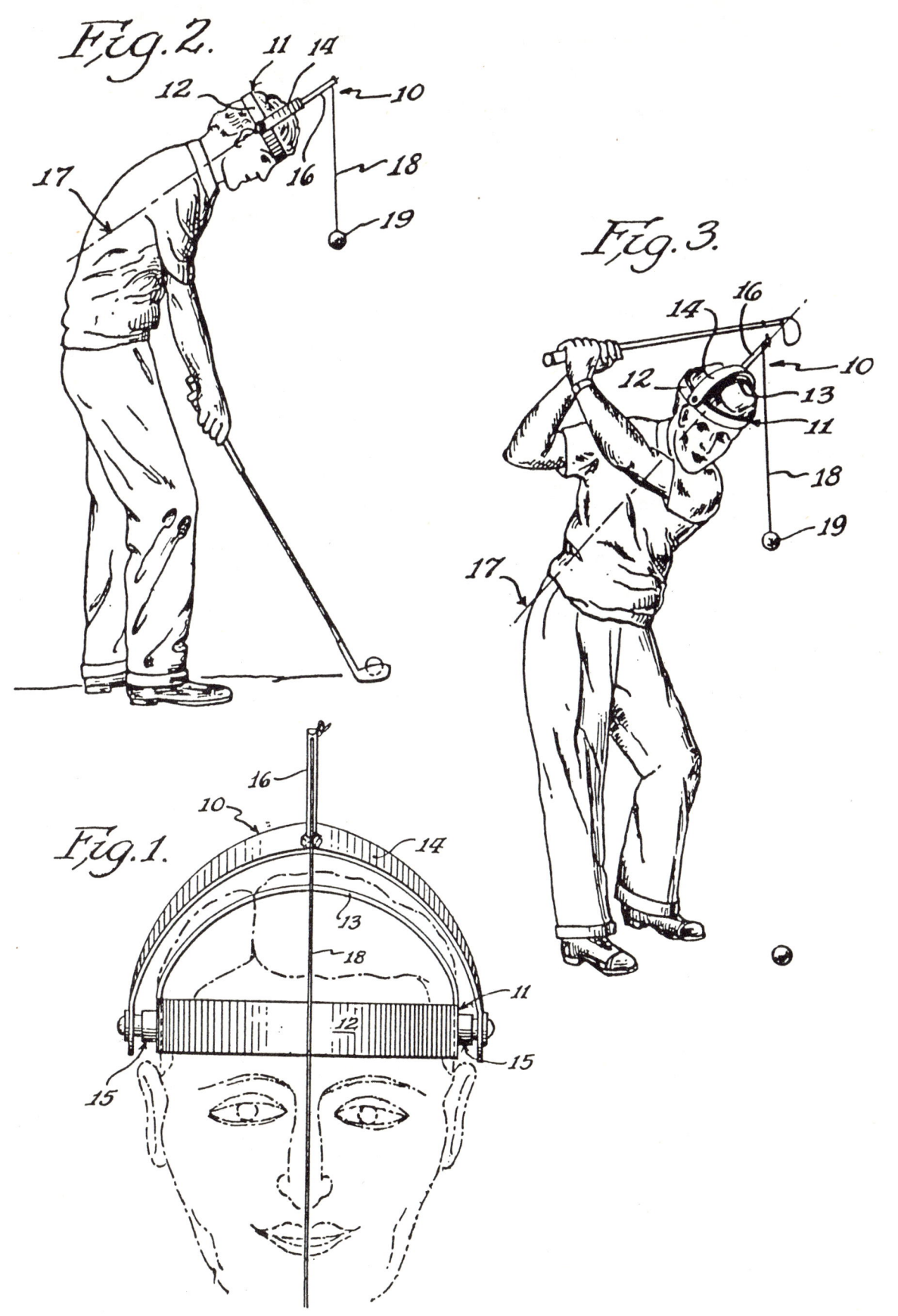

Appliance For Teaching Or Practicing The Game Of Golf

Patent No. 1,459,705 (1922)

Charles Ashton Henry Bullock of London, England

It is the object of the invention to provide a device which can be attached to the head of a person, this device including a plate with a support thereon for a rod adjustable in angular position. The use of this rod alone is valuable in indicating to the person practicing with the device whether or not his head is kept stationary while making a swing of the arms and body. A further object of the invention however is to combine with this appliance a captive ball suspended preferably in an adjustable manner from the rod in such a way that the ball may rest on a floor or other surface with the thread or cord just slack so long as the head of the person using the appliance is not raised during the swing, the ball, however, being displaced by the thread or cord if at any point in the backward or forward swing the head is lifted. The ball in question my be a soft and light ball, for example a soft woolen ball such as is commonly designated a pom-pon, in order that when struck it shall have no considerable momentum imparted to it owing to its softness and lightness, and shall easily be stopped and brought back by the thread or cord.

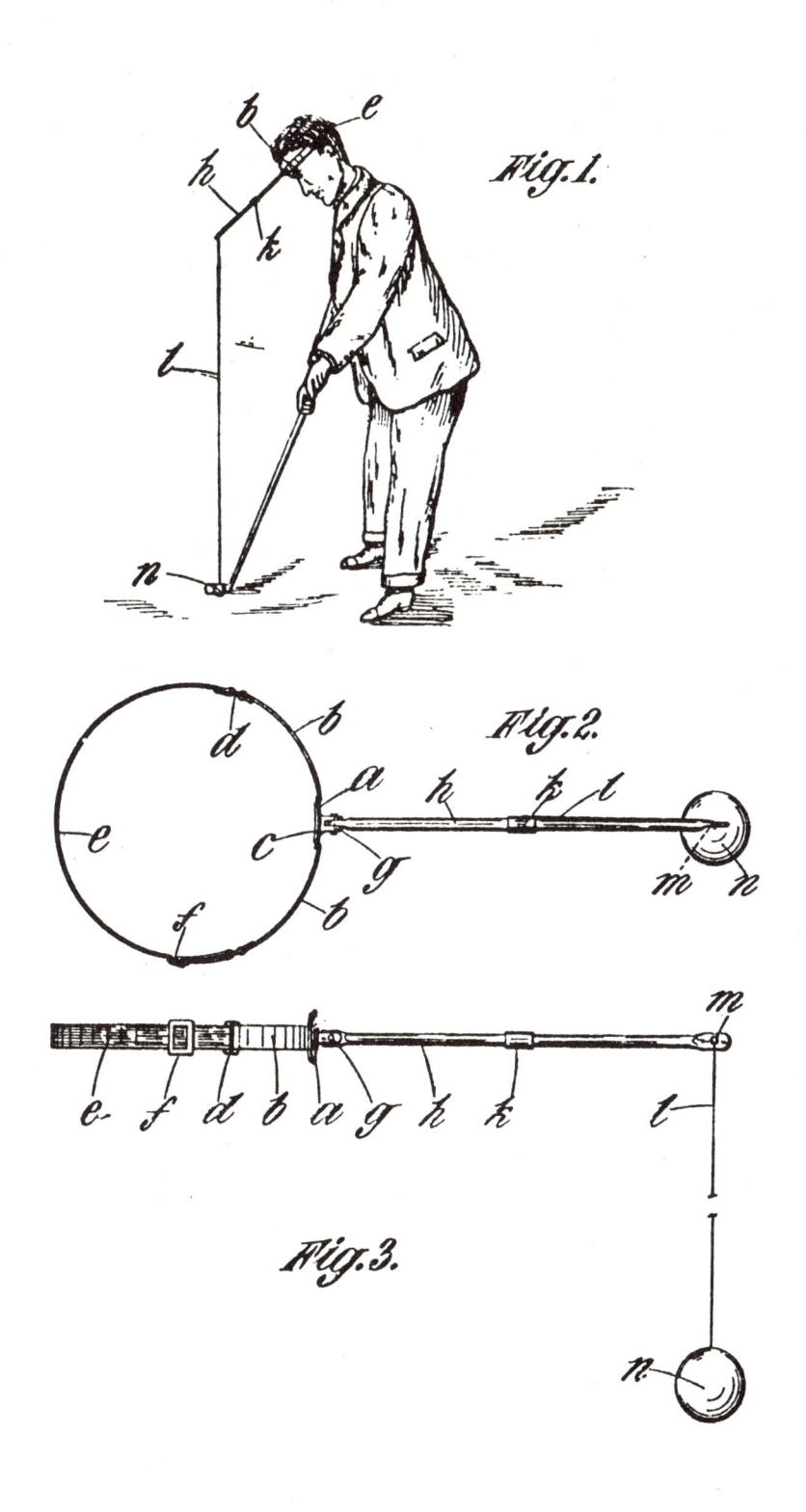

Fig.1.

Fig.2.

Fig.3.

The Patent Duffer

Golf Stance Steadying Device
Patent No. 1,636,086 (1927)
Richard Wolfe of Kenilworth, Illinois

The device is adapted to be positioned in use in contact with the neck of the player, as illustrated at **3** in Fig. 1. It may be placed against the neck and beneath the chin, so that by dropping the head and chin in the position which is normally assumed in addressing the ball, the device is held by friction with the flesh and retained under the chin throughout the stroke.

It will be obvious that should the player turn his head while the device is in the position illustrated, the projections **2**, which are slightly impressed in the flesh of the neck and the chin, will resist such turning movement and draw the flesh of the player in such manner as to immediately make him conscious of the fact that his turning his head. Furthermore the player is conscious by the sense of feeling of the presence of the device in the position illustrated, and is reminded thereby to keep his head down with the chin against the device to retain it in position.

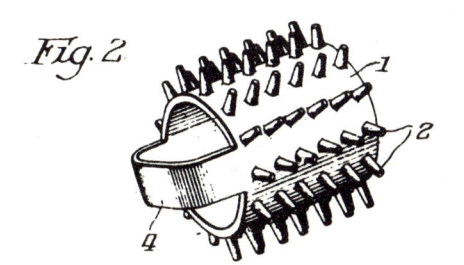

Fig. 1

Fig. 2

The Patent Duffer

Golfer's Head Restrainer

Patent No. 3,713,657 (1973)

Gabriel Presta of Racine, Wisconsin

A golfer's head is shown in FIG. **1** to be in a forward tilted position, and the golfer is wearing the restrainer of this invention. The restrainer has a collar portion, generally designated **12** and extending around the golfer's neck, and it has an upstanding portion, generally designated **13**. Therefore, the restrainer **11** engirdles the golfer's neck, and is releasably attached thereto, and the restrainer positions and holds the golfer's head in a forward tilted position so that the golfer is looking directly at a golf ball on the ground in front of the golfer in the normal position for hitting the ball, and the restrainer **11** restrains the golfer from being able to lift his head to the upright position, of course particularly while the golfer is executing the swing. That is, it is desired that a golfer retain his head in a forward tilted position throughout the action of swinging the club, during the back swing of the club, the moment of impact of the club on the ball, and also during the follow-through of the swing. The restrainer **11** of this invention has been found to retain the golfer's head in the desired forward tilted position throughout the swinging action mentioned.

The Patent Duffer 57

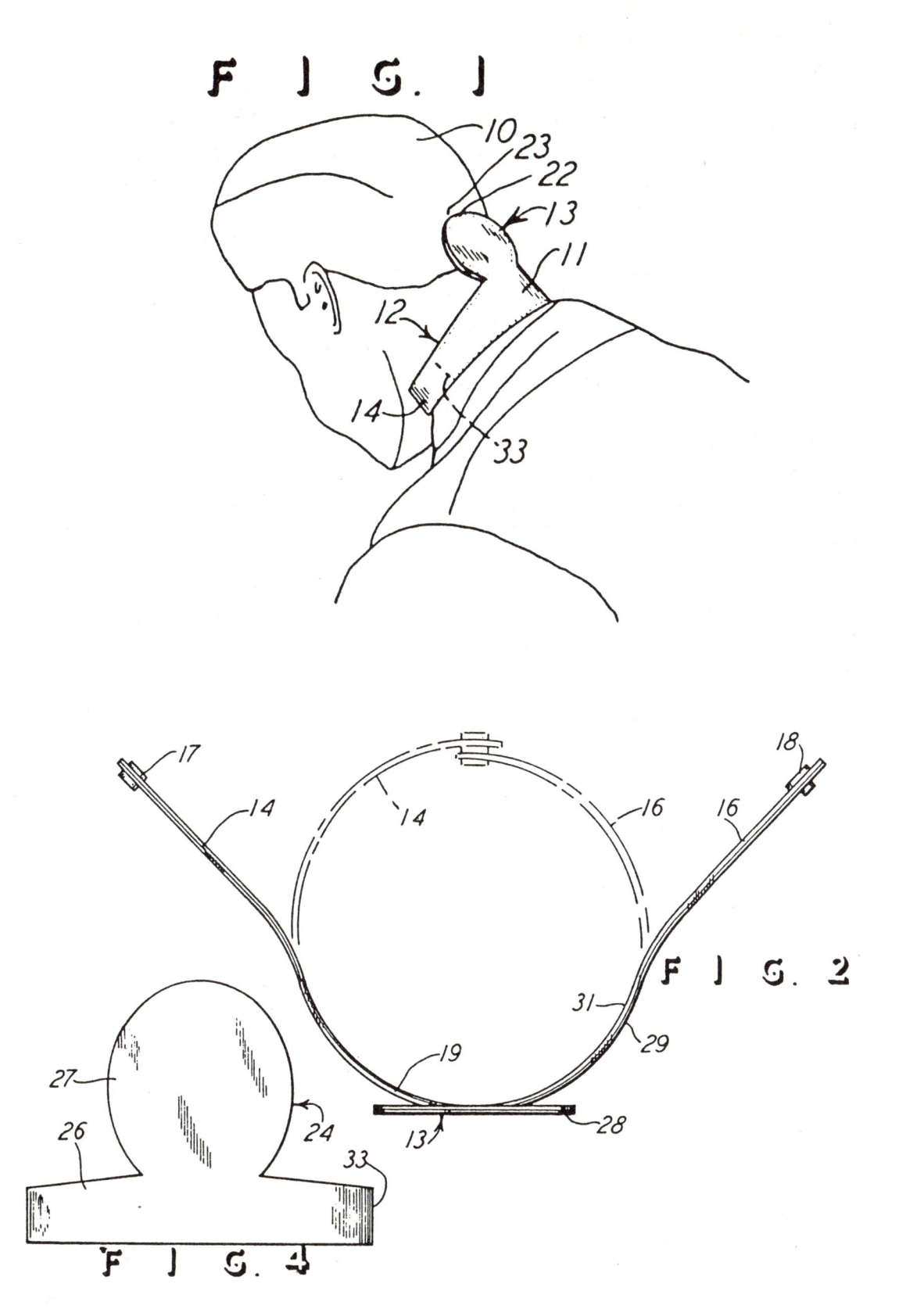

Golfer's Aid

Patent No. 3,063,721 (1962)

Albert Jackson & Sidney Inman of Des Moines, Iowa

To use our device it is recommended that the appropriate bow of the wearer's spectacles be extended through the two slot openings **20** and **21** as shown in FIG. 1. The tube **13** will be yielding held laterally outwardly and slightly downwardly from the head of the user with the ball **17** adjacent the wall **15**. If and when the head is raised and turned, the ball **17**, will however roll inwardly in the tubular member **13** and strike the sounding wall **16**, thereby audibly notifying the user that his head has moved from its position. When getting into position for the shot, the user will lower and slightly turn his head to get the ball to roll to a position adjacent the outer sounding wall **15**. The ball striking the wall **15** will audibly indicate to the user that the ball is in proper outward position. If the user is right handed, the device will be worn on the left bow of his spectacles as shown. Obviously if the user is left handed, he will wear the device on the right bow of his spectacles. When the player wishes to render the device non-operable, the tubular member on the bow is merely swung to a downwardly extending vertical position.

The Patent Duffer 59

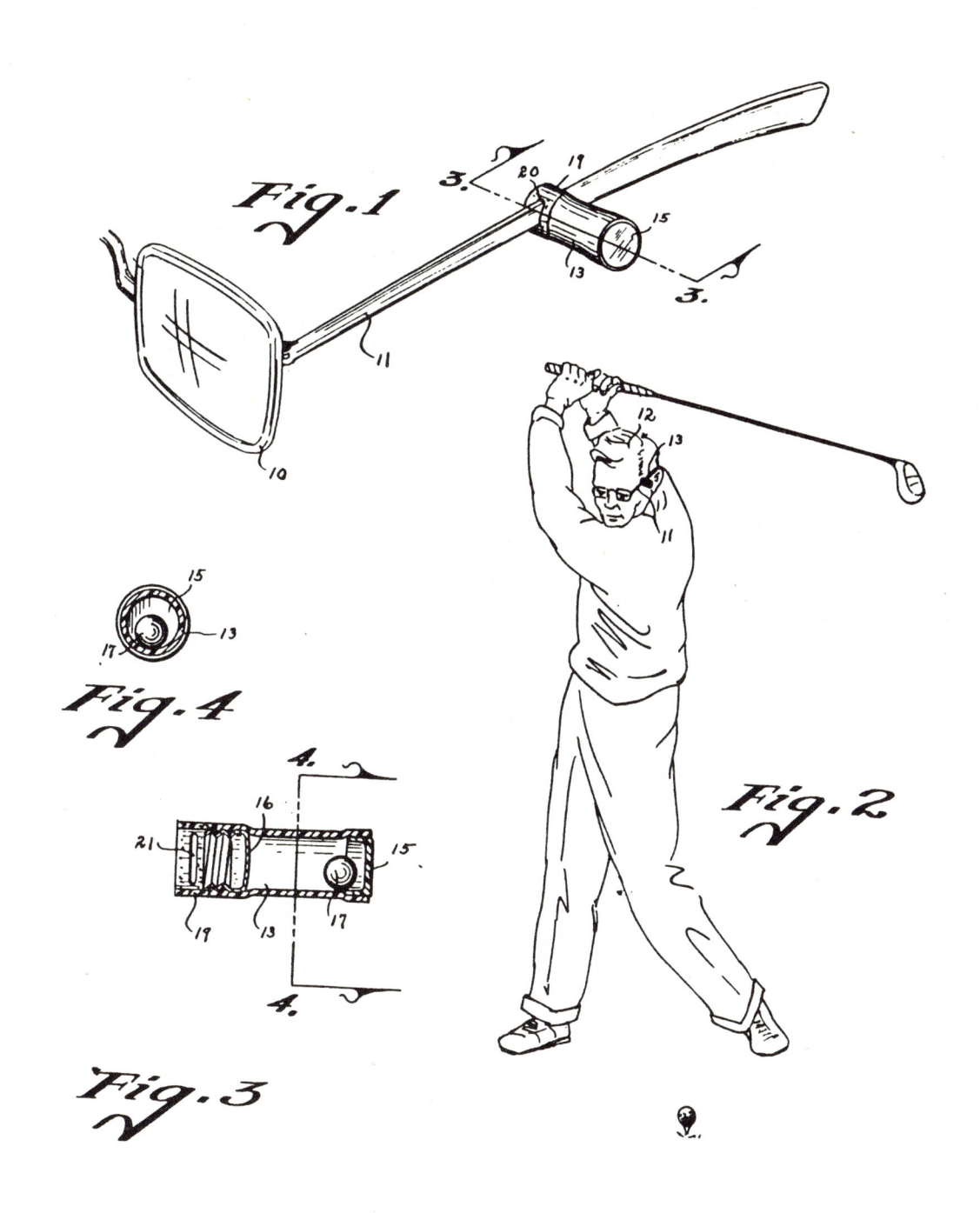

Golfing Aid
Patent No. 3,228,696 (1966)
Charles Hull of Greencastle, Pennsylvania

It is well known that it is frequently difficult to concentrate on the golf ball during the stance in addressing the ball and during the swing, especially when the golfer is under the stress of pressures from competition. It is an object of the present invention to provide a sighting means for a golfer to aid in keeping his head steady to prevent movement during the back swing.

A target sight **29** is provided on the lens **11** and a similar target sight **30** is provided on the lens **12**. These sights are preferably circular, although they may be of other shape, and should be dark and opaque. The sights may be placed on the lenses in any suitable manner such as by painting, engraving or decals. When plastic is used for the lenses, the sights may be etched into the surface of the plastic and then the etched surface may be filled with flat black ink or paint.

When using the sights to sight a golf ball, it will be found that the two sights, if properly adjusted, will blend to appear as a single, hazy, circular shadow encircling the ball. The ideal sights will provide the golfer with what appears as a circular shadow on the ground of about 15 inches in diameter which is just dark enough to be readily noticed when both eyes are focused on the ball.

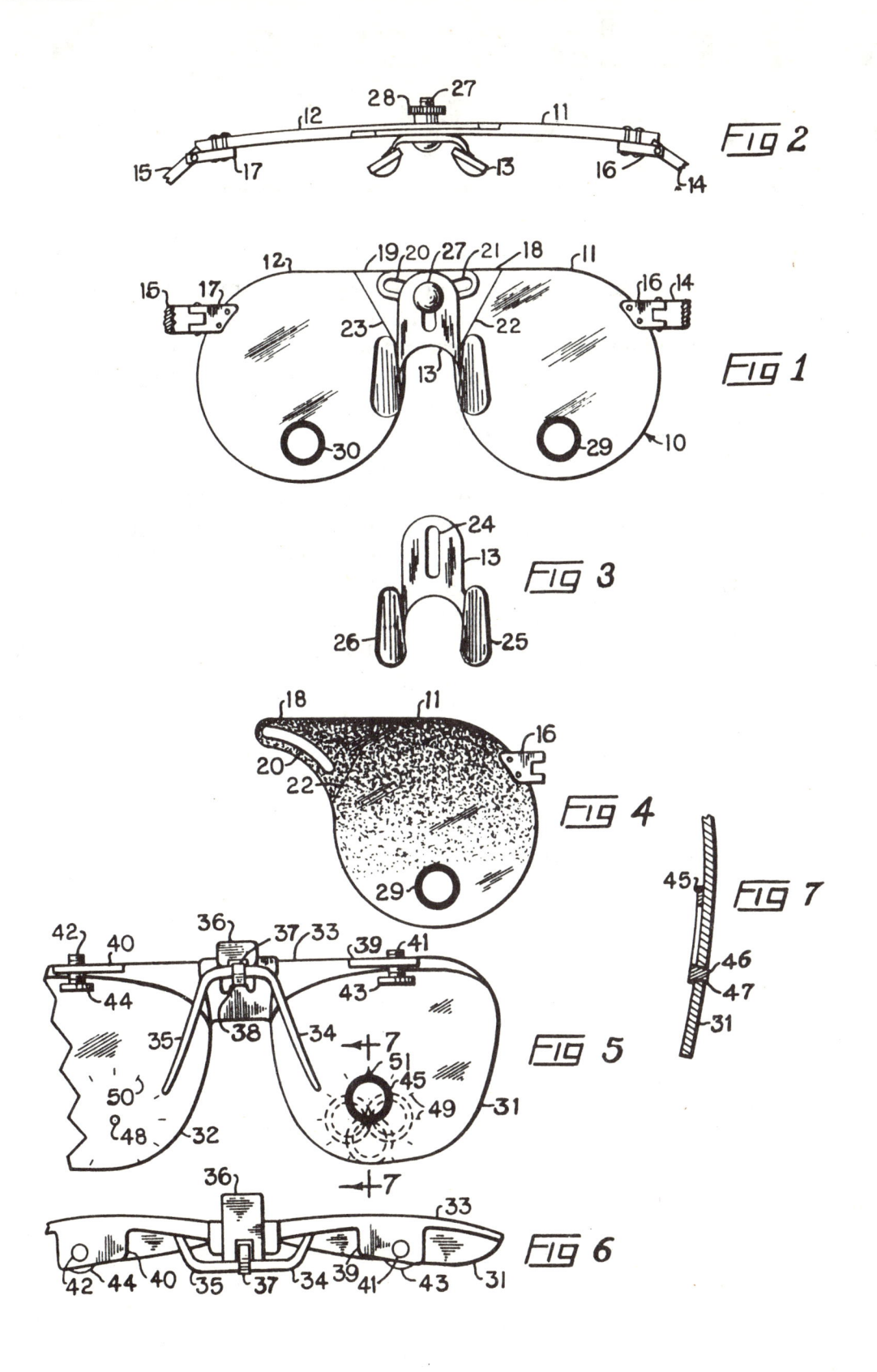

Fig 2

Fig 1

Fig 3

Fig 4

Fig 7

Fig 5

Fig 6

The Patent Duffer   61

THREE
Golfers In Bondage – Not A Pretty Sight

Obviously the golf swing is not an easy movement to learn. Golf professionals all over the country have this fact to thank for their livelihood. It's one thing to understand with one's brain what the body should be doing during the swing, and quite another for the body to do it. For this reason, there is a whole family of golfers who think the answer to grooving a swing is to strap themselves up in a variety of harnesses, belts, cables and other machinery. These masochists obviously feel that if their muscles won't respond to their brains, maybe they will respond to a measure of punishment or constraint or force. Basically we have two different approaches to these training devices; one type tries to limit what you shouldn't be doing, the other type tries to force you to do what you should be doing.

For instance, Andrew Volk of Duluth, Minnesota was convinced that the reason he was topping and sclaffing (his own words) was because his body was turning simultaneously with the downward movement of his arms. To delay his hips until his hands started down, he came up with the **Golf Instructing Apparatus** (page 64). Current swing theory holds the exact opposite opinion, which is the reason you don't see many of Andrew's machines anywhere. It's also probably the reason Andrew never broke 120.

> Golf is an awkward set of bodily contortions designed to produce a graceful result.
>
> *Tommy Armour*

If you don't have a clue as to what the swing should really feel like, try the **Golf Practicing Apparatus** (page 72). George Jenks of St. Petersburg, Florida has come up with the ultimate way to learn to swing a golf club. All you have to do is strap your feet, waist and head to this machine, grip the club, and have somebody turn the apparatus on. It will turn you, twist you, bend you, rotate you, and generally compel you to swing properly. If you can survive – and have a good orthopedic surgeon – you will then become a bionic golfing machine, the ultimate marriage of man and machine. Reportedly, George was last seen working on a portable version of the apparatus which could be used on the course.

Did you ever walk into a clothesline at neck level? That's about the feeling you'll get every time you follow through with the **Training Device** (page 74) of Everett and George Wilson of Duluth, Minnesota. Since the golfing season in Duluth is all of about two good months, these Northern hackers have lots of time on their hands to come up with all manner of golfing bondage.

So if you've tried and tried everything your pro has told you, read all the self-help books, watched all the how-to videos, and your body still won't respond, maybe you should strap yourself into one of these things.

The Patent Duffer 63

Golf Instructing Apparatus
Patent No. 1,703,375 (1929)
Andrew Volk of Duluth, Minnesota

A common fault in the golf swing and one which strongly contributes to slicing, topping, sclaffing, and mistiming is the improper pivoting of the body in relation to the movement of the arms on the downward swing. Particularly in the full swing, as with a wooden club or a mid-iron, the natural tendency at the top of the swing is to turn the body simultaneously with downward movement of the arms. This results in the hands leading the club head in respect to the ball, producing some or all of the faults previously mentioned.

It is a purpose of my invention to provide an apparatus capable of being readily applied to the body and operating to restrain pivoting of the body in a golf swing in a manner to delay body pivoting at the top of the down swing momentarily and just long enough to cause the arms to initiate the down swing independently of the body, that is to say, in advance of any turning movement of the body whence the proper relation is assumed of the arms, body, and club head to the perfect striking of the ball.

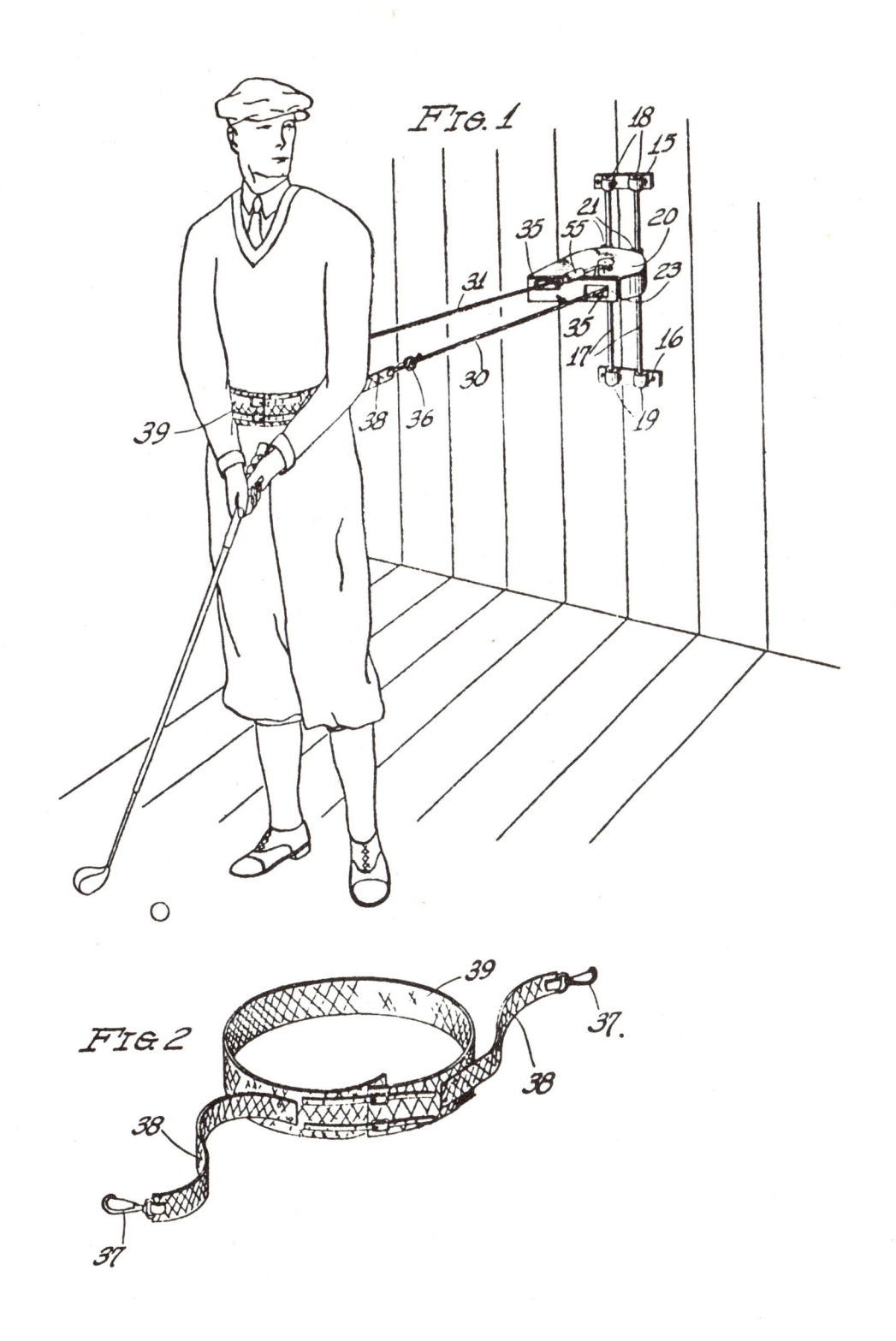

Fig. 1

Fig. 2

Golf Form Apparatus
Patent No. 1,530,519 (1923)
Charles Remington of Indianapolis, Indiana

It is well known that it is the tendency of the average beginner or player who has not acquired proper form, to raise his body when swinging the club back preparatory to striking the ball. In some instances the body is elevated on the toes, and usually the shoulders or upper portion of the body is also raised in bringing the club up. In order to acquire proper form and be able to strike the ball squarely and follow through, that tendency to raise up must be overcome. The feet must remain fixed on the ground, and the upper portion of the body, the waist, shoulders, and head must remain in fixed position. Only a turning movement of the waist and shoulders with the corresponding movement of the legs may be had, while the feet and head remain in fixed position.

It is the object of this invention to provide a brace for holding and maintaining the body from any vertical or upward movement when swinging back for a stroke, said brace permitting the required lateral swing thereof. By swinging the club while held to the brace, the player is taught to swing without elevating the body, so that in actual play the natural tendency to do so will have been overcome.

The Patent Duffer   67

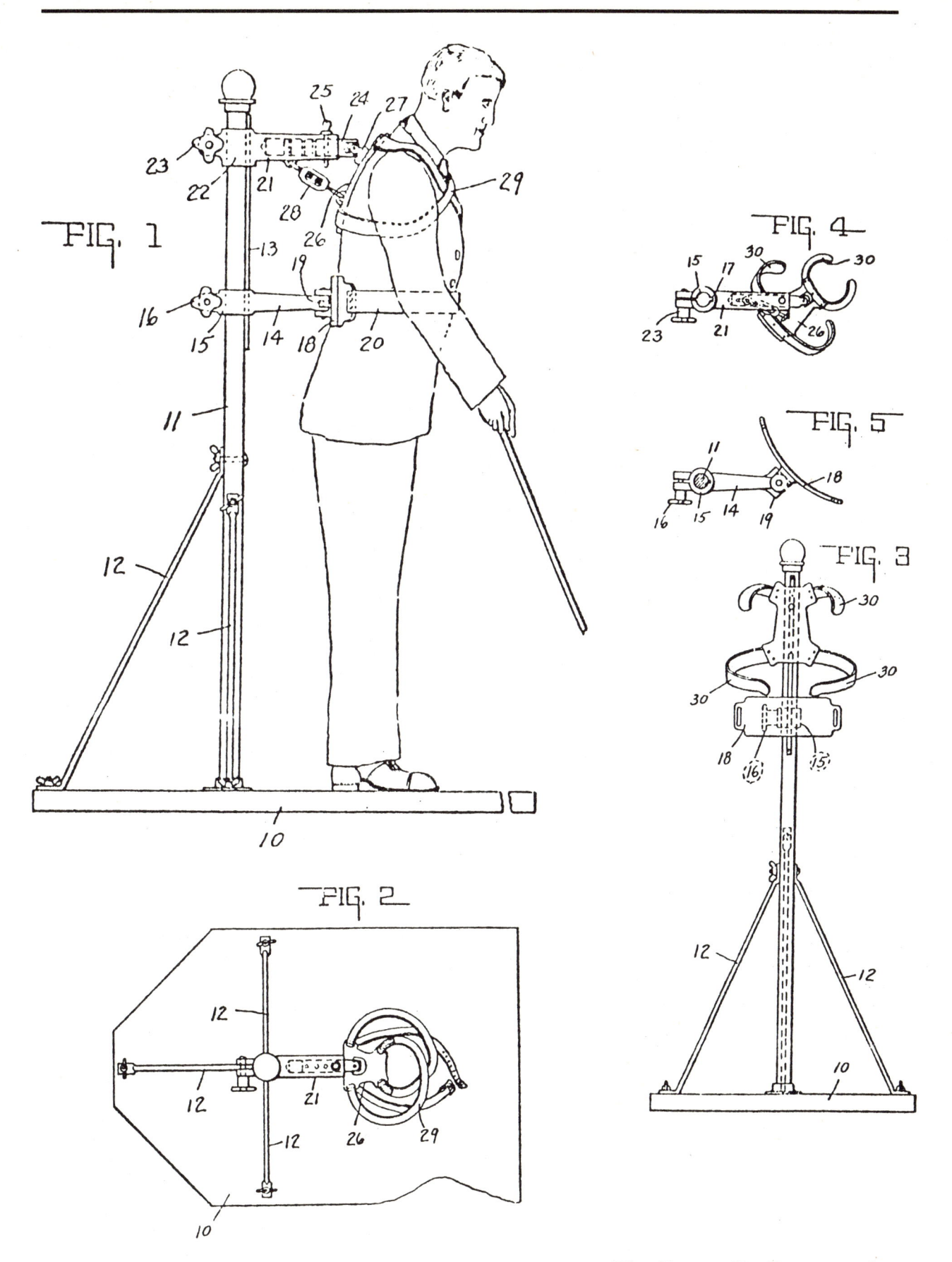

Golf Instructor
Patent No. 1,604,118 (1926)
William Glancy of Morristown, New Jersey

The invention has reference to a novel apparatus for habituating the player to the proper stance and body pose when addressing a golf ball with the club, as well as in the proper body movements which should accompany the swing of the club in order to effect accurate and powerful driving of the golf ball.

In making use of the novel golf instructor, the user first dons the body belt **17**, so that the same encircles the waist, with the guide arms **23** and **25** properly positioned for outward extension from the hips. The side members **10** and **11** of the guide frame **7** being opened, the user positions himself upon the platform **3** and within the embrace of said guide frame. The head brace **36** having been properly adjusted, the user's head is positioned beneath the same, and thereupon, the golf ball **B** or other suitable mark being placed in proper position in front of the user, and the golf club **C** grasped, the user is ready to begin practice.

The head brace **36** together with the proper positioning of the feet compels the player to assume the proper slightly crouched position ready for the swinging of the club **C**. In thus swinging back the club **C**, the player is compelled to turn the body at the waist from left to right, and in so doing causes the guide arm **23** to swing from left to right until stopped at the end of the slotted guideway **15**, thus establishing the desired initial position of the body preparatory to the driving stroke, and to habituate the player in training the eyes properly and constantly on the ball being thus addressed, said guide arm **23** may be interposed between the eye and the ball addressed.

The player having thus been compelled to assume the correct stance and bodily pose preparatory to the driving stroke, now swings the club **C** downward and upward from right to left through the arc of movement proper to the driving stroke. It will be evident that in making the swing, the guide frame **7** in cooperation with the guide arms moving therethrough will compel the player to make the proper body turning movements, without undue side sway or undue lifting or falling of the body, while at the same time the head brace **36** will aid the player in holding the head still and steadied against the temptation to undesirable turning movement.

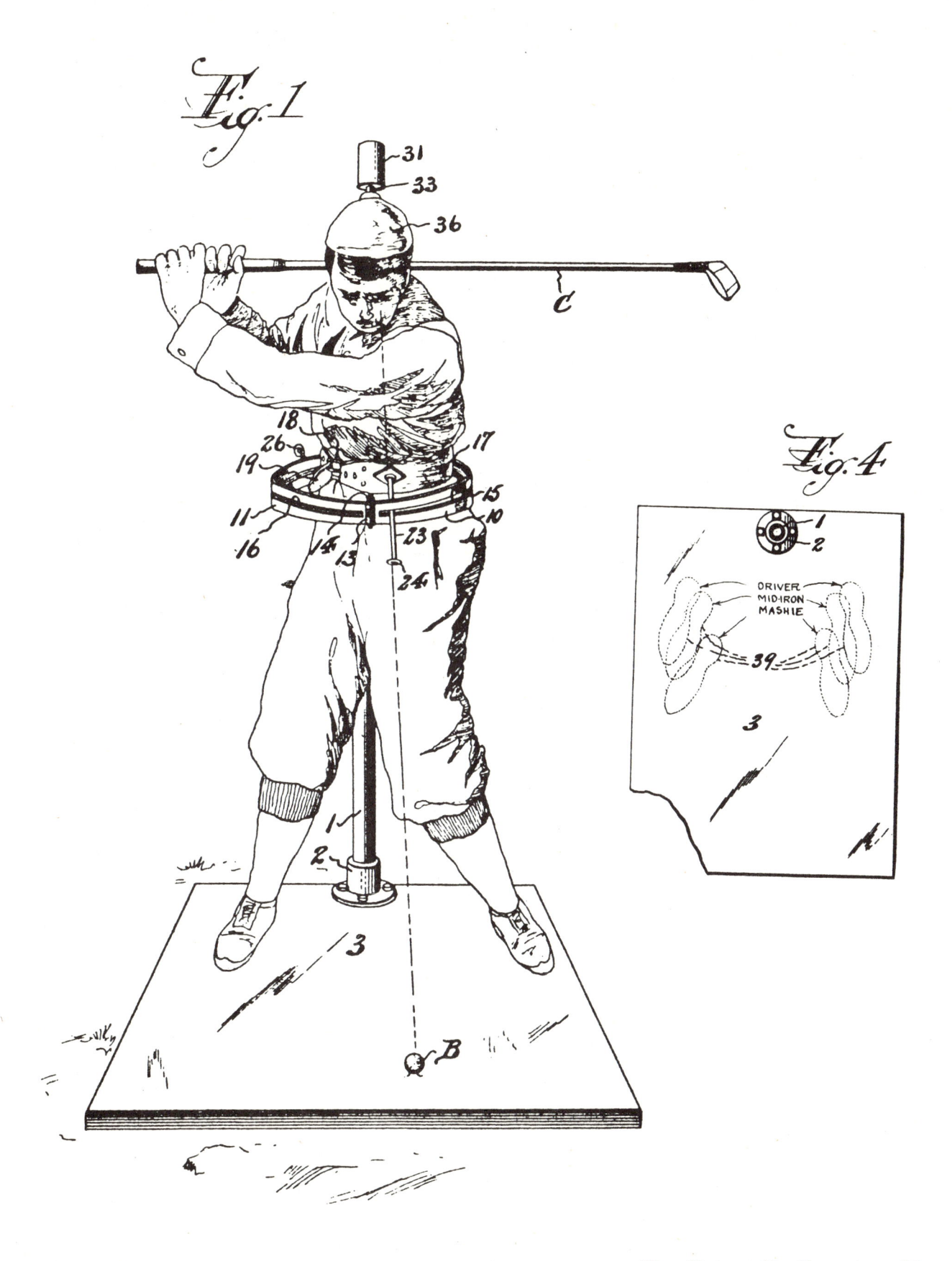

Fig. 1

Fig. 4

Golf Teaching And Playing Device
Patent No. 1,944,942 (1930)
Robert Macdonald of Chicago, Illinois

One object of the present invention is to provide a novel and practical device for guiding a golf club throughout the swing thereof in executing a golf shot, and to enable a player to get the "feel" of the club in its various positions throughout the swing.

In the use of the device as illustrated in the drawings, a player may take a position within the guides and frame, as shown in Figs. **1** and **3** of the drawings and from the position shown in Fig. **3**, with the club at the top of the swing, the club may be brought around through the desired path of movement and carried through to the completion of a full stroke, the gate **17** yielding as above described in a manner to permit the passage of the club shaft in its "follow through" movement to pass through the plane of the guide member **11** and to a position within the confines of the guide. The inner rail or guide **22**, during the swing movement of the club serves as a second point of contact with the club shaft in a manner to indicate or determine the angle of the shaft during the swinging movement of the club.

FIG. 1

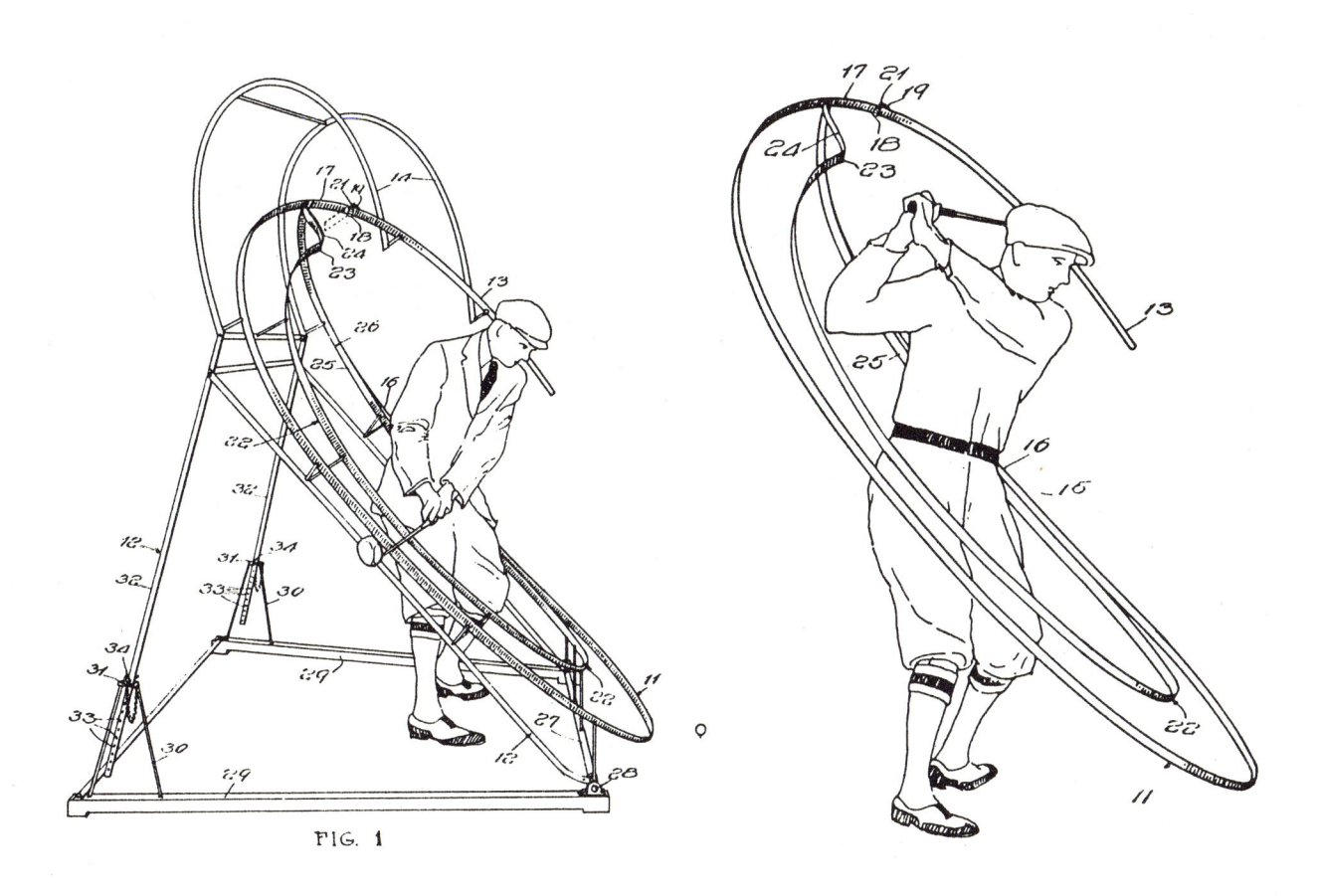

FIG. 3

The Patent Duffer   71

Golf Practicing Apparatus
Patent No. 2,626,151 (1953)
George Jenks of St. Petersberg, Florida

It is an object of this invention to provide a golf practice device which coordinates the individual motions of the principal parts of a golfer's body and thereby teaches an ideal golf swing.

While the average patent description of most inventions is about 4 columns long, Mr. Jenks uses 14 columns to describe the operation of this contraption. Basically it is a completely motorized swing trainer. All one has to do is hold on to the club for dear life when the machine is turned on, and the invention does everything else, from holding the head still to turning the hips and swinging the club all at the proper moment and speed. The complete description has been reproduced in the Appendix for those who might want to build one of these.

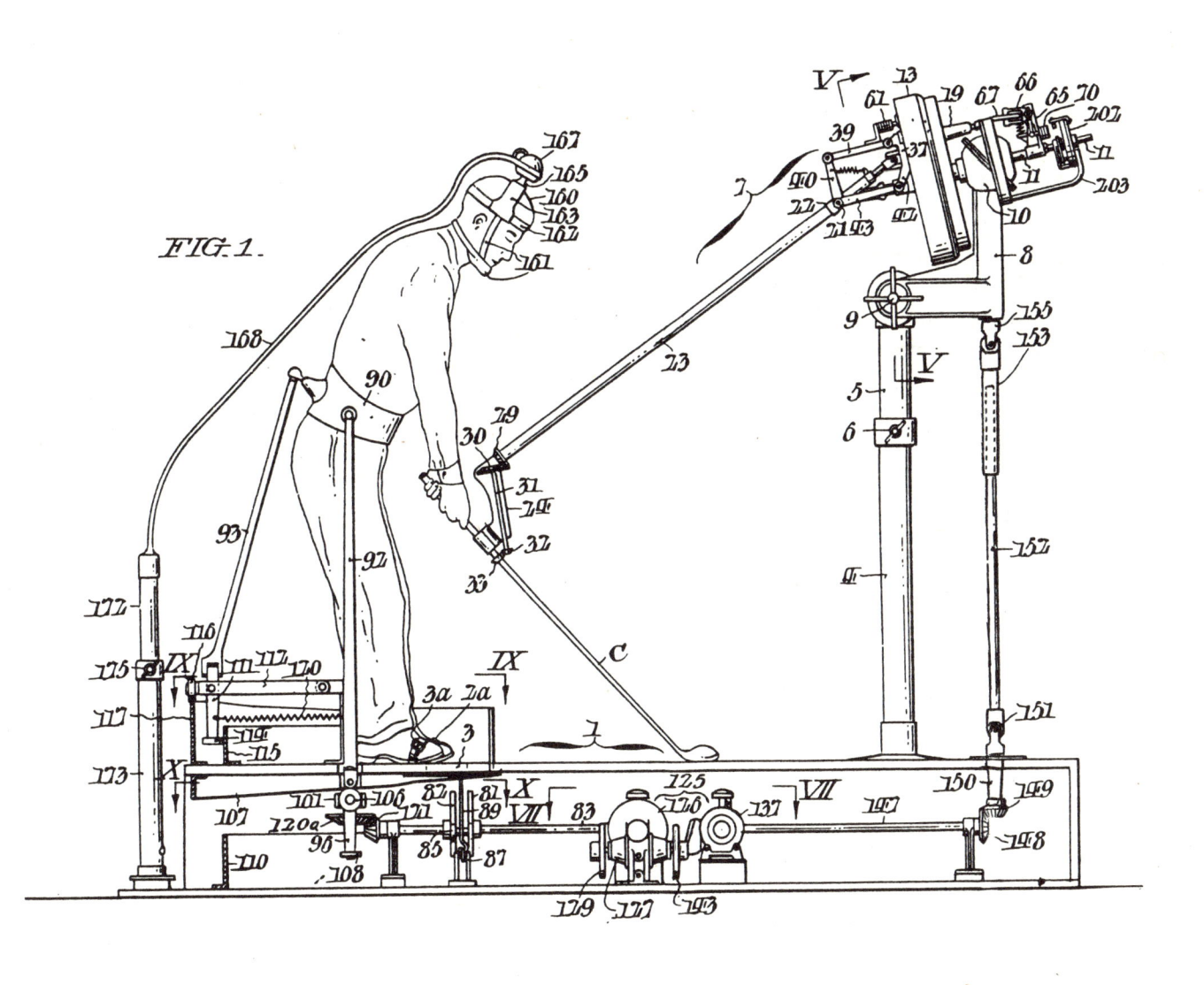

FIG. 1.

The Patent Duffer

Training Device
Patent No. 1,962,256 (1934)
E. Nelson & George Wilson of Duluth, Minnesota

The principal object of the present invention is to provide a training or exercising device which will materially assist, if not actually force, the practicer to swing at and hit the ball in the scientifically correct manner by preventing movement of the head except pivotally, and by causing a proper action stress which certain otherwise dormant muscles essential to the correct swing must overcome, and thereby become properly exercised and developed.

To the extreme outer end of the extension **3** is attached as by a suitable ball and socket joint **9** the helmet **10**, this latter preferably being of the ordinary padded football type of headgear. The advantage of such a structure is obvious when the facts are considered, as before stated, that one of if not the most essential feature of a correct swing necessitates only pivotal movement of the head. However at the conclusion of the swing it is quite desirable that comparatively free upward motion of the head be permitted, so that no undue stress results from anchoring of the head in the proper position.

The Patent Duffer 75

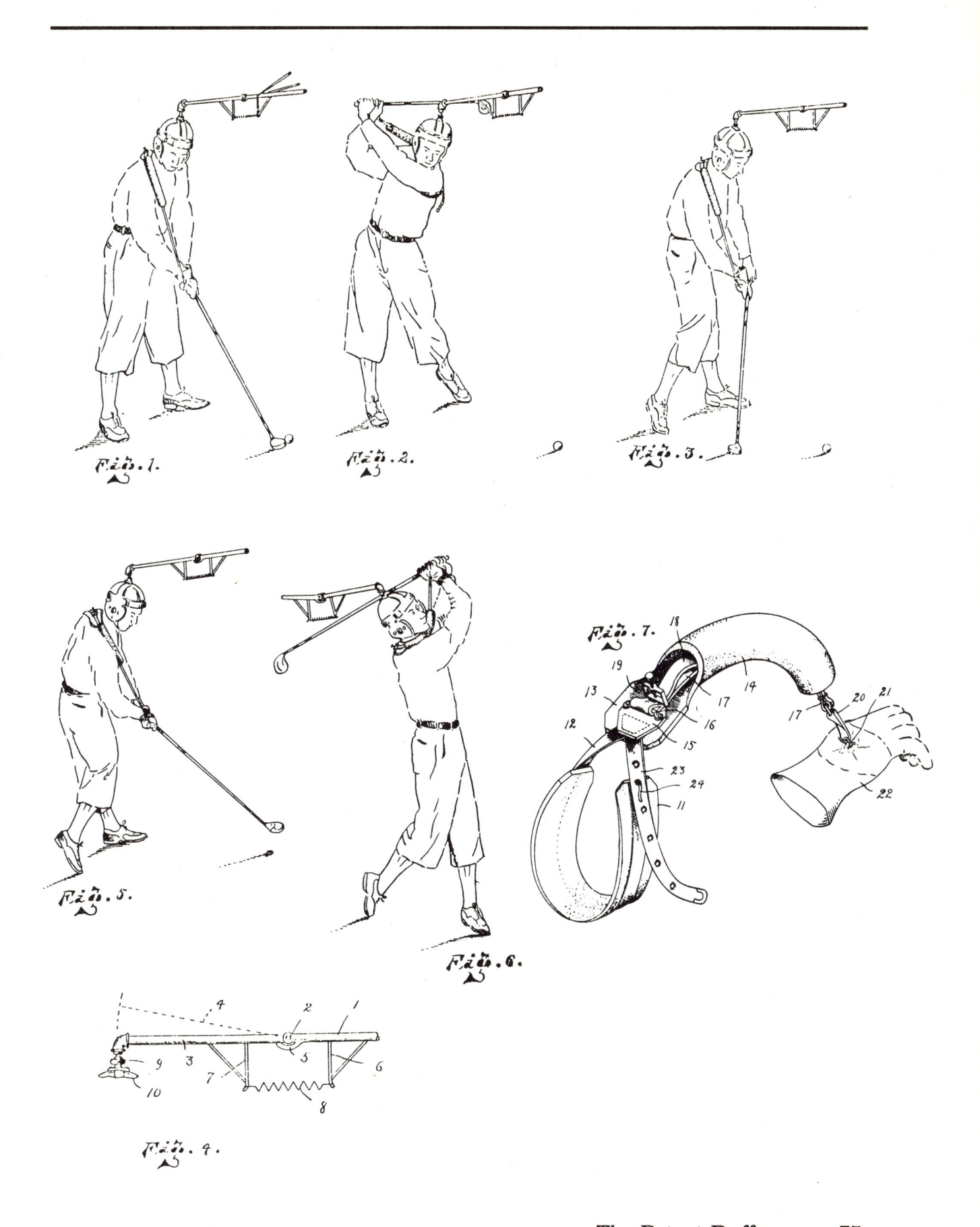

FOUR
Save Your Strength – Don't Bend Over

There's no question golf is a physical game. First you have to lift a heavy bag and cooler out of the trunk and carry them all the way to the clubhouse. Then you have to hoist all this equipment up and put it in the golfcart. You're already breathing hard and you haven't even swung a club yet. Then you start to play, and some courses don't allow golf carts on the fairway so there is all that walking to the ball. Putting isn't that strenuous, so if we subtract 30 strokes or so from an average of 110 strokes a game, we come up with 80 times the club is swung with considerable effort. Say you take two full-speed practice swings for each shot, that's another 160 swings, so we're talking about 240 all-out swings. Thinking about it in fitness jargon, that translates into 24 sets of 10 repetitions each. Now think about all the bending over that's involved – tying your spikes, teeing up the ball, picking the ball up out of the hole, picking up the flag-stick. The people who say you don't have to be an athlete to play golf just don't know what they're talking about.

In the all-American tradition of laborsaving devices, some industrious golfers have striven to eliminate that most dreaded aspect of the game – bending over. Think about it for just a minute. You start the game by bending over to tee up the ball. In a complete round, that's 18 bend-overs right there, or quite a few more, counting mulligans.

Victor Armstrong of Short Hills, New Jersey has stooped to conquer this particularly vexing problem. While the golfer stands in an upright position, this clever **Device For Setting Golf Balls And Tees** (page 80) automatically sets a ball on top of a tee, and inserts the whole thing in the ground. Like magic, never once do the golfer's hands leave his arms, or fall below his knees for this operation.

> If you watch a game, it's fun.
> If you play it, it's recreation.
> If you work at it, it's golf.
>
> *Bob Hope*

Obviously, you need to bend over at least 18 times a round to pick your ball up out of the hole. Well, Lewis Coleman of San Diego, California is one man who has evidently bent over once too often. With his **Ball Projecting Cup** (page 78) he hopes to eliminate this particular twist from the game. If his device was installed at your course, you would simply press the bottom of the cup with the end of your putter, and the spring loaded cup would rocket your ball into the air where it might easily be caught. Just be careful about how hard you put the flagstick back in.

And talking about flagsticks, that's another piece of equipment that has to be picked up all the time. Ever had a partner who feels it's never his turn to pick up the flagstick even if he putted out first? He's not lazy, just smart; he know's how tiring it is to constantly bend over, and is just conserving his strength. A weary Roger Baird, Jr. of Henrico, Virginia must have a partner like this, as he has created the **Golf Flagpole Retriever** (page 82). With this cage-like device attached to the flagstick, you simply hook it with the putter and lift the whole thing up without ever bending a knee. That's another 18 total bend-overs eliminated.

So let's see now, if every course were equipped with a ball projecting cup, the flagsticks all had retrievers, and you had your automatic device for setting a golf ball, that's 54 total bend-overs a round you could save. Just for fun, put the book down a minute and bend over 54 times. Now you know why you're so tired after 18 holes.

Ball Projecting Golf Cup
Patent No. 3,792,861 (1974)
Lewis Coleman of San Diego, California

The ball ejecting golf cup of the instant invention has been designed to provide a means whereby a golf ball may be quickly upwardly ejected from a golf cup to an elevation above the ground sufficient to enable the golf ball to be grasped by a golfer without bending down toward the ground.

After the cup has been recessed in the ground in the manner illustrated, a golf ball such as ball **32** may be played into the cup **10** with the ball coming to rest in the upwardly opening recess defined by the grid or spider **26**. Then, the lower handle end **54** of an inverted putter **56** may be hand depressed downwardly into the cup so as to engage the lower end of the inverted club with the top of the ball. Further movement of the club downwardly will therefore cause downward displacement of the ball supporting and ejecting structure including the grid or spider and the lower portion. Thus, the spring will be compressed and the undersurface of the upper plate will engage the suction cup. Then upon removal of the lower end of the inverted club the suction cup will retain the plate in its lowermost position until such time as sufficient air bleeds through the vent passage to enable the spring to overcome the holding force of the suction cup whereupon the spring will project the lower portion and the grid as well as the ball supported therefrom upwardly with force great enough to propel the ball a distance from the ground whence it may be caught with a cap or other means.

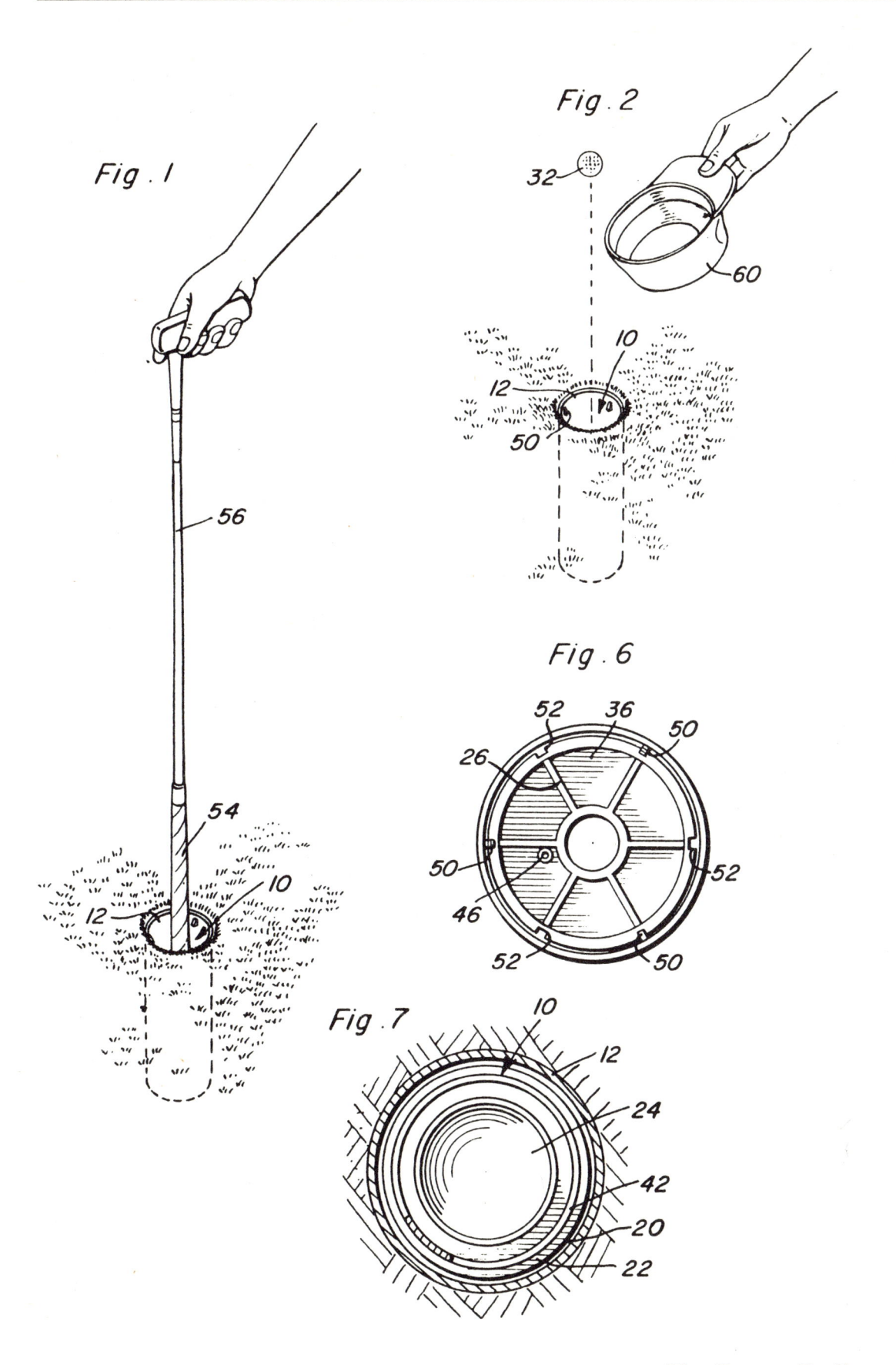

Fig. 1

Fig. 2

Fig. 6

Fig. 7

The Patent Duffer 79

Device For Setting Golf Balls And Tees

Patent No. 2,609,198 (1952)

Victor Armstrong of Short Hills, New Jersey

Ordinarily, a golf player must first place a tee in position, and then place his ball on the tee. This frequently requires much stooping, squatting, or bending of the body and in some cases, for example, convalescents, elderly people, or those having certain physical handicaps, this part of the game proves an annoyance.

Accordingly, one of the objects of the invention is to provide a device which will enable a golfer, by a single operation, properly to place a ball on a tee, ready for driving, without bending or stooping, thereby making it possible to accomplish this objective with the golfer standing in a substantially erect or fully erect position.

When the device is to be used, a tee **T** may be placed in the slot **4** and the golf ball **B** centered upon the head of the tee. Upon finger pressure being applied to the plunger through the button **8**, the plunger head **6** will descend toward the ball and hold the ball in the seat **6a** to clamp the same to the tee, as shown in Figure **3**. The device is then moved toward the ground at the selected location and with the ball constituting a coupling between the plunger and the tee, and downward force applied to the entire assembly will drive the tee into the ground. Finger pressure on the button **8** may then be released so that the cupped clamping head of the plunger will move clear of the ball. The entire device may then be moved in a lateral direction parallel to and rearwardly of the slot to disengage said slot **4** from the head of the tee, leaving the ball mounted on the tee and ready for driving.

Fig.2. Fig.1. Fig.3.

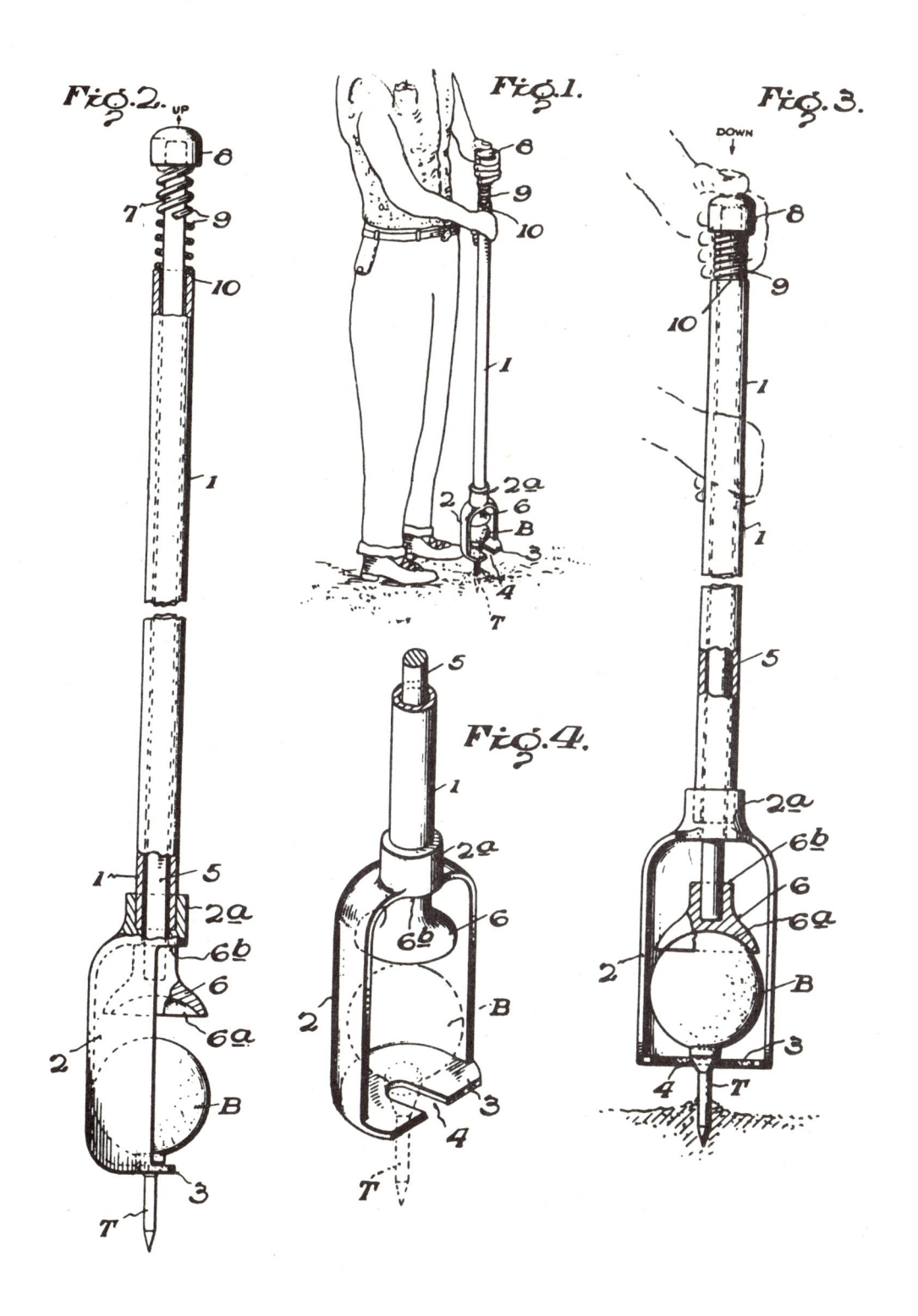

Fig.4.

The Patent Duffer 81

Golf Flagpole Retriever
Patent No. 3,310,026 (1967)
Roger Baird Jr. of Henrico, Virginia

Golf rules require flag poles be removed while golfers putt out. Golfers without caddies normally drop the pole onto the green, complete their putting and then one of the group has to stoop or bend over to pick up the pole and return it to an upright position in the cup. The object of this invention is to provide a device which enables golfers to retrieve a golf flag pole, from a lying on the green position, without the golfer having to bend over to reach the pole on the green. My device, allows golfers to hook or snag the flag pole assembly with use of their putter as a hook on an extended handle.

FIG. 3 shows a golfer **7**, using his putter shaft **8**, and putter blade **9** as a hook on an extended handle and hooking into rod-like members of cage-like enclosure of my retriever. This golfer is ready to raise the flag pole, **6**, by flexing his right wrist and elbow. After raising the pole, by actions of his right arm, the golfer can grasp the pole **6** or the flag **5**, and thus readily, without stooping or bending, return the flag pole to its upright position in the cup **15**, of **FIG. 2**.

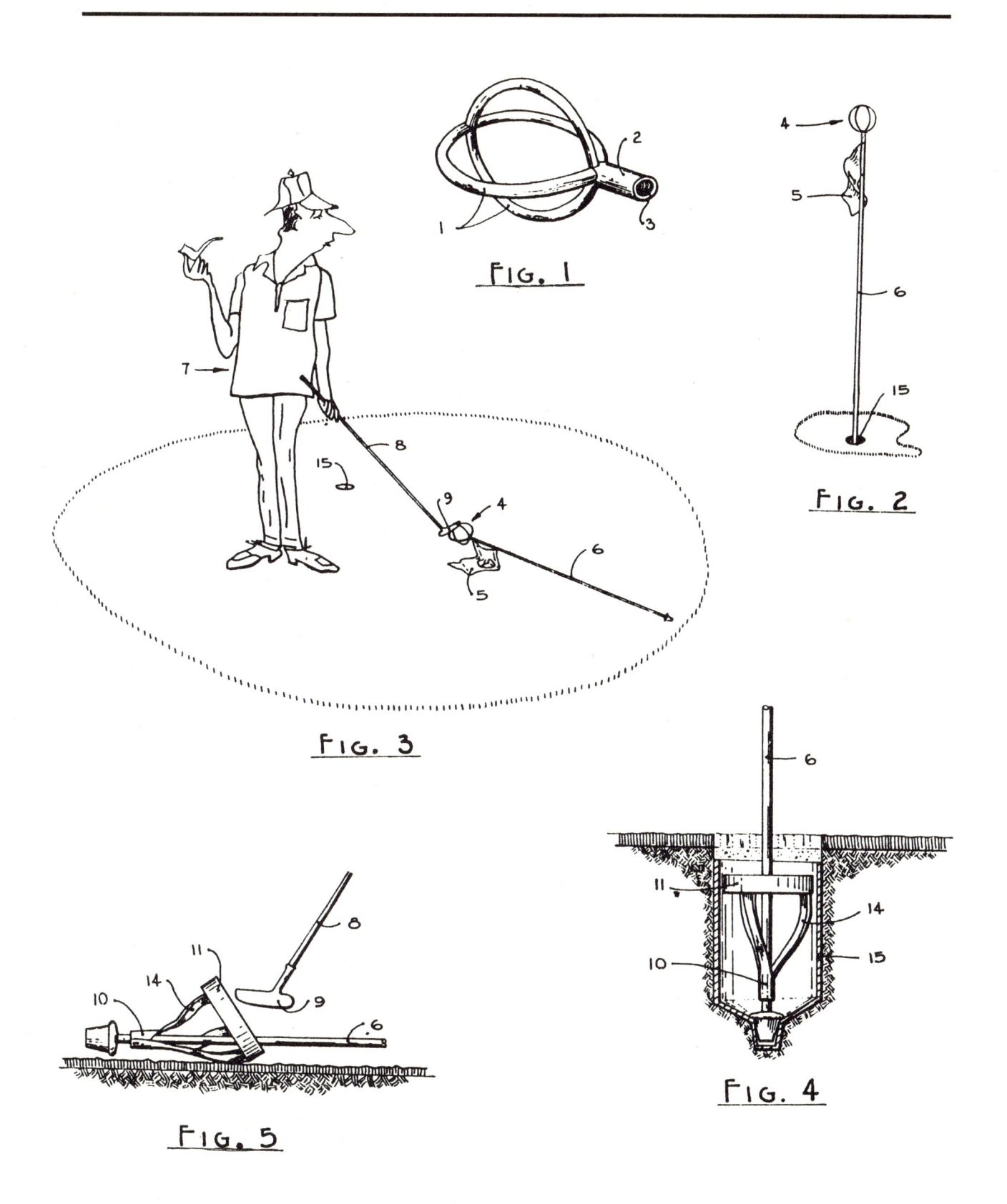

FIG. 1

FIG. 2

FIG. 3

FIG. 4

FIG. 5

The Patent Duffer   83

Golf Club

Patent No. 1,960,110 (1934)

Albert Iles of Hoylake, England

The object of the invention is to provide a golf club which in addition to its ordinary use in the playing of the game is adapted to assist in the picking up of golf balls by a player either from the green or out of a hole.

According to the present invention a golf club has an opening in the sole of the head which is capable of expansion to allow a ball to pass there-through, and of contraction after such expansion to retain said ball above the opening.

The inner portion **3** has a recess **7** formed on its inner surface for accommodation of part of the disc **4** when bent upwardly as shown in dotted lines, to allow passage through the sole of a golf ball **8**. Thus when it is desired to pick up a golf ball, the sole of the club is pressed over the top of the ball, so that the disc or washer **4** is bent upwardly to cause enlargement of the opening **9** therein, whereon the ball passes through the sole into the position shown in **Figure 1**, where-upon the disc **4** returns to its normal position and retains the ball within the opening **10**. The club may then be lifted and the ball removed from the club head.

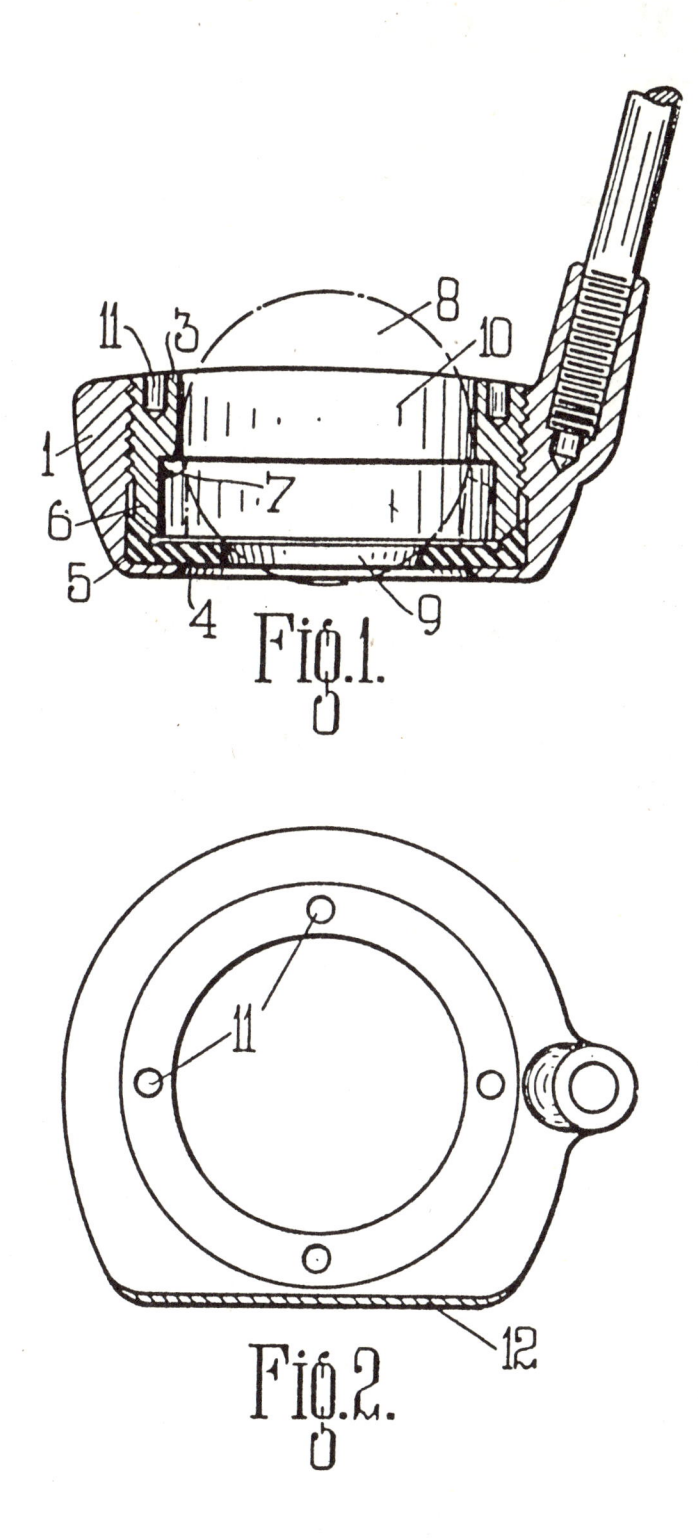

Fig.1.

Fig.2.

The Patent Duffer 85

Golf Ball Retriever
Patent No. 3,169,790 (1965)
John Kaanehe of Honolulu, Hawaii

During a game of golf it becomes necessary to retrieve the golf balls many times during the course of play and often the ball cones to rest in places where the same cannot be retrieved by ordinary means. Accordingly an object of my invention is to provide a novel golf ball retriever, whereby a golf ball may be readily retrieved from normally inaccessible places.

The manner in which the golf ball retriever is used is believed obvious from the foregoing description, for example, golf balls are retrieved simply and easily by swinging the retriever toward a golf ball **B** to provide a scooping action, see FIGURE 3. Thus, as illustrated, by this action a golf ball is scooped up in an upward swinging motion of the retriever by the golfer to the left and with a naturally resulting tilting of the head portion **13** to the right so the ball will roll easily into the retriever over the feathered edge **25** of the sill **19**.

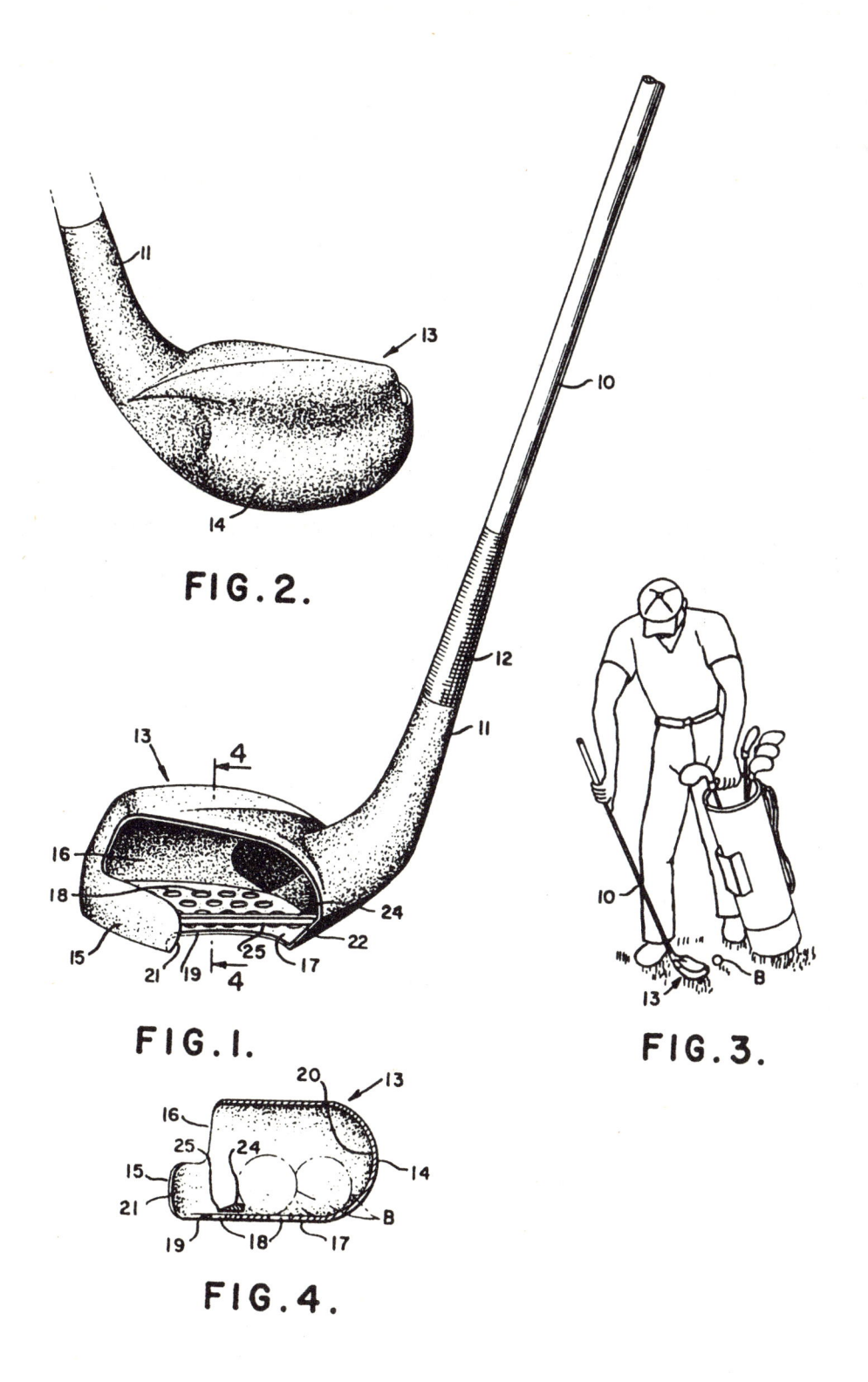

FIG. 2.

FIG. 1.

FIG. 3.

FIG. 4.

The Patent Duffer   87

Golf Tee Holder And Carrier
Patent No. 1,948,284 (1934)
August Breitbarth of Valparaiso, Indiana

The purpose of my invention is to provide a self-contained golf tee holder that is readily attached in a detachable manner to a golf bag; that provides a carrier stem of sufficient length so that the user need not stoop down to put the tee into use; that near the lower end of the stem a wire loop is pivoted to freely swing all around the stem when the golf ball is hit by the player; that enables the user to place the golf ball on the wire loop before the stem is pressed into the ground; that when not in use to form a tee the wire loop can be folded upward against the stem to not project from it as the holder is suspended from the golf bag; and that by reason of a shaped knob attached to the upper end of the stem the entire device is readily handled without inconvenience and without ever stooping down to put it into use, as is common with devices proposed heretofore.

The combined support and carrier comprises a long stem **1** which may be tubular or solid. It may be approximately thirty-one inches long so that the player need never stoop in putting the device into use. Golf tees proposed heretofore have comprised short pins on top of which the golf ball is placed. Such tees cannot be used without the player bending over so as to reach the ground to place the tee in position to receive the golf ball. This needless effort becomes wearisome to such an extent as to seriously interfere with the recreative value of the sport

The stem is pressed into the ground as deep as desired, as instanced at **5**. The ball **8** is to be positioned at varying distances above the ground according to the wishes of different players and the stem is pressed into the ground variably without having the sleeve **11** engage the ground. The ball **8** may however be positioned still closer to the ground at a slight angle as shown by the dotted line **21** on Fig. **1**. This will lower the carrier **6** to the dotted line **22**.

The Patent Duffer

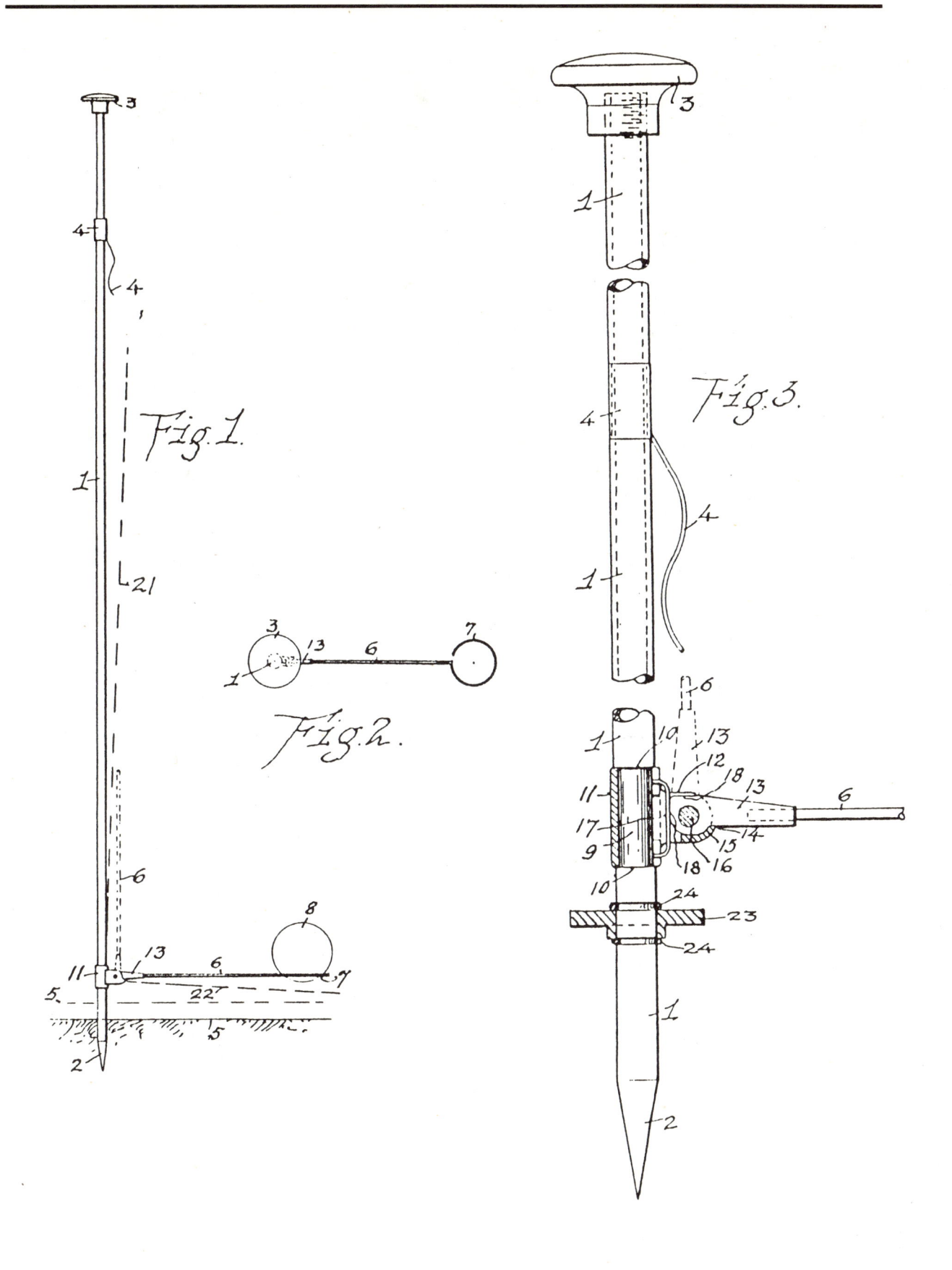

FIVE

Grips & Gloves

Wrapping the handles of various tools and implements with strips of leather insures a firm grip, has been known since Roman times. Whenever critical work is being done, it is obvious that the hands must remain firmly in control of the tool being used.

In some instances when extremely critical work is being done, say during brain surgery, or when one is swinging a golf club, an extra measure of security is needed. If the surgeon's scalpel were to slip to the slightest degree, a lifesaving procedure could quickly become a gruesome disaster. Equally gruesome and disastrous, in some golfing minds, is the occurrence of the golf club slipping upon impact with the ball. If the club rotates one-eighth of an inch upon impact, a golf ball can be 10 yards off its intended target. What about the club flying out of a golfer's hands after an overzealous swing? To minimize these risks, specialized gloves and grips are definitely called for.

Basil Finney of Arlington, California has applied space-age technology to this slippery dilemma. His **Interlocking Glove And Handle** (page 92) utilizes Velcro strips on the glove and handle of the club to guarantee a no-slip grip. It also makes a wonderful tearing noise when your opponent is about to drive.

> Golf is not a game of great shots.
> It's a game of the most misses.
> The people who win make the smallest mistakes.
>
> *Gene Littler*

Can't figure out exactly where your fingers should go on the shaft? William Mohr of Chicago, Illinois seems to have modified a toilet bowl plunger to fit on your club and guide your hands. His **Grip Guide For Golf Clubs** (page 98) might not win any beauty prizes, but it could work if you could stop laughing long enough to use it.

If you favor a punk-rock look on the course, Wilmer Van Denburgh of Richmond, Virginia has the stylish golfer in mind. In addition to being eminently fashionable, all of the zippers, studs, straps, and snaps on his **Adjustable Golf Glove** (page 104) have a specific purpose. It also looks smashing with an all black outfit.

Having trouble keeping your hands dry in inclement weather? If you can find one, why not try the **Dry Grip Sleeve** (page 106). Tobias Koch of Drexel Hill, Pennsylvania has come up with an ingenious solution to a soggy problem; it's a kind of raincoat for your hands that is attached to the grip of the club. Tobias must be a dedicated golfer to think up a device that will let you continue play in a driving rain.

Whatever the solution, all of these geniuses have solved that slippery predicament of how to get a sure grip.

Interlocking Glove and Handle
Patent No. 3,368,811 (1968)
Basil Finney of Arlington, California

The primary object of the invention is to provide means for enabling a player to grip the handle of a sporting implement such as a golf club, in a non-slip grasp that will permit the player to relax the tension of his grip and concentrate on other details of the game or contest, with full confidence that the handle will not slip or shift in the slightest degree from the carefully applied handgrip with which he originally grasped the handle.

These objects are achieved by providing a glove having a patch of fabric material on the palm thereof, which is made with a large number of projecting loops of thread, or the like, which are adapted to be hooked by a large number of hooks projecting from fabric material wrapped around the handle of the implement. This type of interlocking fabric is commercially available under the trademark Velcro, in the form of two cooperating tapes, which are adapted to be sewn to opposite edges of a closure for the purpose of providing a separable fastener.

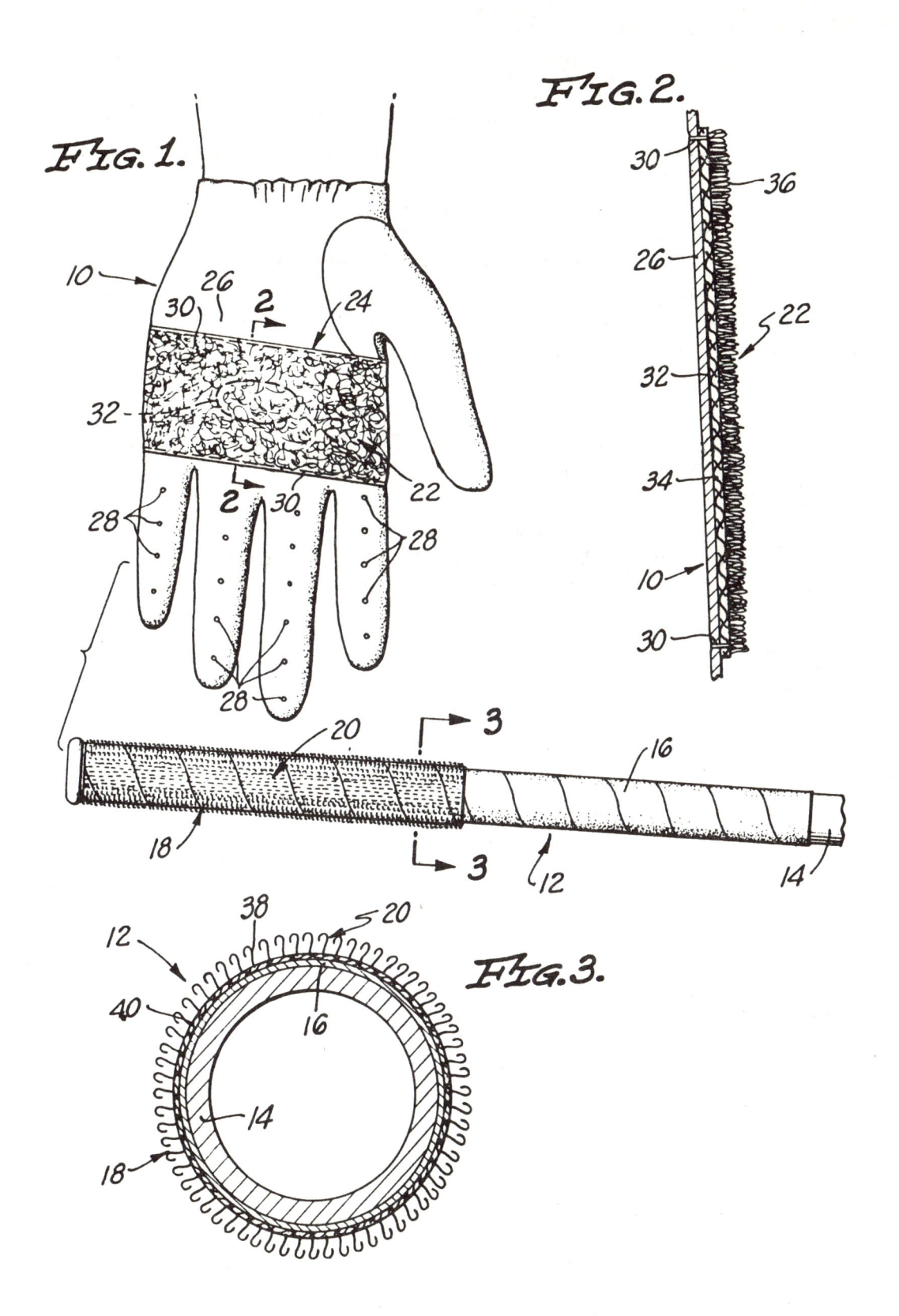

Fig. 1.

Fig. 2.

Fig. 3.

The Patent Duffer

Golf Grip Guide
Patent No. 2,928,678 (1960)
Albert Cutting of Grosse Pointe, Michigan

A primary object of the present invention is to provide means detachably associated with the handle or grip of a golf club shaft to aid the golfer in consistently positioning his hands on the shaft in desired relation to the club head and to help him in maintaining his hands in such position throughout his swing.

Another important object of the present invention is to provide thumb cups attached on the handle or grip of a club shaft and within which the thumbs of a golfer can be placed and to provide a loop through which the little finger of the left or right hand can be inserted, thereby enabling the golfer to maintain a firmer grip on the club and to prevent his hands from slipping and to keep the club shaft from turning in the hands during the golfer's swing. By adjusting the thumb cups to the right or left, the tendency to hook or slice can be overcome.

The Patent Duffer   95

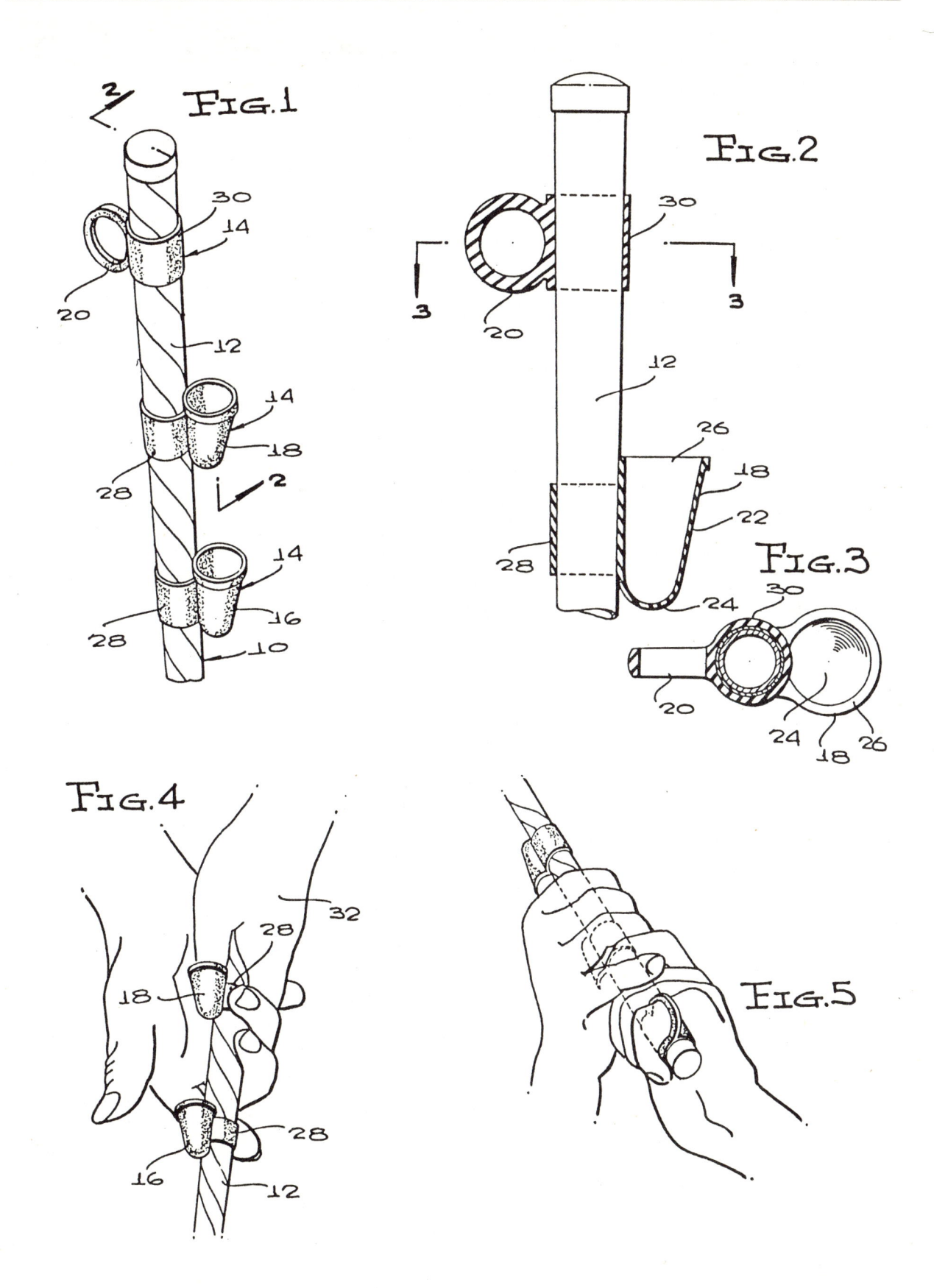

Grip Attachments For Golf Clubs
Patent No. 2,780,464 (1957)
Merwin Ashley of Arlington, Massachusetts

As is well known, the proper gripping of a golf club shaft is usually found awkward and unnatural for beginners, and even experienced golfers are prone occasionally to grip the shaft with their hands improperly oriented with respect to the striking face of the club. Another fault, equally common, is occasioned by relaxing the grip and re-gripping the club shaft as the club is swung, usually at the top of the back swing when the direction of the club is being reversed to strike at the ball.

In use, the handle end of the golf club shaft **21** is successively threaded through the tubular end portions **12** and **11**, which are stretched and rotated as may be necessary to bring the portion **11** tightly about the shaft adjacent to its handle end with the strap **10** extending substantially parallel with the shaft in position to insure proper grip when the strap is engaged over the last three fingers of the player's left hand adjacent to the knuckle joints. Thus it will be seen that with the strap firmly fixed in position on the shaft, the golfer may again and again grip the shaft in exactly the same position in relation to the club head by merely inserting the last three fingers of his left hand under the strap **10** until the strap engages over the first phalanges of the three fingers. To complete the grip of the left hand, the thumb is placed against the shaft and the index finger is gripped over the inner terminal end of the strap **10** to press the strap down toward or against the club shaft, thus tightening the strap over the other fingers.

Fig. 4
Fig. 1
Fig. 5
Fig. 3
Fig. 2

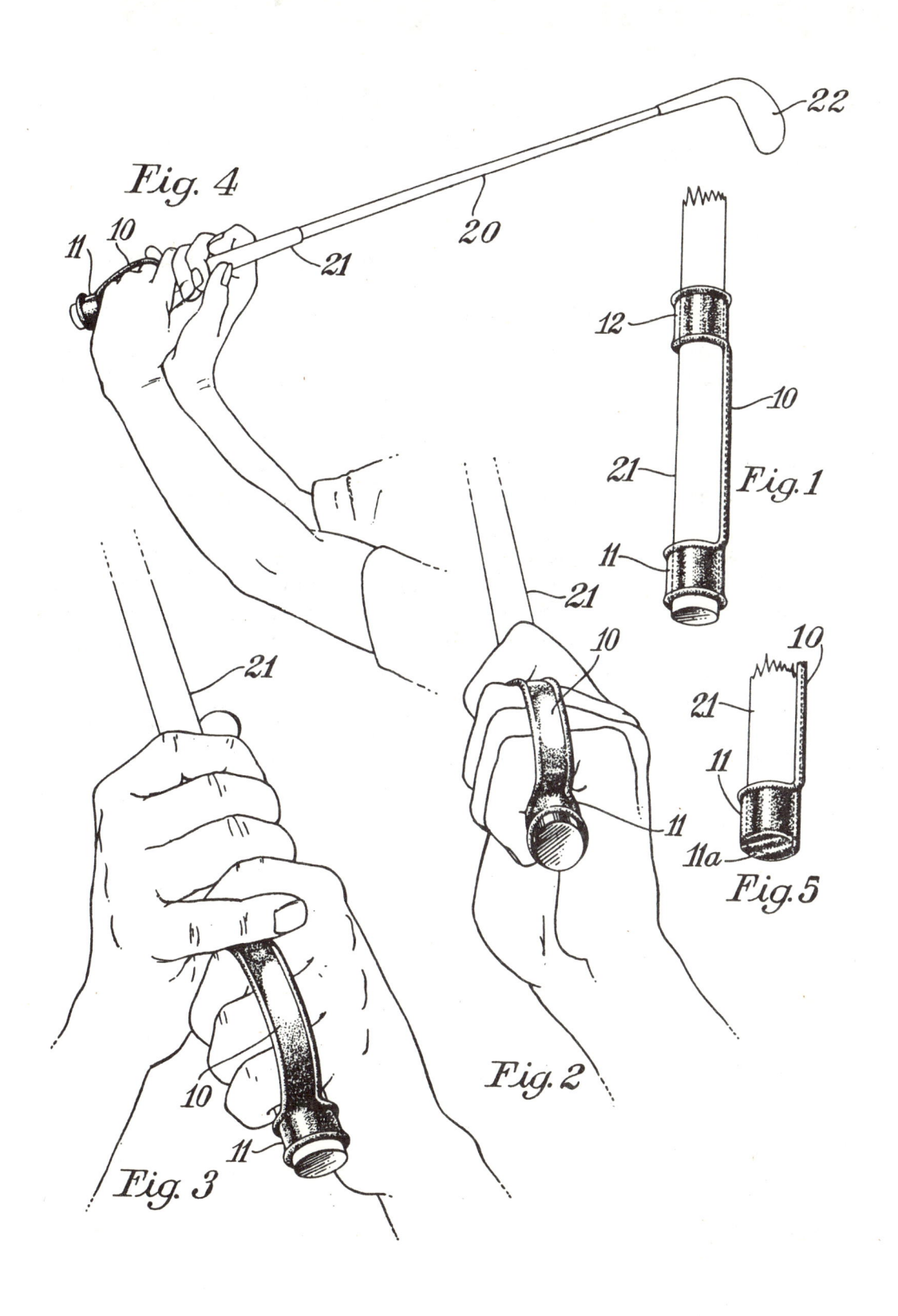

Grip Guide For Golf Clubs
Patent No. 1,843,039 (1932)
William Mohr of Chicago, Illinois

It is an object of this invention to provide a grip guide which aids to a degree not heretofore known in preventing the turning of the club in the player's hands during a stroke.

Still another object of this invention is the provision of a grip guide for golf clubs and the like which causes a proper distancing of the player's hands from the shaft of the club, and results in a proper orienting of the club face.

It is still a further object of this invention to provide a golf club grip guide which forces the player to embody more wrist action in his swing, increasing the wrist action up to but not in excess of the proper amount.

A still further object of this invention is the provision of a grip guide for golf clubs which embraces at least a portion of a user's hand, and while the device is sufficiently rigid for causing the hand to properly grip the shaft of the club, yet the device is not so rigid as to cause discomfort or injury to the hand.

Once the players's lower hand is seated within the member **7**, this lower hand will automatically be caused to properly grip the golf club shaft, and with one hand properly gripping the club it is a simple matter for the player to properly grip the club with his other hand. Of course, the devices are preferable made in various sizes to accommodate variously sized hands.

FIG.-1 FIG.-2

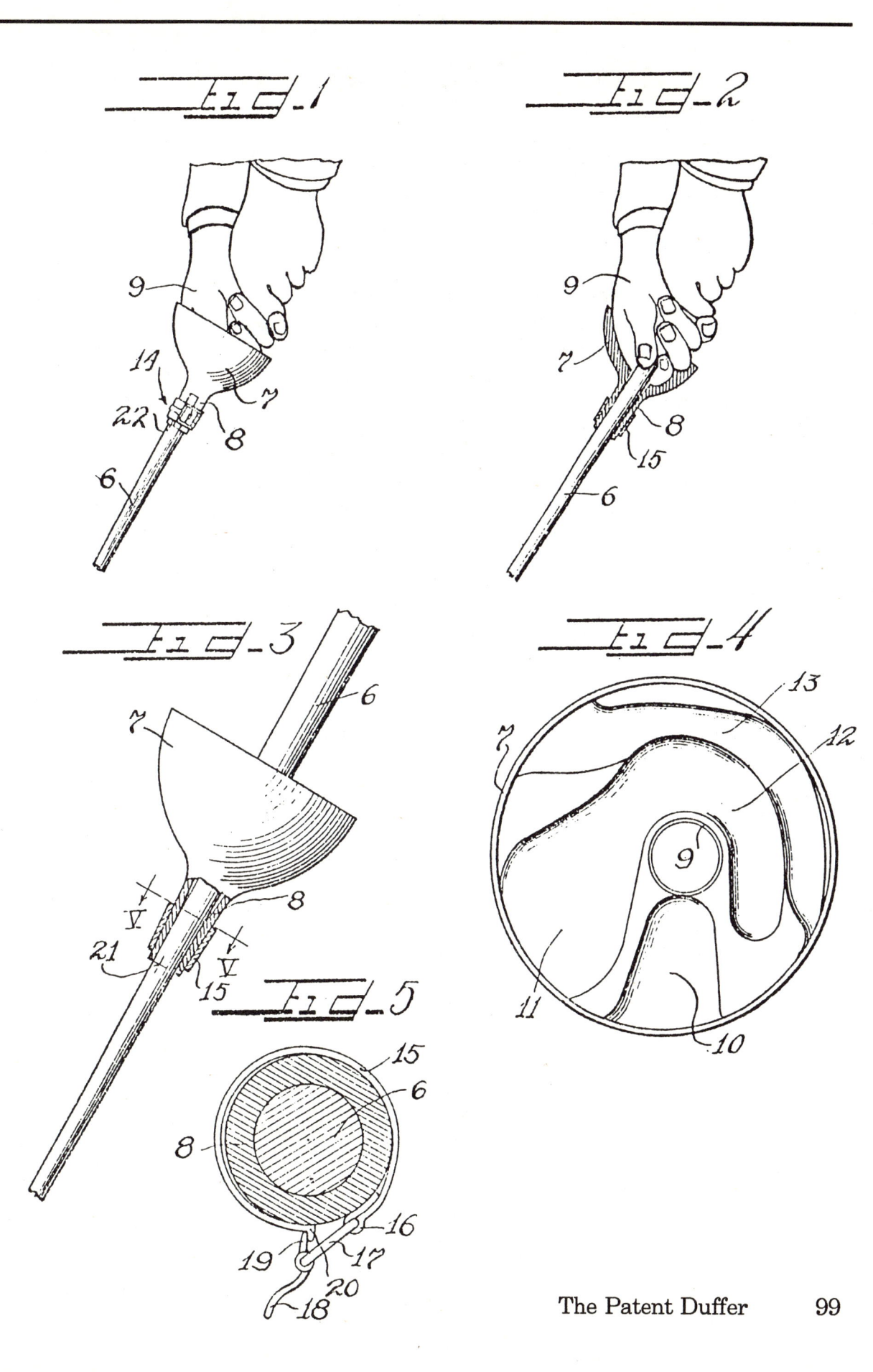

FIG.-3 FIG.-4

FIG.-5

The Patent Duffer   99

Wristband Grip For Golf Clubs
Patent No. 2,288,150 (1942)
Anthony Wyman of Orange, New Jersey

This invention relates to a wrist band grip for golf clubs and has for an object to provide a strap adapted to straddle the butt end of the club shaft and pass around the back of the golfer's hand so that at the top of the back swing the tendency of the butt end of the shaft to swing or pivot in the hand will pull the strap against the back of the hand and cause a pulled cocked wrist at the top of the swing to prevent overswinging and eliminate loss of control of the club.

In operation during the back swing of the club, the butt end **20** will tend to pivot outwardly in the palm and this tendency will be resisted by the club straddling portion **13** with a resultant pull of the strap against the back of the hand at the wrist of the golfer to produce a pulled cocked wrist at the top of the swing.

Fig. 1.   Fig. 2.

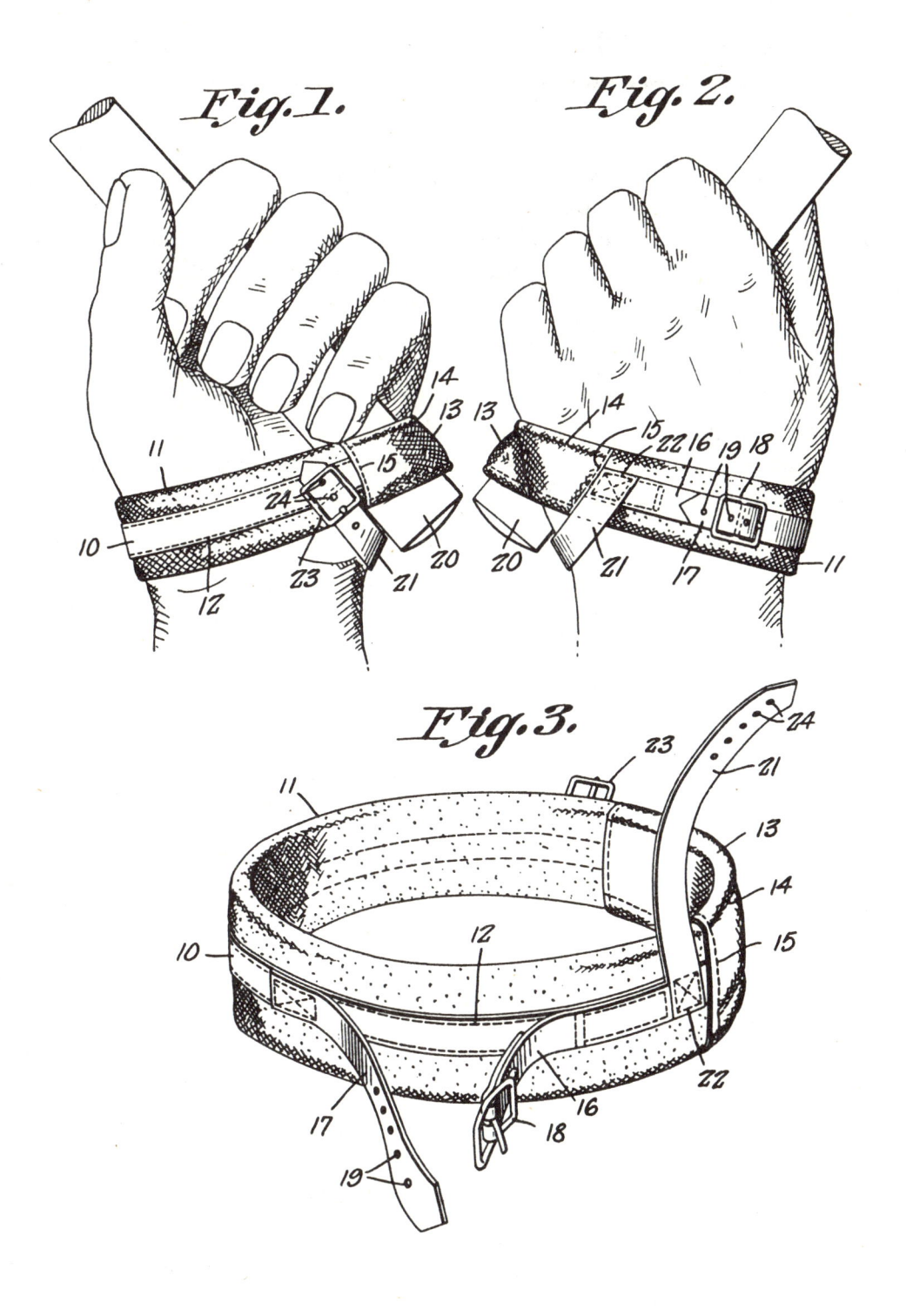

Fig. 3.

The Patent Duffer   101

Nonslip Golf Glove
Patent No. 2,474,030 (1949)
Charles Braswell of Long Beach, California

The primary object of the invention is the provision of flexible equipment or a frictional device for use in the hands of a golf player to tighten the grasp on the grip-handle of the club, thereby eliminating tendency of the club to turn, relieve the player of muscular strains in the fingers and hands, and to assure a proper grip with the club in correct position for easy manipulation and delivery of a stroke.

As indicated in the drawings, the fingers of each hand are inserted in the tubular open end fingers, the intermediate strap is wrapped around the grip or handle of the club, as seen in Figure 3, with a frictional grip, and the handle of the club is grasped by the covered fingers, as shown in Figure 1.

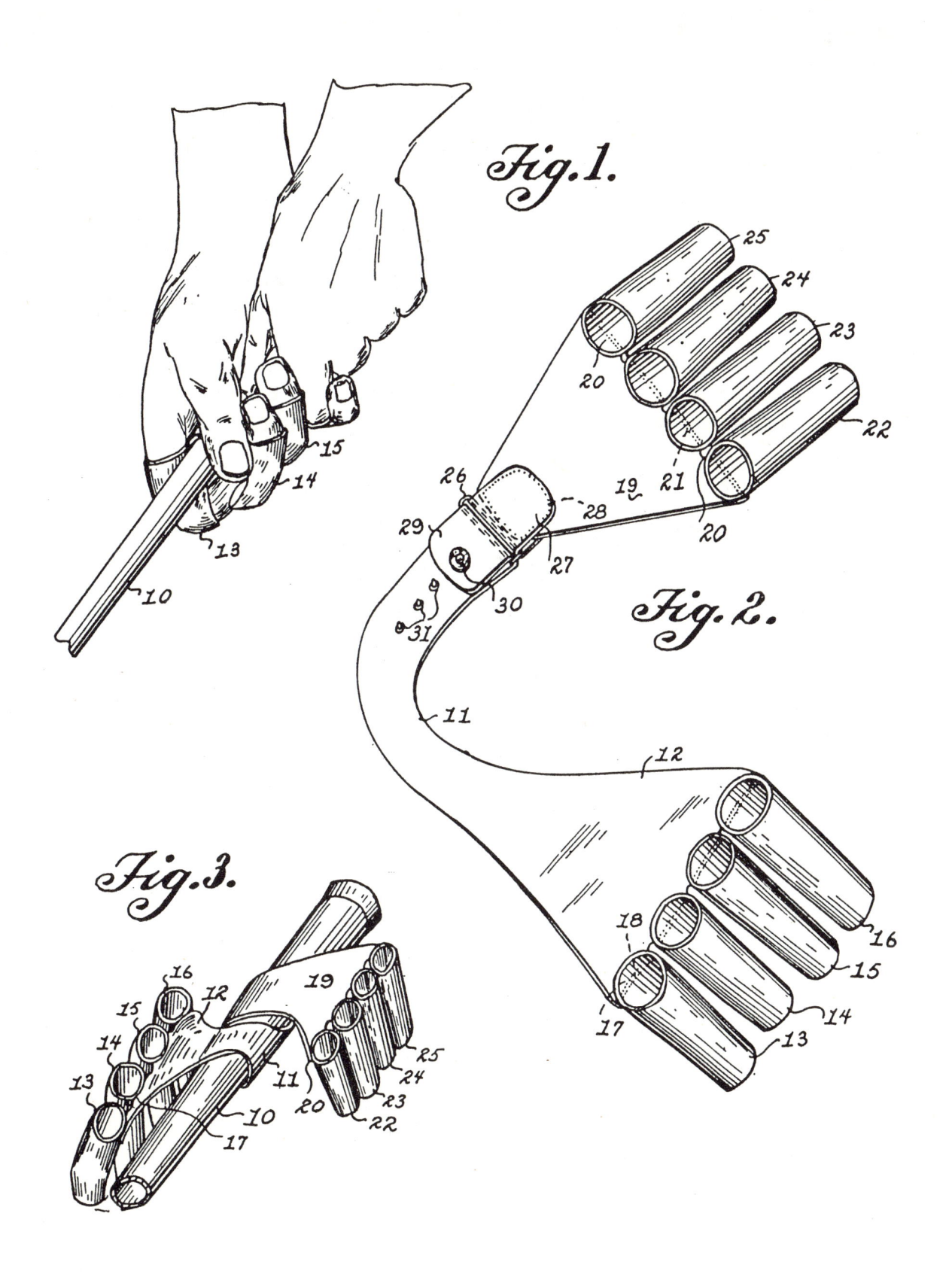

Fig. 1.

Fig. 2.

Fig. 3.

The Patent Duffer 103

Adjustable Golf Glove
Patent No. 2,700,159 (1955)
Wilmer Van Denburgh of Richmond, Virginia

The invention consists principally in a gripping member adapted to receive and properly position a golf club handle in the user's hand. The gripping is adjustable on a glove to lie at any desired angle across the wearer's palm and in any selected position toward or from the fingers.

As shown in Fig. 2, the palm portion of the glove is completely cut away to expose the bare palm of the wearer. The finger, thumb and wrist encircling portions serve the function of holding the back portion or panel 2 in relatively fixed position on the back of the wearer's hand.

A palm piece or gripping member 10 (Fig. 2) is provided and is of somewhat elongated shape to extend transversely across the palm of the hand. The palm piece or gripping member 10 may be of any desirable material but is preferably of a relatively stiff material capable of being readily bent about the handle of a golf club but sufficiently stiff to at least partially retain the bend to define a concave groove extending lengthwise of the palm piece and generally across the palm of the hand. Such curved configuration of the palm piece 10 defines a transverse concave groove adapted to receive and properly position a golf club in the user's hand. The palm piece 10 may be made of leather, reinforced or impregnated fabric, or a suitable plastic material.

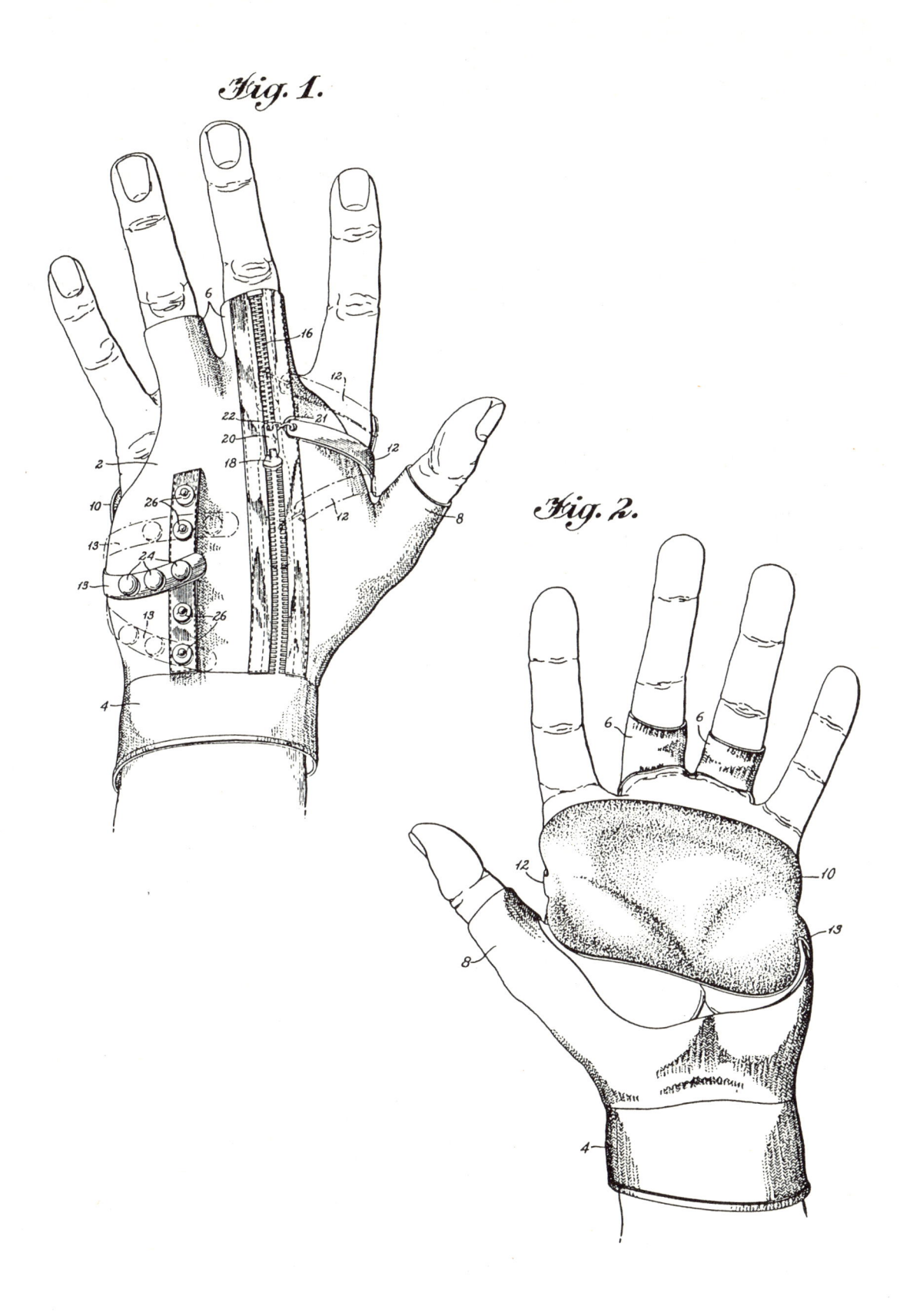

Fig. 1.

Fig. 2.

The Patent Duffer 105

Dry Grip Sleeve
Patent No. 3,397,891 (1968)
Tobias Koch of Drexel Hill, Pennsylvania

It is very difficult to hold onto a golf club and swing it properly when the shaft of the golf club is wet, such as when the golf game is being played in the rain. Wet weather does not deter the enthusiastic golfer from playing, and this is especially so when the rain starts during the course of a match.

The golfer may use a towel to dry his hands and dry the club shaft, but as the game proceeds the shaft becomes wet and slippery and very difficult to control. In some cases, the golf club may become so slippery as to slip entirely out of the hands of the golfer during the course of the swing and fly out of his hands, presenting considerable danger to the other golfers and caddies in the immediate vicinity.

Accordingly, it is an object of this invention to provide a dry-grip sleeve which keeps dry the shaft of a golf club and the like.

The Patent Duffer

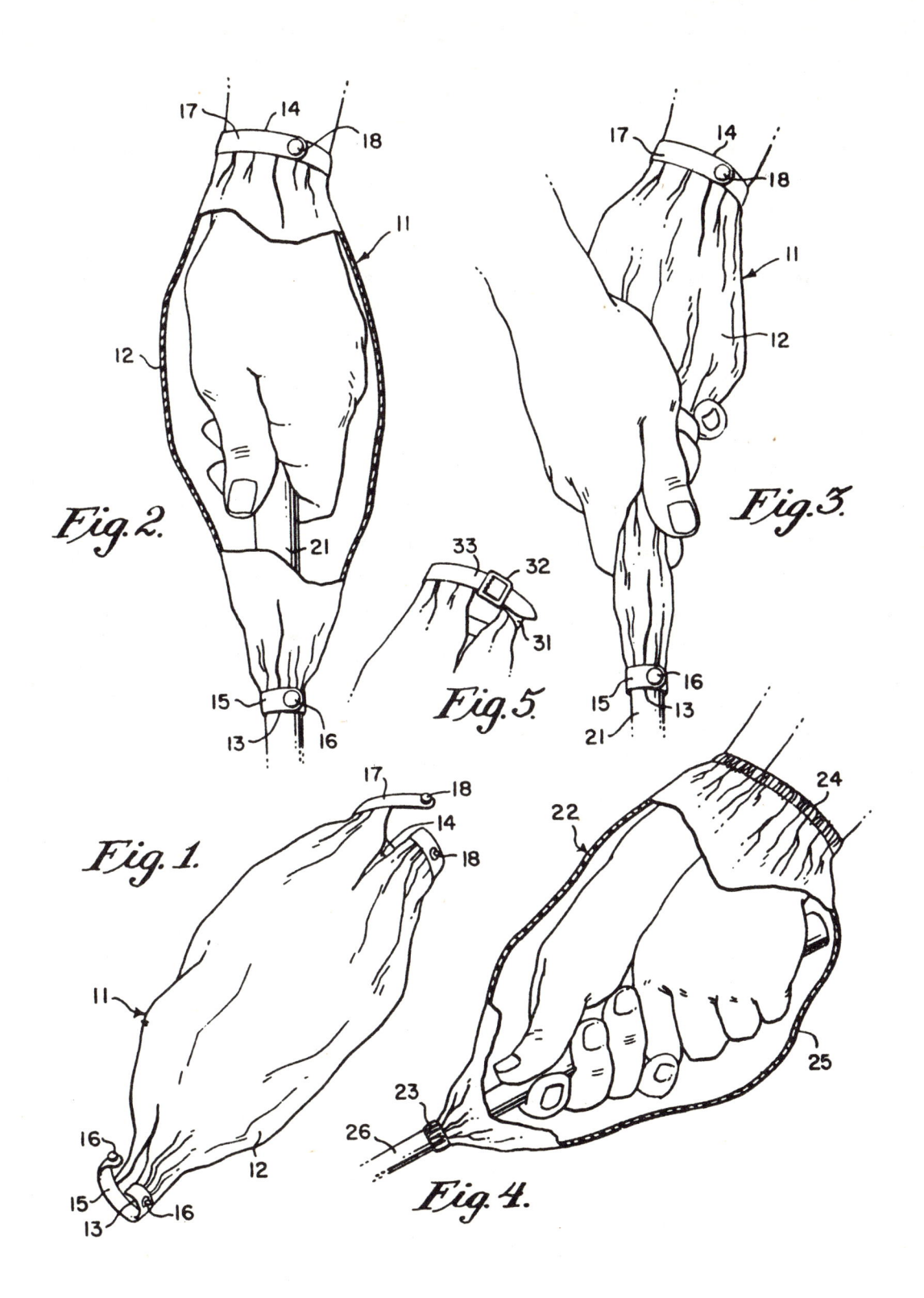

SIX
Feets Don't Fail Me Now

Of all the movements of the various anatomical parts common to the golfer, the proper function of the feet seem sadly neglected. Your head, your left arm, your wrist position at the top, your hips, all these parts have probably been the beneficiaries of countless tips, but when was the last time somebody gave you a suggestion about what to do about your feet? Logically, it seems obvious that the foundation of a good golf swing is built from the feet up, but aside from strapping on the spikes, how much attention is given to how the feet are supposed to work?

If any thought at all is given to the feet, it probably occurs when one is tempted to use the "foot wedge". For those steadfast and true golfers who may be unfamiliar with the "foot wedge", it is chiefly employed by golfers who don't abide strictly by the rules of golf, and employ their feet to extricate their balls from nasty lies when their opponents aren't looking. Ernest Savoy of Oklahoma City has taken the common "foot wedge" and made it respectable with his **Game And Apparatus For Playing The Same**, (page 116). He calls it a game apparatus, but those of us in the know understand what it is to be used for.

> Show me a man with both feet planted firmly on the ground and I'll show you a man about to swing a golf club.
>
> *Bing Crosby*

Now when your ball has found some impossible rough, instead of just kicking the ball and hoping to catch a good one with your toe to extricate yourself, you can select from a set of inserts with different lies to attach to you shoe.

Have a problem because your left toe leaves the ground on the back-swing? If you do, you probably need more help than anything you'll find in this book, but Harlan Hornbarger of Miami, has the cure for this particular problem with his **Golfer's Foot Holding Device** (page 110). If you don't mind wearing a manacle around your shoe on the range, this piece of equipment might do you some good.

Want to know how to really pivot your feet correctly? Guy Paulsen of Longmeadow, Massachusetts has come up with a **Golf Practicing Apparatus** (page 118) that makes it a cinch to learn what to do with your left foot. All you do is step onto this device and swing normally. The invention will automatically pivot your left foot.

With all these different contraptions which hold the toes or heels down, pivot the feet at the correct time, and tilt the feet in the right attitude, no one should have an excuse not to learn some fancy footwork. The only golfer who won't find any help here is the clumsy member of your foursome who has two left feet.

Golfer's Foot Holding Device
Patent No. 3,606,341 (1971)
Harlan Honbarger of Miami, Florida

The golfer with the faulty swing that results in a slice usually sways and fails to shift his weight properly to the forward foot because of his inability to keep the forward or lead foot contained in one position on the ground on the forward swing. The present invention contemplates the containing of the forward foot by this device during the complete swing of a golfer to prevent sway and improper weight shifting that normally result in a bad golf shot.

Therefore, it is a principal object of the present invention to provide a golfer's foot holding device which contains the golfer's forward foot during a golf swing yet permits the proper lifting of his heel and shifting of his weight as required in a good swing.

In the normal use of my device **10**, the golfer addresses a golf ball in the usual manner to determine the approximate location of his left foot. He then inserts the spike **12** into the ground at that location lays that portion of the elongated member **10** having end portion **18** on the ground and places his leading foot thereon. He then wraps both portions of the elongated member **10** about his shoe and presses the "Velcro" fasteners together to form a tight loop about the shoe. Now as he swings his club, the leading foot is prevented from leaving the spot in which it rested at the address, yet in his back swing, he is able to lift the heel of the foot and in his down swing, he is able to shift his weight to that foot and in his down swing, he is able to shift his weight to that foot in his follow through as required in a proper swing. Upon continued use of my device **10**, his muscles will acquire a memory so that in time he can discard the device **10** and swing properly without moving his leading foot in his down swing and follow through which can only result in a bad shot.

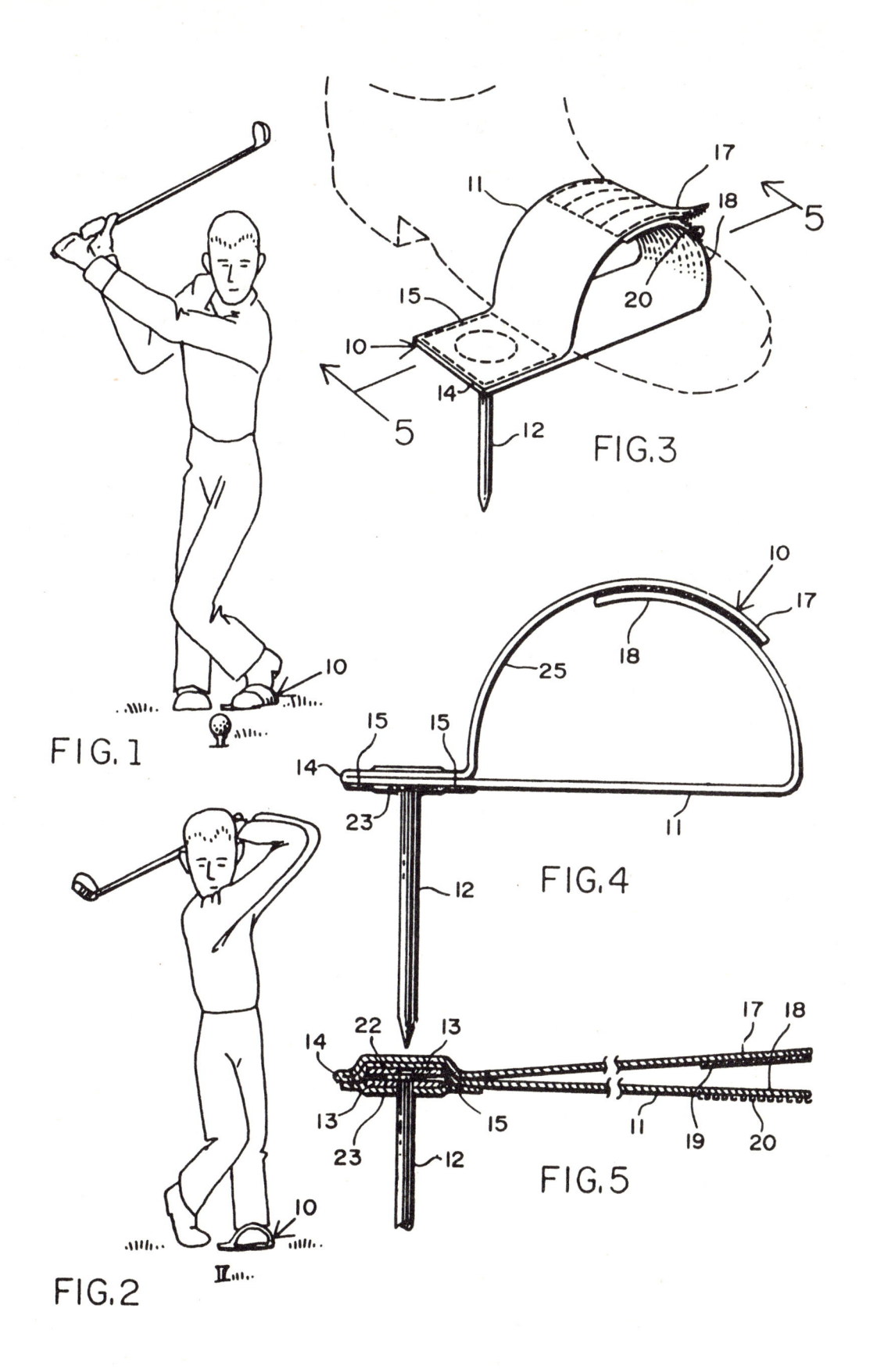

FIG. 1

FIG. 2

FIG. 3

FIG. 4

FIG. 5

The Patent Duffer   111

Golf Training Device
Patent No. 3,614,107 (1971)
James Kinsey of Fort Wayne, Indiana

The golf training device limits movement of the golfer's foot so that during the backswing and power swing, the pivot foot is confined to rolling from the inner edge to the outer edge of the shoe. This is accomplished be means of a locator which is either a permanently fixed post or a post which can be removably imbedded in the ground and has a locating surface against which the back of the shoe is brought. An attachment which is received on the golfer's shoe has a projection which bears against the lower edge of the locating surface, thus preventing lifting of the shoe and thereby maintaining the proper foot position of the golfer at his pivot foot during both the backswing and the power swing.

In operation, the golfer simply slips the attachment **52** into his shoe. After the attachment **52** is slipped in place, the golfer takes his stance with the pivot foot heel resting against the surface of the accurate guide surface **72**, and the pin **86** is disposed below the lower edge **88** of the guiding surface **72** and is engageable therewith. The ball is then placed and the driver begins his normal backswing, proceeding as indicated in FIGS. **1D** through **H**. In the process of so doing, a weight shift occurs to the inner edge of the shoe as the backswing develops, then during the down stroke the weight shift proceeds with opposite rolling action so that the driver ends up with his weight resting more on the opposite or outer edge of the driving shoe. But at no time will the pivot foot lift as indicated in panel **1d** since the pin **86** engaging the lower edge **88** will prevent the pivot foot from doing so.

FIG. 1a — LT. HEEL FLAT

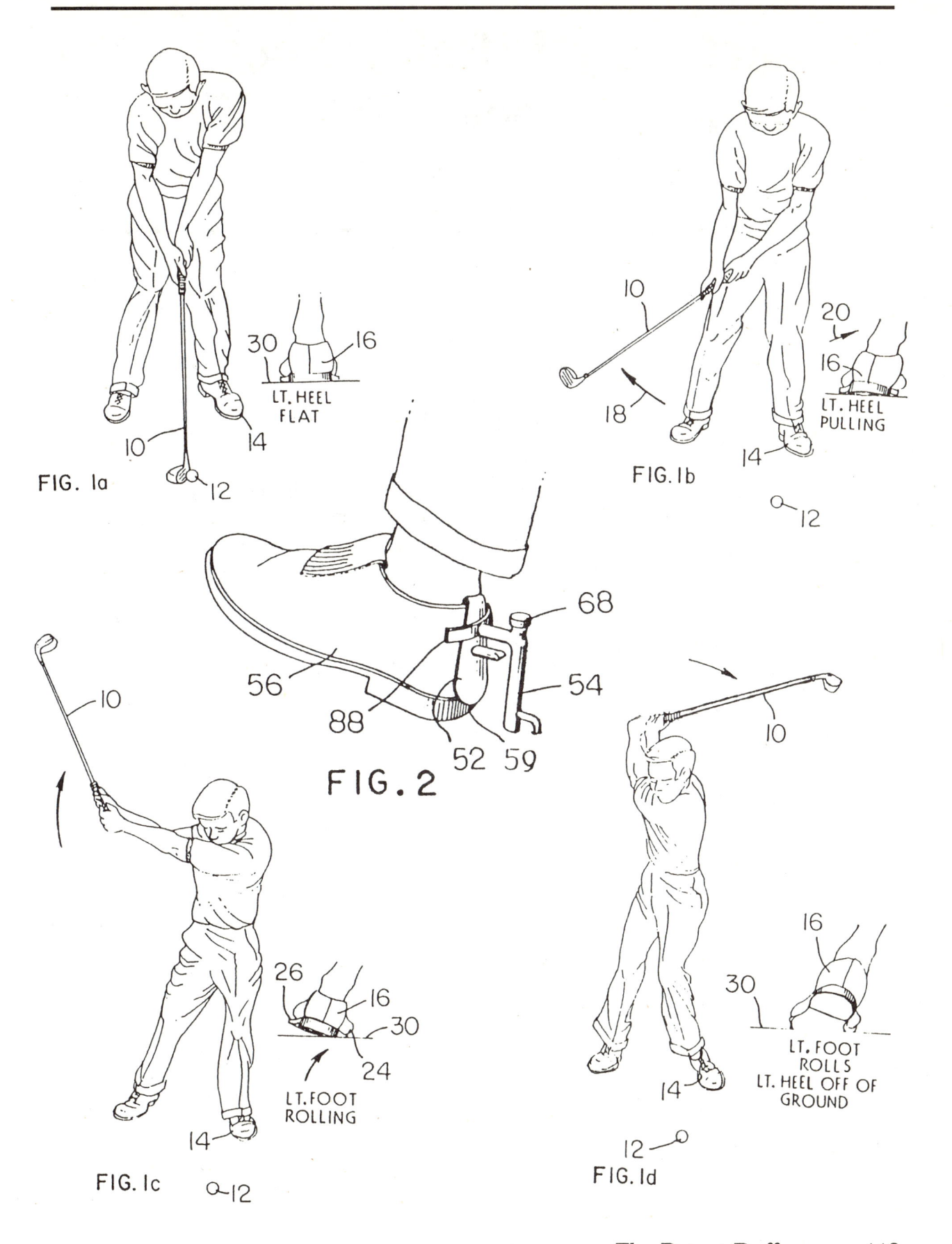

FIG. 1b — LT. HEEL PULLING

FIG. 2

FIG. 1c — LT. FOOT ROLLING

FIG. 1d — LT. FOOT ROLLS LT. HEEL OFF OF GROUND

The Patent Duffer   113

Magnetically Liftable Foot Positioning Block For Golfers
Patent No. 3,275,320 (1966)
John Hydock of Byesville, Ohio

In using the novel anchor block, the player takes his stance addressing the ball either on the tee or in the fairway, and then places the block under the right foot with the right side of the right shoe sole overlapping the inclined face **14**, as shown in **FIGS. 1-3**, and with the longitudinal edges **15** and **16** at the right angles to the intended line of flight of the ball. This tilts the right foot and causes a corresponding slight inward bend of the right knee.

As the golfer moves the club through the back swing to the top thereof, the tilt of the lower right leg and the inward bend of the right knee keeps the weight of the body properly balanced on the right leg, without allowing rearward swaying of the body and over-swing at the top of the back swing.

A magnet **18** is embedded in the outer surface of the front side **14** of the block, preferably midway of the ends **12**, with the upper surface of the magnet exposed and substantially flush with the block surface. The purpose of the magnet is to enable the golfer to pick up the block without stooping over, merely by contacting the steel head of any of the golf "irons" and lifting it up to the level of the hands.

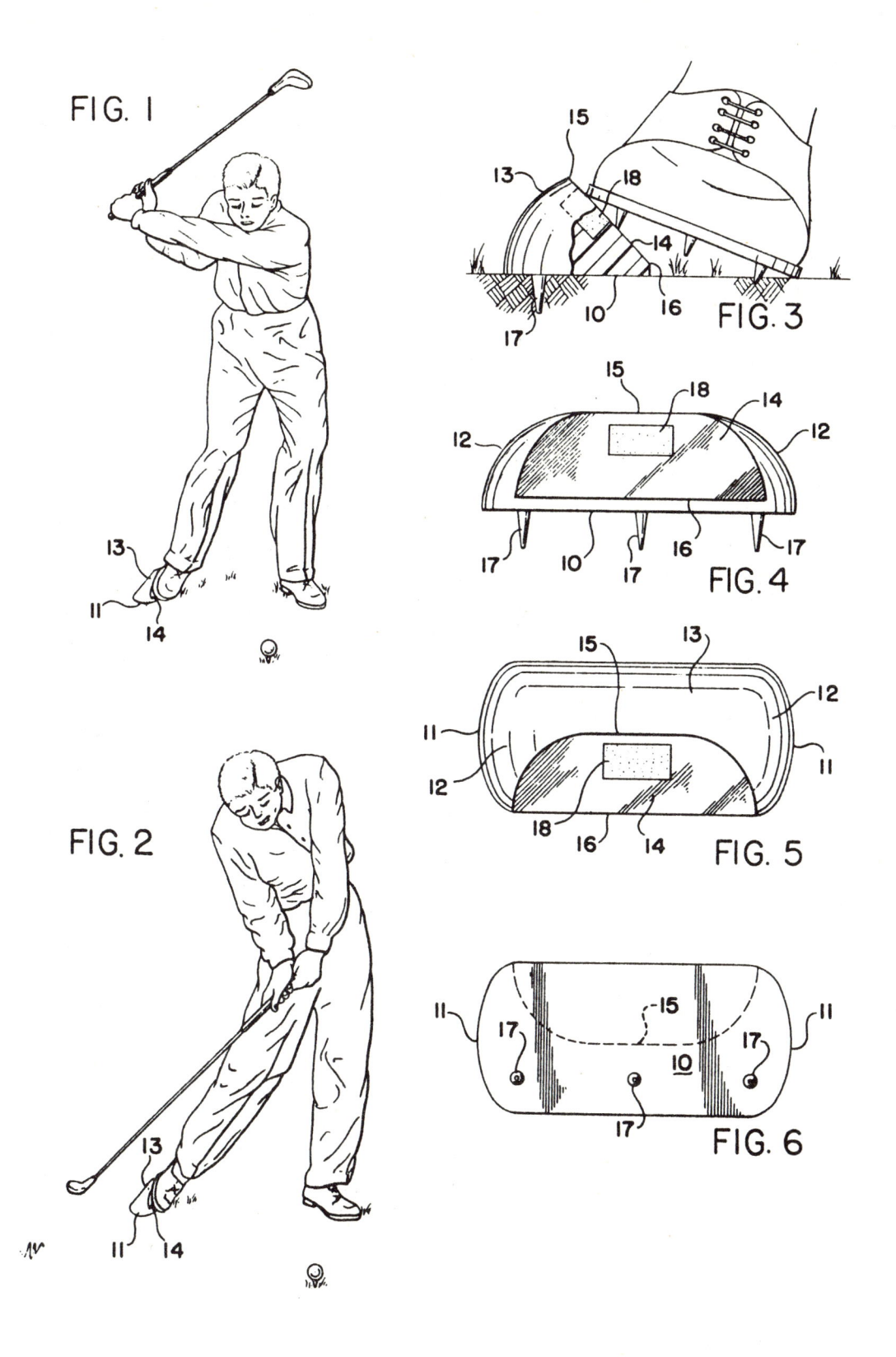

FIG. 1

FIG. 2

FIG. 3

FIG. 4

FIG. 5

FIG. 6

The Patent Duffer 115

Game And Apparatus for Playing The Same

Patent No. 2,220,291 (1940)
Ernest Savoy of Oklahoma City, Oklahoma

The invention embodies a device to be applied to the shoe of the player for supporting a selected striking head that is to be brought, by the swinging of the foot, forcibly into contact with the ball for propelling the same over the golf course from tee to green.

In the present instance three types of striking heads are shown, the one shown in Figure **5** having the edge **16** of such a pitch that the striking head will function somewhat in the nature of the well-known "mashie" golf club; while the head shown in Figure **6** has its striking surface **16** at a pitch so that said head will function very similar to that performed by the well-known "putter" golf club; while the striker head shown in Figure **7** has its striking surface **16** at a pitch so that said head will function substantially in a manner similar to that performed by the well-known "niblick" golf club.

In driving from the driving tee, the ball **17** is teed up in the usual manner and the driving head **15** properly positioned on the attachment **6**. The player then with a swing of the foot in an obvious manner, drives the ball **17** from the tee **18**. Following this the player changes the striker head and substitutes the same with a suitable striker head, depending upon the particular "shot" he wishes to make, it being obvious, for example, that when "putting" the ball, the player will use the striker head, the striking face of surface **16** of which is disposed at a pitch corresponding to the pitch of the head of the well-known "putter" golf club.

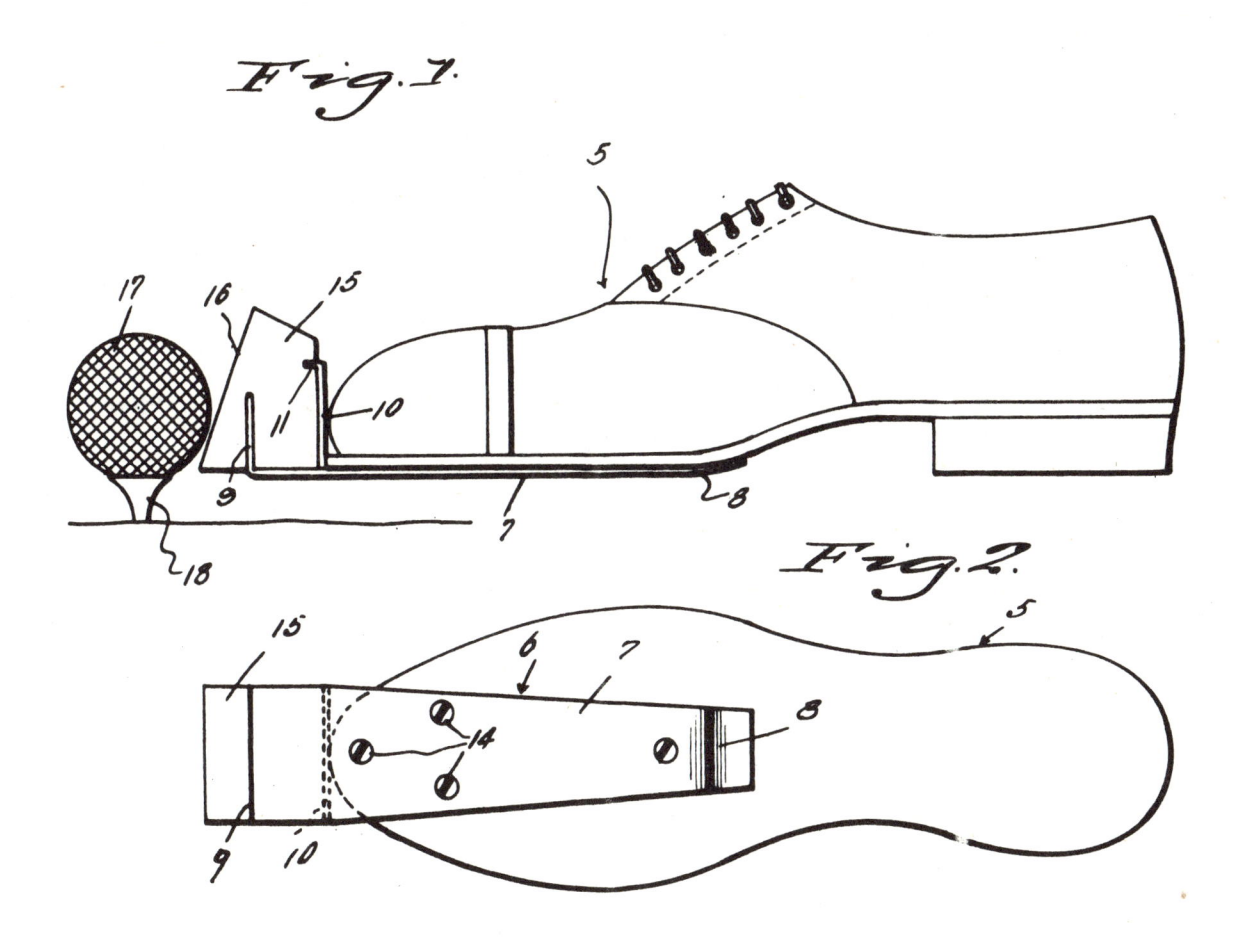

Fig. 1.

Fig. 2.

Golf Practicing Apparatus
Patent No. 2,189,613 (1940)
Guy Paulsen of Longmeadow, Massachusetts

This invention relates to a golf practicing apparatus and has for its object the provision of an apparatus which may be used either indoors or out for training a student of golf in the proper body swing for any of the usual types of golf strokes. The arrangement is based on my theory that if the student is given a proper stance and is by training accustomed to a proper "feel" of the feet in the movement of making each stroke then the correct pivotal motion of the body at the waist and swing at the shoulder will unconsciously follow until the proper coordination of these movements will become more natural and uniform for every type of stroke.

It is the particular object of the present invention to provide such a support for the feet of the student that in making a stroke the turning press of the feet on said support will automatically cause the same to assume the proper positions throughout the stroke. To this end the invention consists in the novel combination and arrangement of parts.

The student takes a position with his left foot on plate **1** and right foot on plate **2**. He then swings the club as he would for making a stroke and as his body swings on said drive the turning press of his foot on the left hand plate will rock it inwardly and forwardly causing his left foot to assume the proper position for guiding his waist in a proper pivotal movement. It is this feature of the invention which is particularly important in guiding and instructing the student, namely that the properly guided movement of left foot in making the swing will bring about a more uniform pivotal movement at the waist.

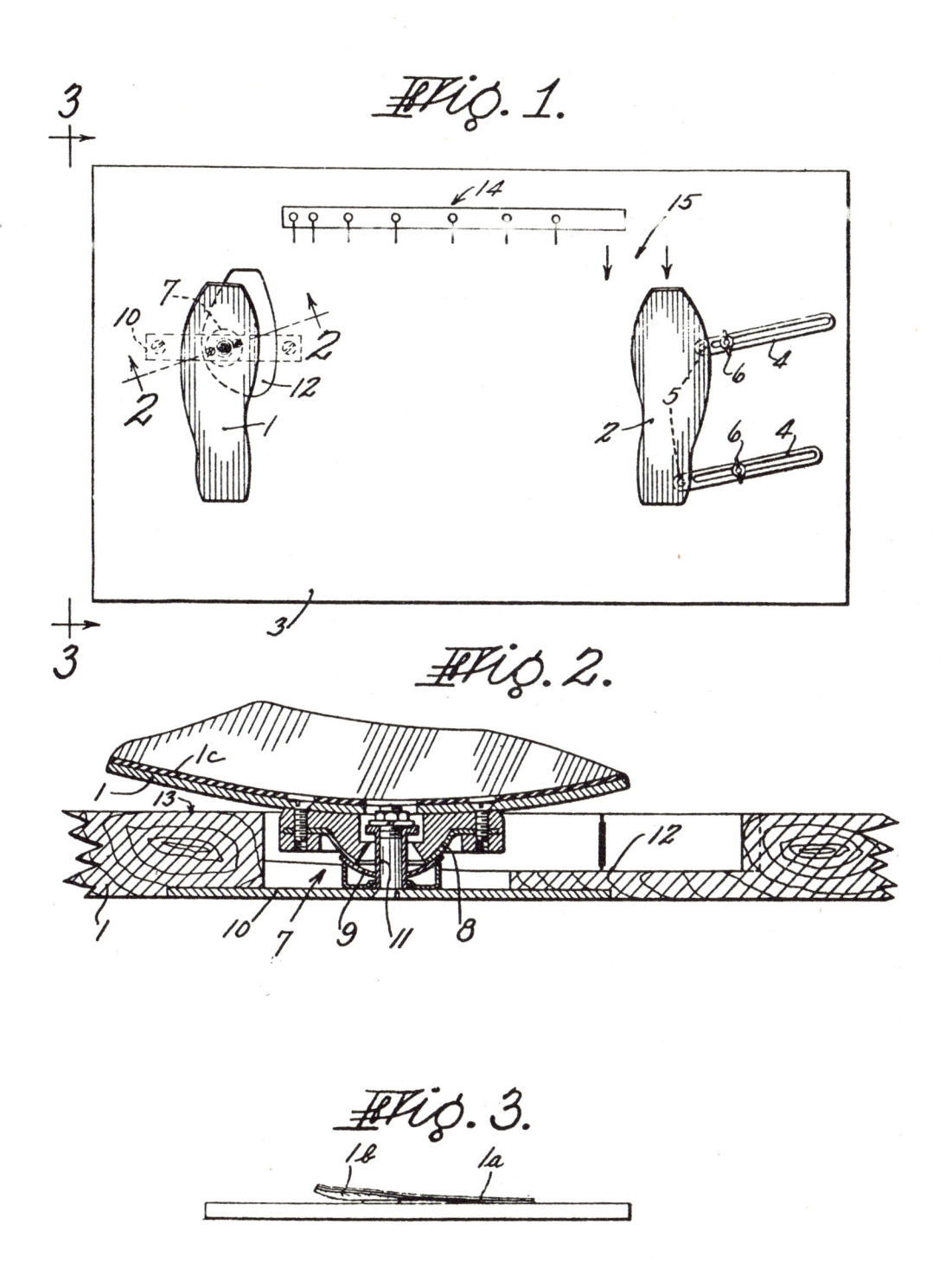

Fig. 1.

Fig. 2.

Fig. 3.

The Patent Duffer

Shoes For Golfers

Patent No. 2,847,769 (1958)

Joseph H. Schlesinger of New York, New York

The present invention relates to means for a golfer to obtain the correct position when his is taking a stance for his golf swing, and particularly takes the form of what the player is to stand on in order to obtain such correct position. The teachings of this invention may be incorporated in shoe structure to be worn by the golfer.

Another object of this invention is to provide a novel and improved means to compel the correct position when taking a stance, of the character as described, so that the player need have no thought or ever be fidgety as to whether his position for the play is correct, because the action of the means involving this invention, is automatic in compelling the correct golf position to be assumed by experts or novices at golfing.

The mentioned correct position of the player accomplished by this invention is shown in Figs. **7** and **8**. Fig. **7** particularly shows the player with his knees bent in towards each other and hence flexed. In Fig. **8**, the player is shown in position with his weight directed back through the heel region. The player's position is of course the composite of both these figures.

With the use of this invention, the accomplishment of correct position for his footwork is automatically and positively secured and requires no special effort. The player is thus given freedom to concentrate on other movements for his play.

The Patent Duffer 121

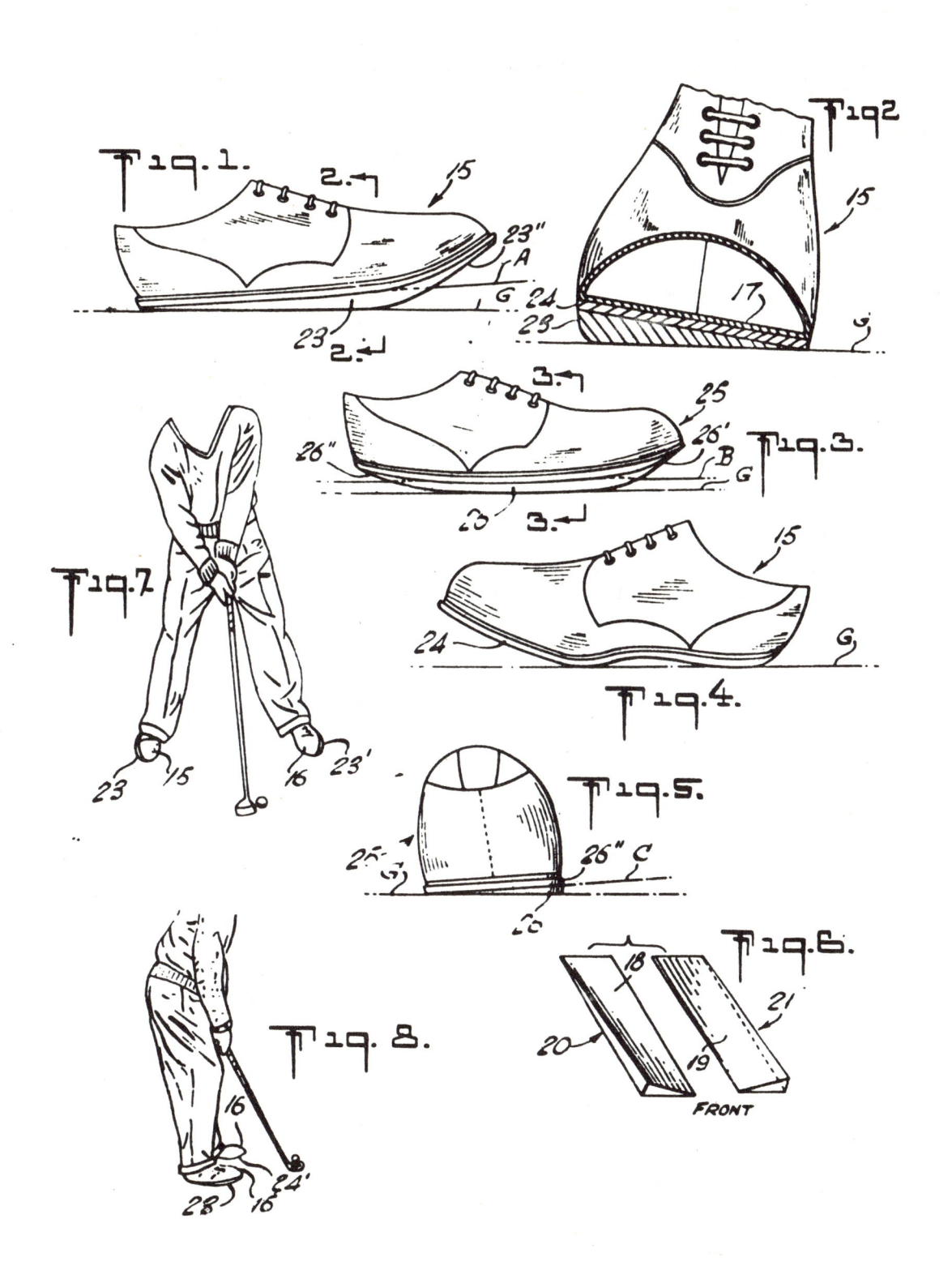

SEVEN
The Law Of The Straight Left Arm

Although there is a wide variety of styles in the swings of expert golfers, close inspection can detect a few details that they all have in common. One of these is the tendency to keep one's head down. Another is the manner in which they keep their left arm straight. One of the easiest ways to pick out the novice at the driving range is to watch his left arm. Invariably the beginner will take the club back and the left arm bends in an uncontrolled manner from the momentum of the club-head.

If you want to have some fun, the next time one of those helpful members of your foursome admonishes you to keep your left arm straight, ask him why. He will probably sputter and get a dumb look on his face and then hem and haw about how that's the way its always been done. It's traditional.

Could it be that some ancient Scot might have had a broken elbow that never healed correctly and his gimpy arm was forever fixed in a rigid posture? Suppose his handicap was 20 or 25 before his accident, and after he was able to play again – with his newly stiffened arm – he was at scratch. His fellow duffers, noticing this vast improvement, all started to keep their left arms straight, with the same success. The technique spread throughout the aboriginal land and *hootman*, another tradition in golf was born.

Why do golfers need to keep the left arm straight, anyway? Obviously, one needs to keep the head down so the eye doesn't wander from the ball. But why keep the left arm straight?

> It took me 17 years to get 3,000 hits in baseball.
> I did it in one afternoon on a golf course.
>
> *Hank Aaron*

After all, we're talking about a swinging motion here, and baseball players wouldn't dream of hitting a baseball with a straight left arm.

Thanks to some simple physics, the answer becomes apparent. The baseball is a moving target that needs to be hit at various locations in relation to the batter's body. Strikes might come inside, outside, high, or low, all with a chance of being hit. With the elbow hinged, the batter is free to adjust the position of the bat to the various pitches by bending his elbow and bringing the bat closer to his body, or straightening his arm for those pitches that are outside.

Golf is a different story. The golf ball is in a fixed relationship to the body, established by the distance one stands from the ball. To connect solidly and consistently with the ball, the left arm needs to be straight at address and maintain this position throughout the swing. This posture establishes a constant-length arc from the back-swing through the hit, eliminating one of the variables which can cause topping, hitting fat, or missing the ball completely.

Thankfully, people like William Koski, and Paul Maguire of Los Angeles realize the severity of this problem. Their **Arm Stiffening Device** (page 130) is a clever apparatus which golfers can inflate around their left arm to maintain the necessary rigidity.

Robert Coupar of Victoria, British Columbia takes his **Golfer's Arm Bend Restraining Device** (page 128) a step further by a clever way to let the elbow bend on the follow through. Whatever the means, these inventors understand the law of the stiff left arm.

Golfer's Arm Bend Indicator
Patent No. 3,419,276 (1968)
Sante Poggioli of Little Neck, New York

It does not require much of a signal to announce to a golfer or to his teaching professional that the golfer's lead elbow is bending. Yet this bending is hardly perceptible to the unaided eye.

To alleviate this condition a training device is shown for use by a golfer to correct bending of the elbow of his lead arm. A two-piece device is connected across the elbow. Relative motion between the pieces allows bending of the elbow so that the golfer's normal swing will neither be confined nor restricted. On relative motion in response to a bending of the elbow, an audible ball and socket sounding device announces to the golfer that this elbow has bent.

Fig. II.

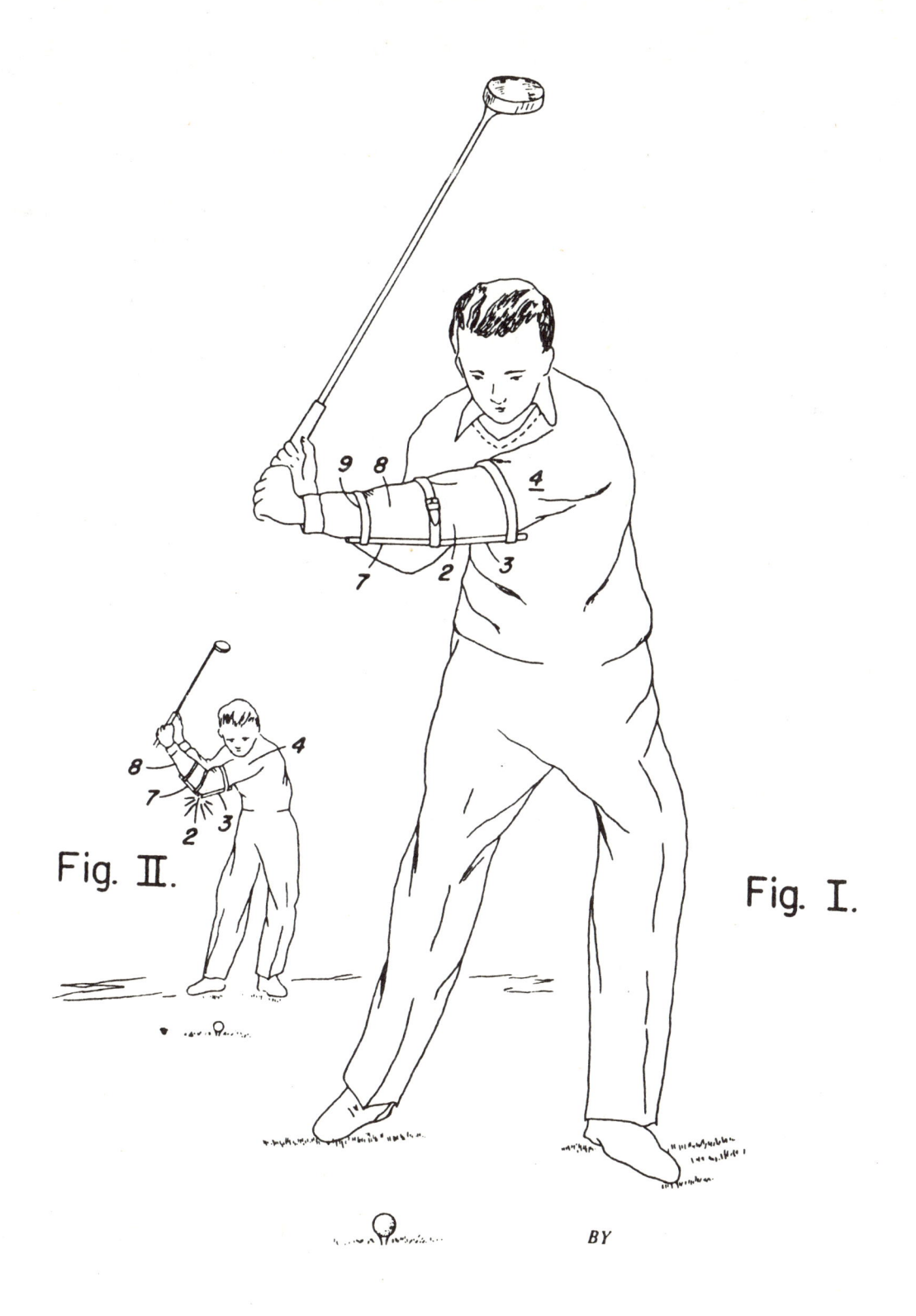

Fig. I.

BY

The Patent Duffer

Golfer's Arm Positioning Device Comprising Elbow Bend Restraining Means
Patent No. 3,419,277 (1968)
Clarence Martin of Greenville, South Carolina

A device for guiding the leading arm of a golfer during the backswing portion of a club swing, in order to assure that proper coordination is obtained. Restraint is imposed against bending of the leading arm at the elbow upon the leading arm reaching the top of the backswing, while the elbow is free to bend during a normal follow-through. Movement of the leading arm against the torso in a rearward direction is restrained in order to assure coordination of a turning movement of the torso with movement of the leading arm.

The Patent Duffer   127

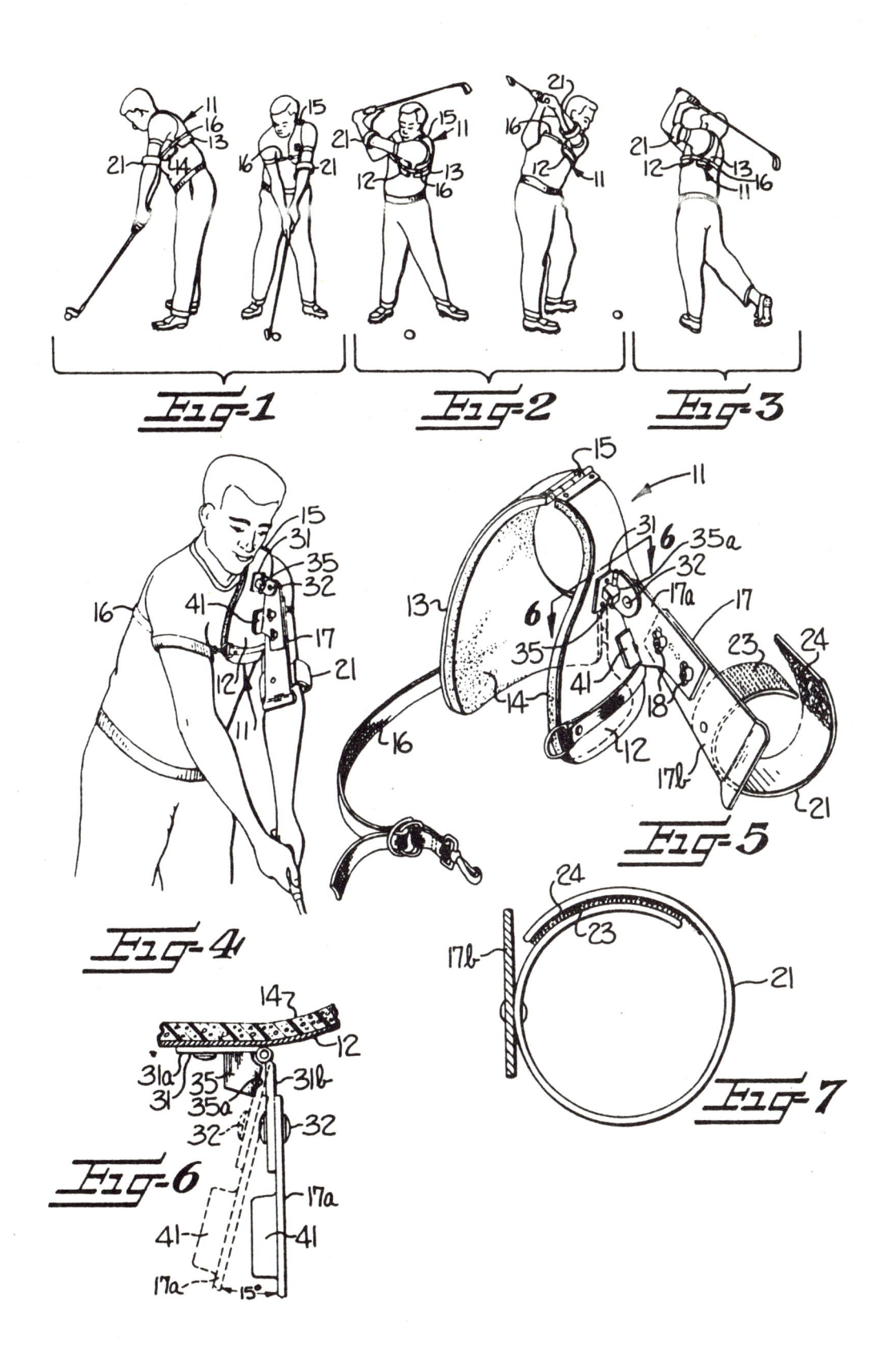

Golfer's Arm Bend Restraining Device
Patent No. 3,339,926 (1967)
Robert Coupar of Victoria, British Columbia

The present invention provides an apparatus to maintain the leading arm in a stiffened condition during the back-swing portion of the golf swing yet, which by utilizing the relative changing position of the wrist to the upper arm occasioned by the pronation of the hand as the arm moves into the follow-through portion of the golf swing, automatically operates to permit the elbow to be bent, thereby permitting the golfer to finish his stroke in the desired relaxed manner.

The present invention also provides a means by way of an audible signal after the club is brought to the top of the back-swing whereby he may momentarily hesitate for a predetermined period of time before swinging his club downwardly to strike the ball. This momentary hesitation is important in developing a controlled swing so that the golfer may concentrate on proper co-ordination of all his movements before swinging his club to strike the ball.

The Patent Duffer 129

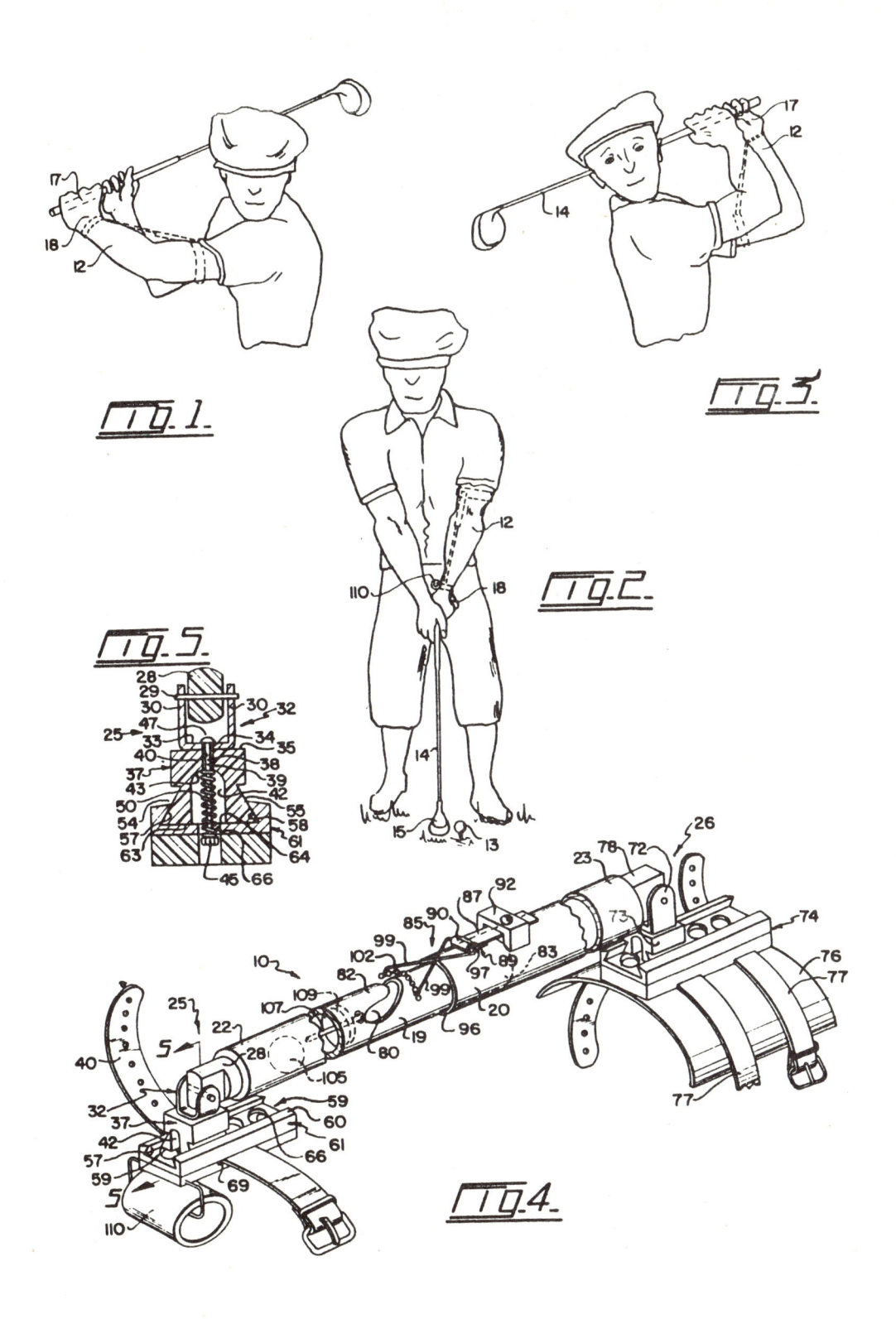

Arm Stiffening Device
Patent No. 2,943,859 (1960)
William Koski of Orange, California
Paul Maguire of Los Angeles, California

The present invention relates to devices for holding the leading arm of a golfer substantially rigid while the golfer is swinging a golf club, and more particularly to such a device which is easy to put on and take off, comfortable to wear, which my be left in position on the arm for an extended period of time without affecting the golfer's game adversely and which is readily adjustable.

The device includes an elongated tubular inflatable sheath **12**, a liner element **14** and a valve element **16**.

The sheath **12** includes an inner layer **18** and an outer layer **20** preferably formed from an air impervious flexible, substantially inelastic material such as, for example, polyethylene or polystyrene plastic. The layers **18** and **20** are, sealed to provide a substantially air tight sheath. In addition, portions of the respective layers are sealed to one another to form ribs **22** paralleling the central axis of the sheath.

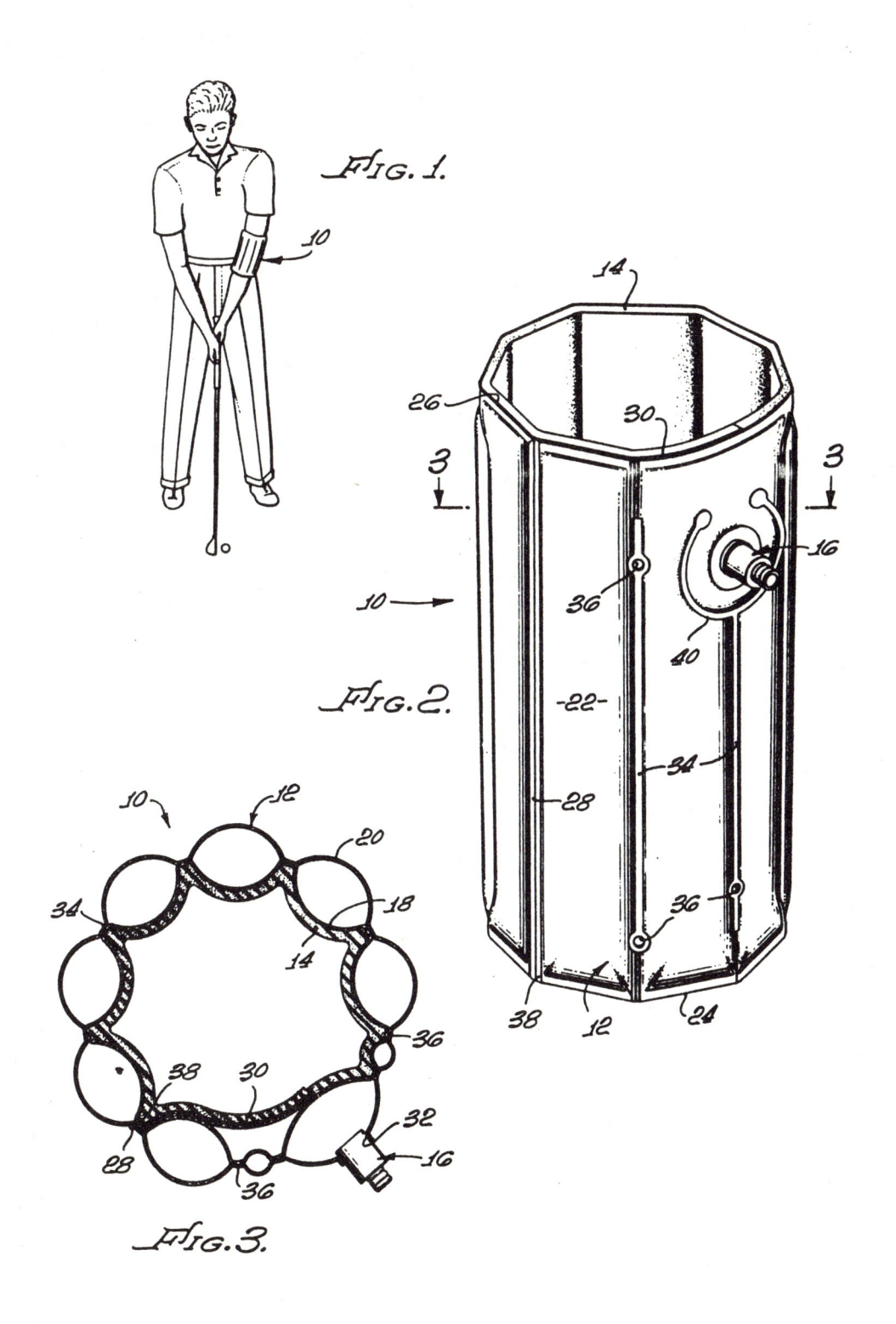

Fig. 1.

Fig. 2.

Fig. 3.

The Patent Duffer 131

EIGHT

The Drive For Distance

One of the never-ending quests of, amateur and professional golfers alike, is the continuing search for more distance off the tee. For the amateur, a drive that is twenty yards longer can mean a two-club difference in his approach shot. Think about what your game is like now and imagine what you could shoot if you were twenty yards closer to the green on each drive. Is there any other shot in golf that gives the same exhilaration as cranking one out 275 or 300 yards off the tee?

Professional golfers are incredibly protective of their favorite driver. Many pros will squire their driver and putter back to their hotel rooms for safekeeping overnight. These are the two clubs which have the greatest impact upon their scoring, and are the most personal in terms of feel. The pro's love affair with his big stick is a curious one. On one hand, they are protective and solicitous of their favorite wood, and on the other hand, they are forever trying out different models on the practice tee. At every tournament, reps from the various club companies have a big selection of drivers that the touring pro will try out in a search for those added yards, and just the right feel. Unfortunately, this same amorous ambivalence has been the cause of quite a few marital slices.

Graphite, titanium, cobalt and other exotic materials from the space program have all been added to the quest for the ultimate driver. Before the technology for spinning graphite into fibers was invented, Philip Samson of London, England invented a driver with a woven fabric face that was impregnated with a resin mixture. His **Golf-Club And Other Sporting Implement** (page 138), for which he received a patent in 1914, was technologically way ahead of it's time.

> I've never been so drunk I couldn't drive.
> Of course my putting suffered a little.
>
> *Dean Martin*

Woven graphite heads have only recently come on the market using the same basic ideas.

An exotic material of days past was mercury, an extremely heavy and liquid metal. Thomas Davis of Brooklyn, New York, used these qualities to invent a driver containing a shifting quantity of the stuff. In his ingenious **Golf Club** (page 140) the mercury is in the handle portion at the top of the back-swing, and is supposed to shift to a reservoir in the head on the down-swing. This shifting mass is supposed to be responsible for an increase in club-head speed upon impact with the ball. If this sounds like a great idea and you're tempted to go out and put one of these together, be advised that the club doesn't conform to USGA rules. You would also have to issue an environmental impact statement to the EPA because mercury is a toxic substance, and if you ever lost your temper and threw the club into the lake you could be prosecuted.

Exotic materials aren't the only solution to increased distance. William Witherspoon of Greenbelt, Maryland, has taken the concept of bulge and roll to new extremes with his **Golf Club** (page 136). This odd-looking, round-headed club is supposed to have a psychological effect upon the user. The theory is that, with a round face on the driver, the golfer will not slow the club down in an effort to square the face of the club to the ball. Although it has been reported that this is Gerald Ford's favorite driver, this fact has not been confirmed.

Whatever the means, spring-loaded faces, exotic materials, psychological clubs, the drive for more distance is definately on.

Golf Club
Patent No. 925,389 (1909)
Charles Royce of Montclair, New Jersey

My invention relates to an improvement in clubs used for golf and like games, and the purpose of it is to impart resiliency to the face of the club and thus to increase the distance to which balls can be driven thereby.

It consists in providing the face of the club with a cover-plate or pad of celluloid, rubber other suitable material, which is backed on its inner side by plugs of elastic material.

It also consists in making these plugs in the form of balls which are set in sockets in the body of the club; also in making the balls of rubber bands or threads wound tightly together; and also in making the balls of such rubber threads of bands wound under tension.

Fig. 1.

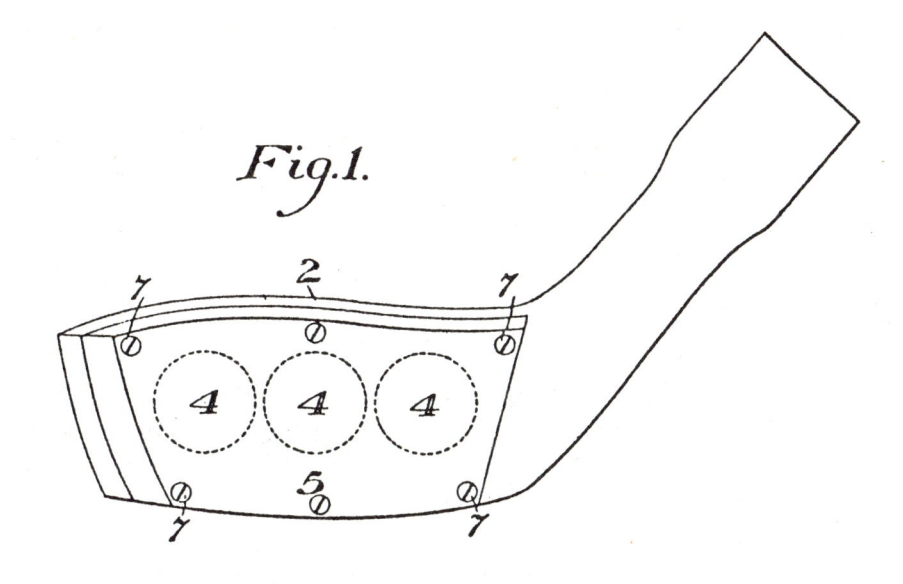

Fig. 2.

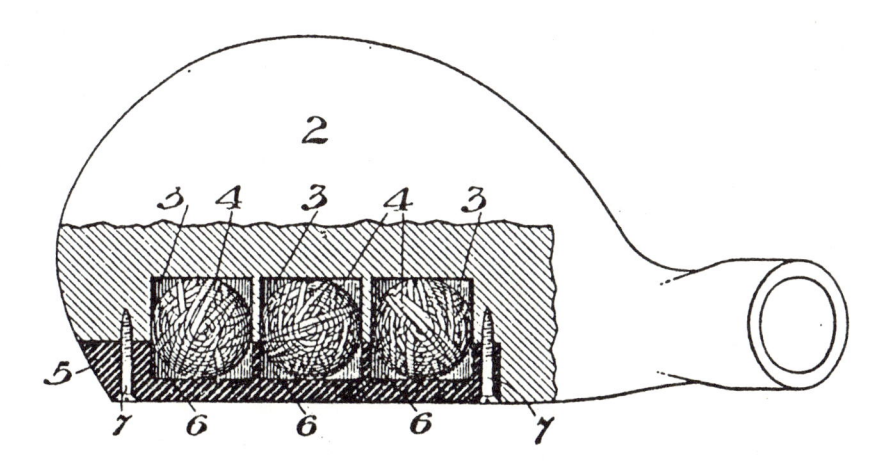

Golf Club
Patent No. 3,759,527 (1973)
William Witherspoon of Greenbelt, Maryland

There is a tendency of many golfers to release the wrist-cock much too early in the down swing, and lose vital club head speed at impact with the ball. I have found that this action, hitting from the top of the back swing, indulged in by many golfers, occurs from an image formed in the mind of the golfer at the address position with the ball, before initiating his swing. He realizes that the club head has a nearly flat striking surface with which to strike the ball. and he feels that, before he can hit the ball in the proper line of flight, he must make an attempt to square or realign, in the down swing, that nearly flat striking surface to the ball before impact. Even knowing his objective throughout the swing, namely to retain the wrist-cock for as long a time as possible before impact, and let the centrifugal force of the club face at the proper alignment, there is a reflex which takes over and slows his hand speed, and causes a manipulation of his wrists and hands too early, with a fear that the club face will not be aligned in time to hit the ball. This action reduces the vital club head speed.

The purpose of this new club head design, which is to be used for actual point-to-point contact with a golf ball or training aid simulating a golf ball, is to develop the proper muscular co-ordination for a more natural wrist release and remove the fear that the club head will not be aligned properly at impact with the ball.

FIG.6

FIG.1

FIG.5

FIG.3a

FIG.3b

FIG.3

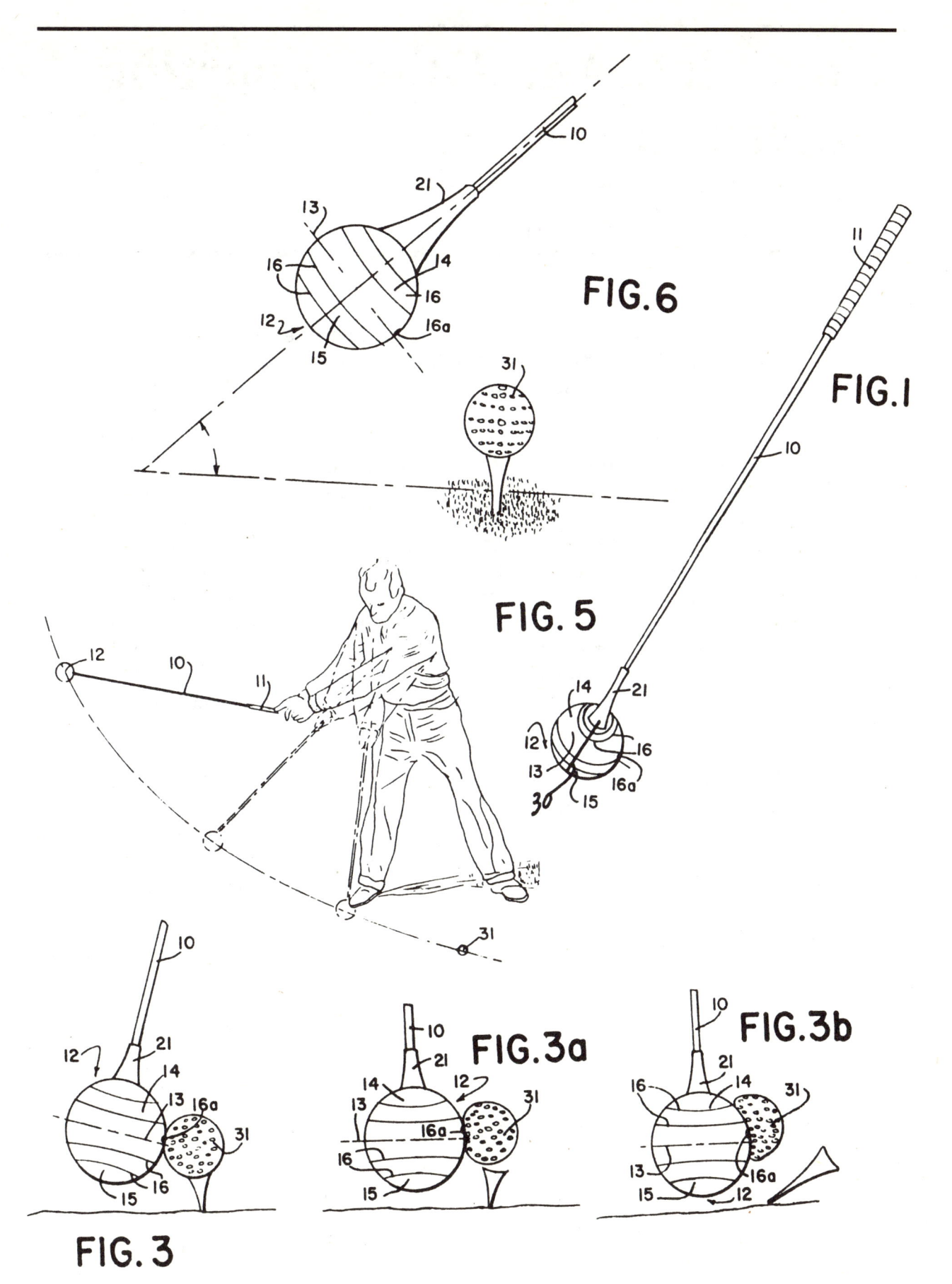

The Patent Duffer 137

Golf-Club And Other Sporting Implement

Patent No. 1,094,599 (1914)
Philip Samson of London, England

I have found that a ball can be driven considerably farther with a club having the facing specified herein than with other clubs. The said facing consists of a fabric which possesses the required resiliency and which also has on its striking face the necessary formation of surface to reduce "slicing" and "pulling" and is of such a nature that it will be only momentarily and not permanently deformed by impact with the ball and remain unaltered and give its full value in all kinds of weather.

In carrying this invention into effect I form the facing from strands of the desired material which strands are interwoven or intertwined in such a manner and are of such dimensions as to give approximately a surface formation (for instance such as shown in Fig. 22) which has only previously been obtained by cutting or shaping a surface which did not inherently possess the desired formation. This surface as will be seen, is not perfectly smooth, but consists of elevated and depressed portions that impart to it a somewhat checkered or matted appearance.

The fabric obtained by the intertwining of the strands is, or the constituent strands are, impregnated, that is to say, saturated, with a binding substance which is waterproof and when combined with the fabric provides sufficient elasticity to give the length of drive and sufficient hardness to prevent substantial deformation of the striking surface.

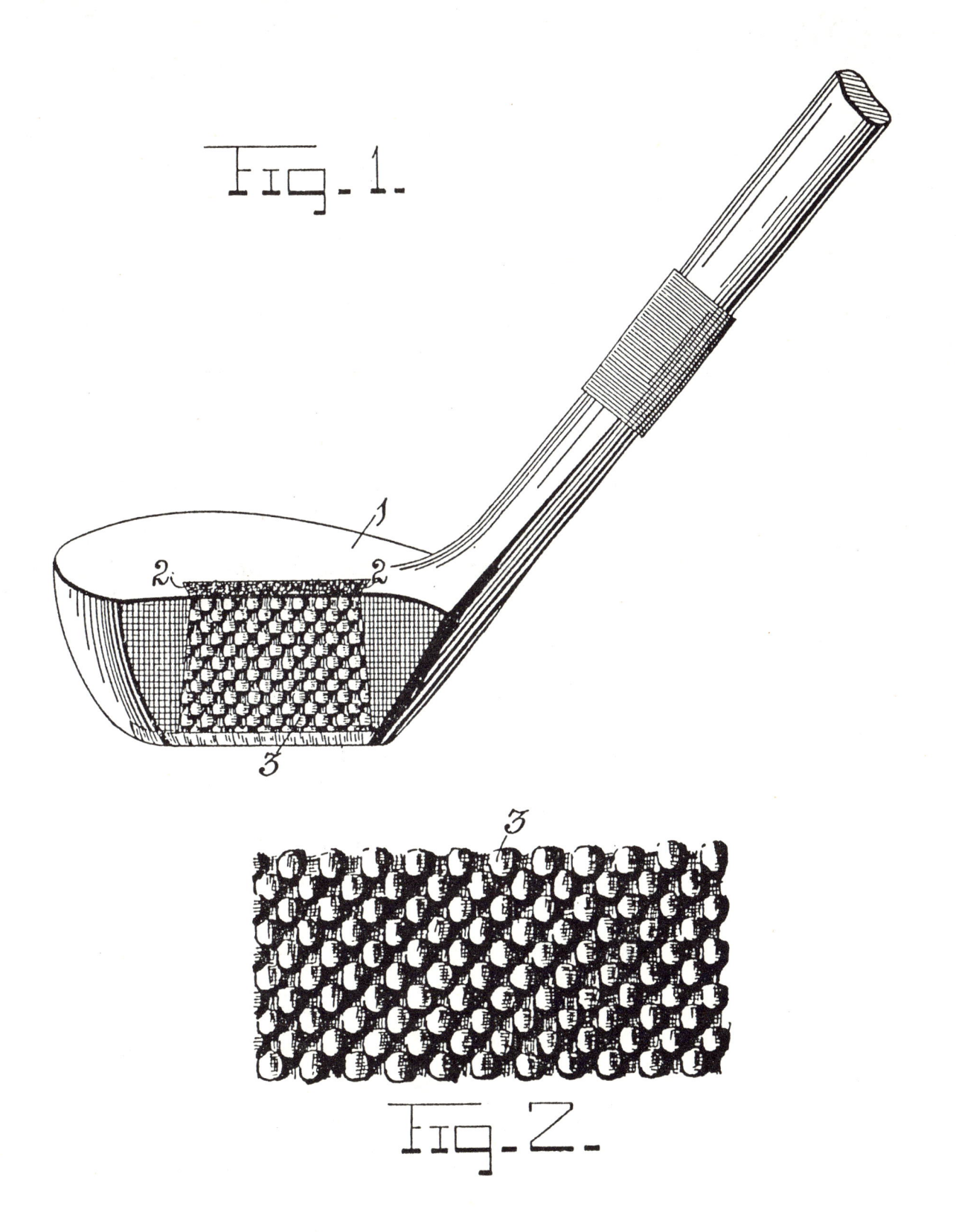

Fig. 1.

Fig. 2.

The Patent Duffer

Golf Club
Patent No. 1,561,595 (1925)
Thomas Davis of Brooklyn, New York

It is well known that the so termed "carry through", is exceedingly important and yet difficult of attainment. The amateur or student starts the club from the shoulder with certain vim and velocity, but as the club approaches the ball, the head of the club is slowed down until the contact is at a force less than that desired. The swing is neither complete nor artistic and this so called "choking" of the stroke is noticeable even in players of long experience, the "choking" resulting most often from nervousness or overanxiety.

Into the canal **12** and well **13**, I place metallic mercury, the quantity used being that quantity which will be contained almost fully within the well. The mercury can readily pass through the channels or canals and when the club is lifted, the mercury will be wholly within the stem **2**. The downward movement of the club, in making a stroke will cause the mercury to rush into the well, encouraging the user of the club to continue the swing to its full extent.

The Patent Duffer 141

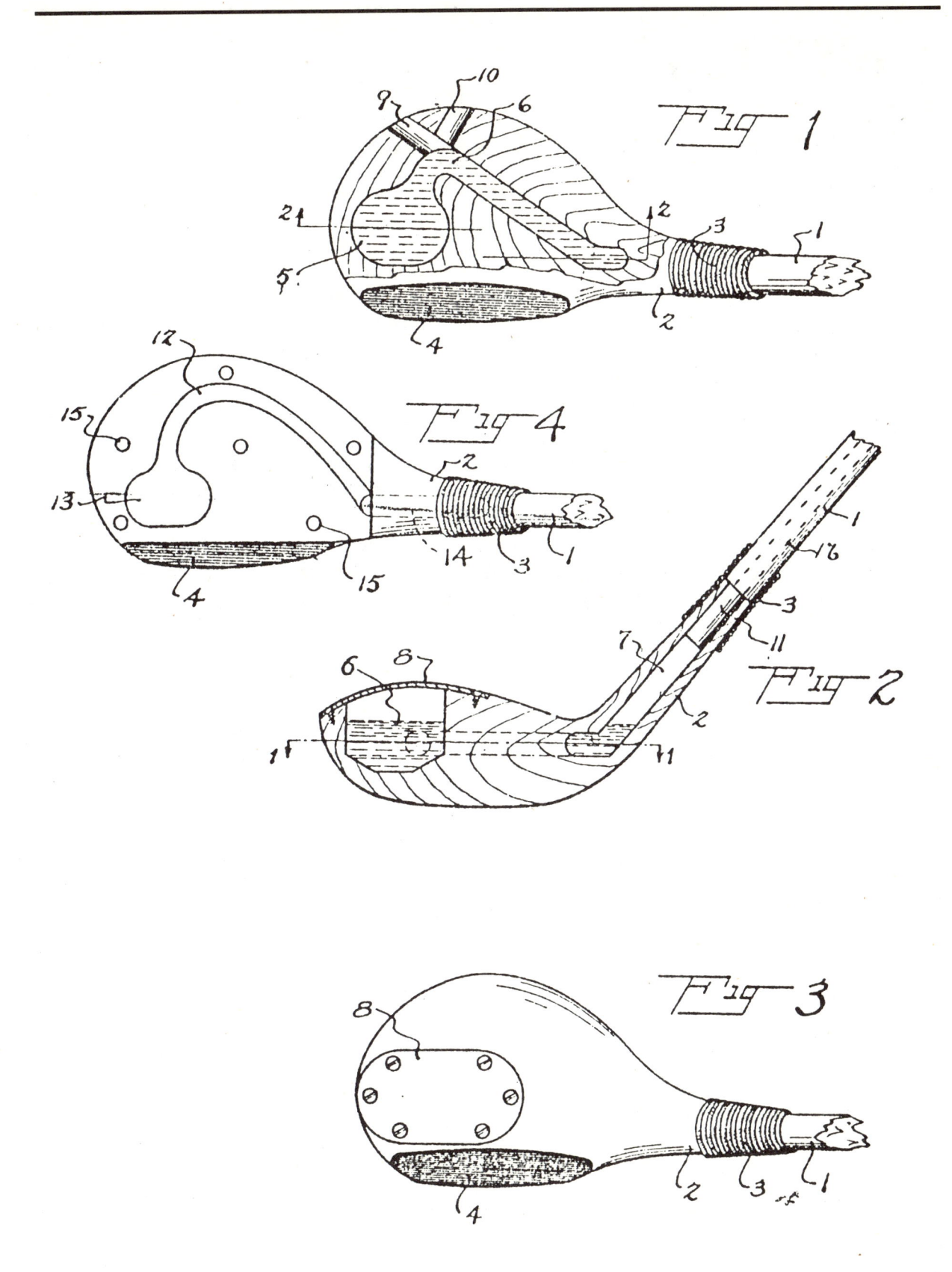

Golf Club
Patent No. 2,026,749 (1936)
Ray Pester of Grayslake, Illinois

The primary object of the invention is to provide a new and improved head for wooden clubs so that the impact face of the head may be manipulated to change the angle thereof and thereby make the wooden club applicable for various uses including a driver, brassie, and spoon.

Upon turning the thumb not **20**, the stem **18** will be given rotative movement, and due to the cooperation of the head **17** with the bore **16**, the pin **14** will be given rotative movement. Rotative movement of the thumb nut **20**, therefore, causes rotative movement of the pin **14**, and due to the engagement of the worm **13** with the teeth **12**, the member **6** of the club head will be caused to turn and vary the angle of the impact face **1**. The angle will be set to conform with the type of club to be used whether it be a driver, brassie, spoon, or any other club.

The Patent Duffer 143

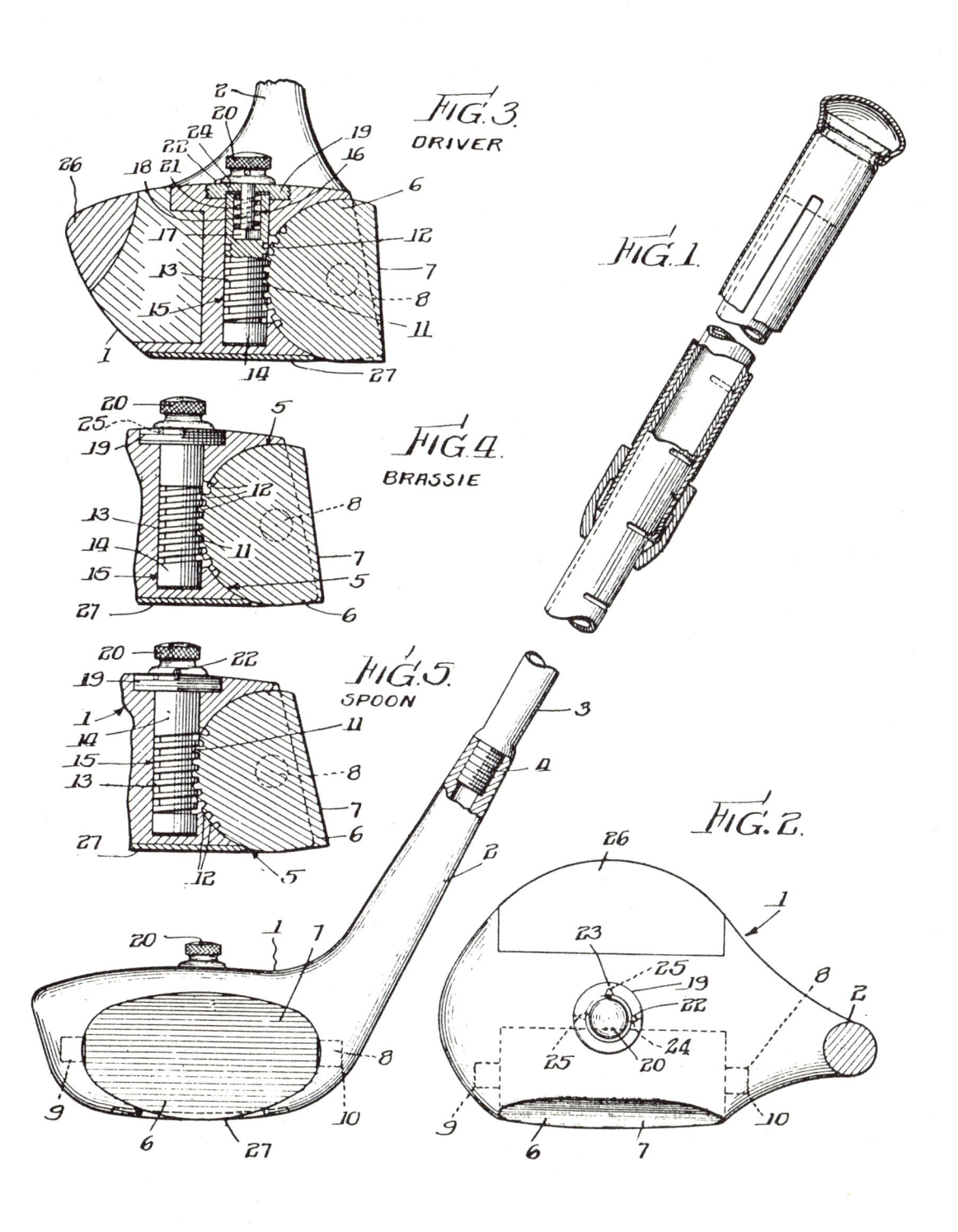

Golf Club
Patent No. 769,939 (1904)
Charles Clark of Lynn, Massachusetts

The head **h** of the driving member normally occupies a position substantially flush with the striking-face of the head **a**, so as to engage the ball, projecting, however, ever so little, and when brought severely into engagement with the ball the spring will be suddenly compressed and will quickly react and thrust the driving member outward and give to the ball an additional drive by materially accelerating its speed. The spring-actuated driving member or plunger is the essential element of the accelerating device in this instance.

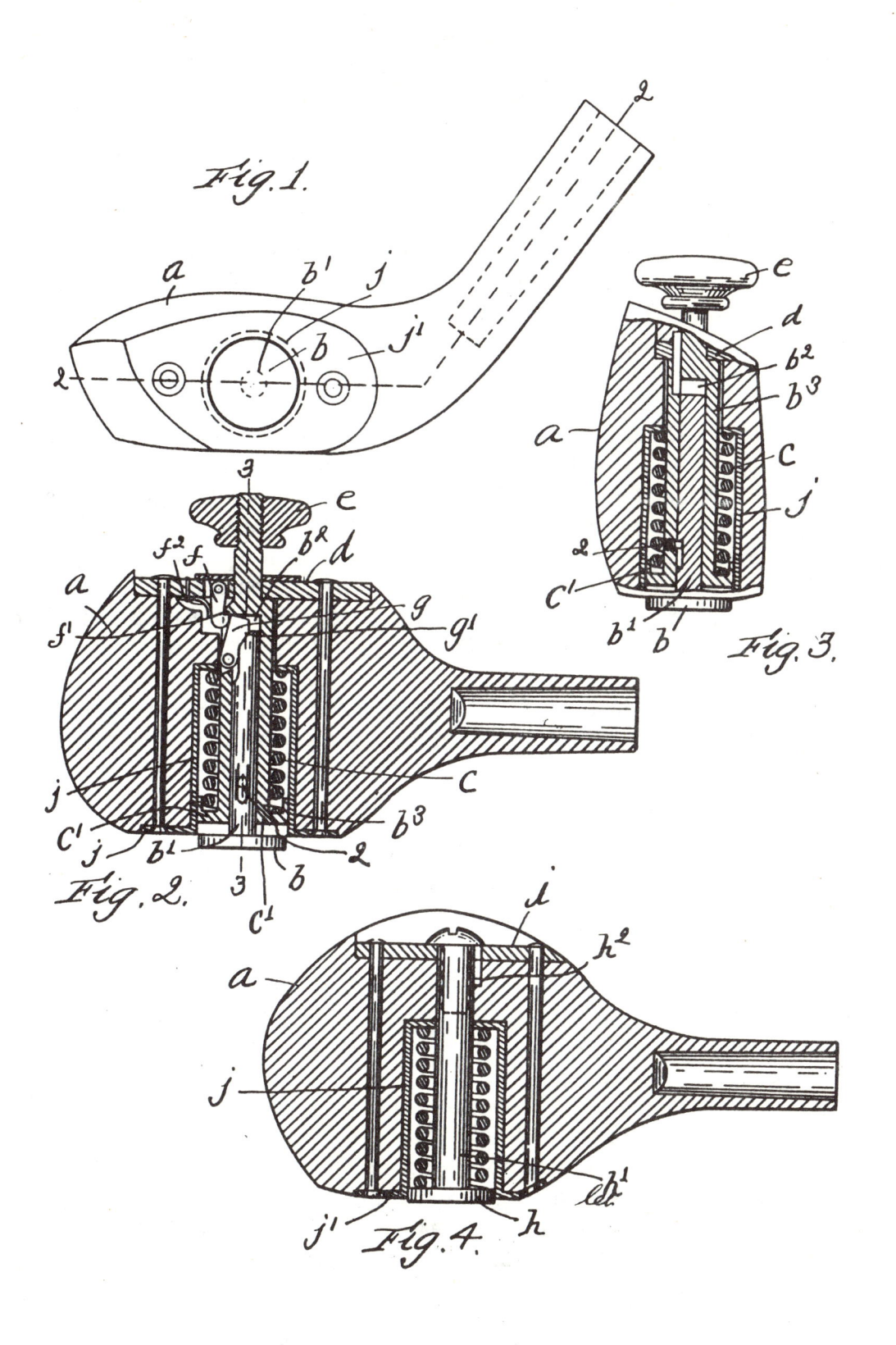

Fig. 1.

Fig. 2.

Fig. 3.

Fig. 4.

The Patent Duffer

NINE

Golf Balls

For well over 400 years, golf was a game largely confined to wind-swept coastal areas in Scotland. For generations, those venerable Scots used the same type of ball for their ancient game. The "feathery", as it was known, was made from three or four lobe-shaped strips of leather. The pieces were soaked in an alum solution, sewn together with waxed thread, and stuffed with boiled goose feathers (about as many as would fit in a top hat). A special stuffing iron was used to pack the feathers tightly together, which the ball-maker placed against his chest for greater leverage. Once the balls were packed, the hole was sewn up and the ball was left to dry. The feathers would expand and the leather would shrink as the ball dried, leaving a hard, solid sphere. Finally, the ball was oiled to make it waterproof, chalked or painted for visibility, then signed with the ball-maker's signature. Since a good ball-maker could only make about three or four a day, the cost was relatively expensive.

In 1848, a new type of ball was introduced that would change the game forever. This new ball was much easier for the average player to hit, flew appreciably farther, and lasted many rounds longer than the previous "featheries". This revolutionary new ball was the inimitable "gutty". Robert Patterson, a Brit, first came up with the ball after soaking a stick of gutta-percha in warm water, and shaping a spheroid from the rubbery mass. The first balls were smooth, and would fly off the club like a shot before ducking swiftly to the ground. It was soon discovered that used balls, which were nicked and scored, flew much longer and straighter than the newly-molded ones, so the manufacturers intentionally began to dimple the surfaces. The "gutty" soon drew scores of new players to the game, and took golf from the exclusive domain of the Scots to worldwide popularity.

The next revolution in ball-making took place in the United States. We have Coburn Haskell of Cleveland, Ohio to thank for being a golfer who was in the right place at the right time. In 1898, Coburn was visiting a friend at the Goodrich Rubber Company in Akron when he chanced upon some narrow rubber stripping the company made. The thought immediately struck him to wind the strips around a rubber core to produce a new lively ball.

> If you think it's hard to meet new people,
> try picking up the wrong golf ball.
>
> *Jack Lemmon*

Initially, getting the strips evenly wound around the core was a problem, but a machine built by the Goodrich Company finally solved the problem. These "Bounding Billies", as they were called, went a good twenty yards farther than the previous "guttys". Except for changes in the cover materials, this basic three-piece ball design is still used by the ball manufacturers. Cover materials have gone from gutta-percha to balata, to the new synthetics like Surlyn and other plastics mixed with lightweight metals.

The search for a ball that goes farther, feels softer, is more forgiving of mis-hits, and is able to bore through the wind better, goes on to this day. The USGA's Initial Velocity limit (which restricts a ball's speed at impact to 255 feet per second) has been reached for a number of years. Ball manufacturers have recently been concentrating on the aerodynamics of the covers. By the number and shape of the dimples, the ball-makers can control how high or low the balls fly, so a particular ball may be tailored to each person's game.

Our focus in this chapter will be on some of the more imaginative configurations the simple sphere has taken. For example, have you ever hit a ball and when you walked over to where you know it landed, there was no sign of it? Philip Kane of Kane, Pennsyvania was probably the victim of this situation more than once, since his everlasting contribution to the game is a **Golf Ball** (page 158) that contains a replaceable smoke bomb inside. The golfer lights the fuse on the ball and drives without worry about where the ball ends up, since a plume of smoke will be emitted when it lands. It should be noted that after a few courses burned to the ground, this ball was banned from play.

Ever had a record round going and you get to the 16th hole just as darkness falls? Most people would have to quit. Charles Smith and Hugh Jamieson of Los Angeles wouldn't think of going in just because of a little darkness. Their bright gift to golf is the **Electroluminescent Game Ball** (page 154) which glows in the dark for extended play.

So whatever your choice of balls, – smoking balls, balls that glow, two-piece balls, three-piece balls, oranges ones, white ones, whatever – remember, when you play, just go out and have a ball.

Method Of Toughening Golf Ball Covers

Patent No. 2,805,072 (1957)

Wendell Smith of Nutley, New Jersey

I have discovered a highly effective way of irradiating the covers of golf balls without objectionably injuring the rubber windings. More particularly, I have found that by using high-voltage electrons as the means of irradiation it is possible to successfully irradiate the covers of golf balls in such a manner as to substantially enhance the toughness, scuffing-resistance and cutting-resistance of the covers without objectionably injuring the rubber windings. Still more particularly, I have discovered that by employing high-voltage electrons having a voltage between 200 and 800 kilovolts, and by applying an irradiation dosage equal to from 5×10^{-5} to 2×10^{-3} coulomb per square inch of cover surface area, the cover of the golf ball can be irradiated so as to have considerably enhanced toughness, scuffing-resistance and cutting-resistance without objectionably impairing the properties of the rubber threads of the windings.

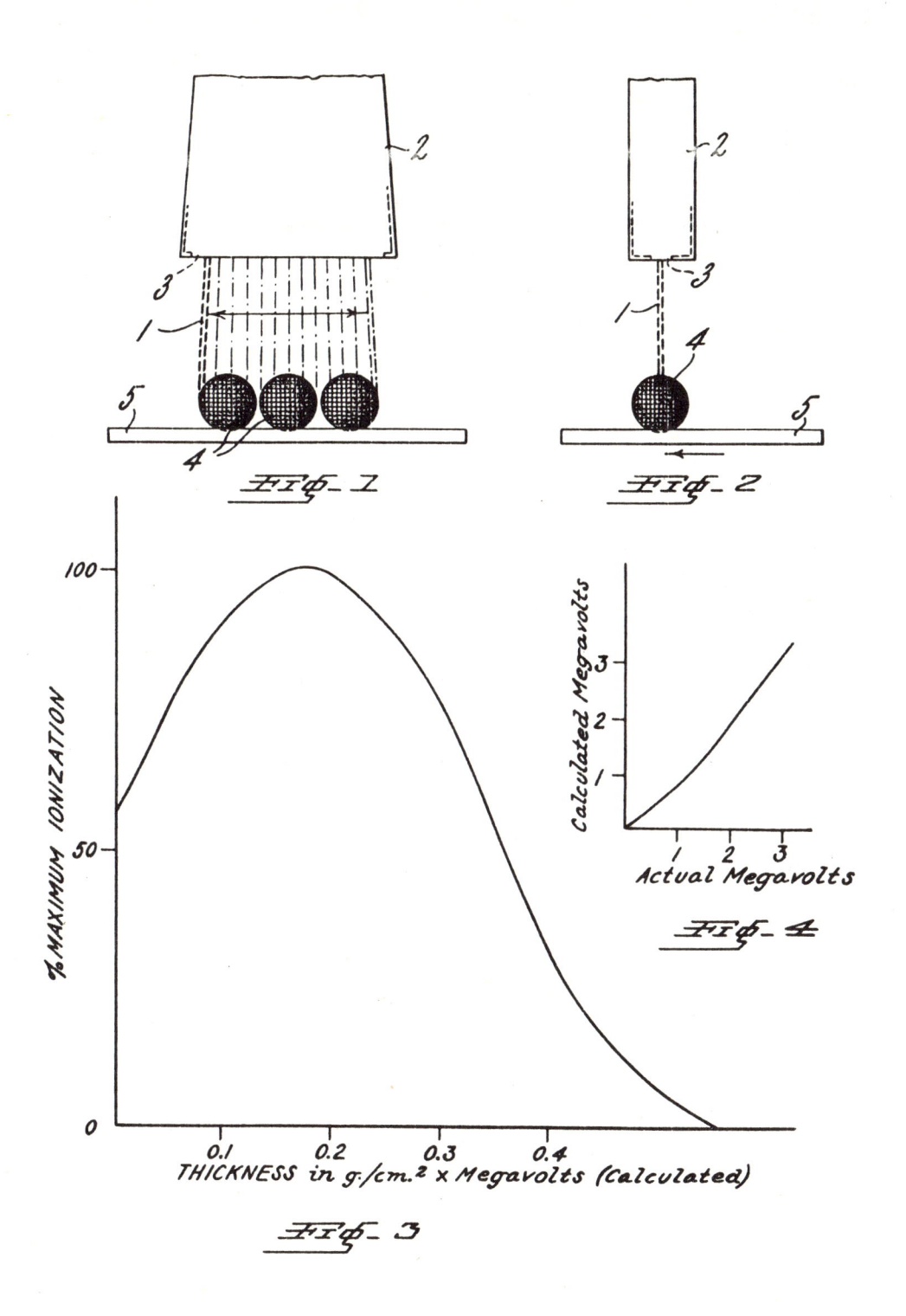

Fig. 1

Fig. 2

Fig. 3

Fig. 4

The Patent Duffer 149

Practice Golf Tee Including Mirror Means

Patent No. 3,459,428 (1969)

Nathan Miller of Lynbrook, New York

As best seen in FIGURE 1, the ball is adjusted on the tee so that the mirror is substantially normal to a line extending from the eyes of the golfer to the ball. It will be observed that variations, particularly in a vertical plane, from the precise normal position are permissible so that, for instance, a golfer may adjust the ball so that the eyes, when directed toward the ball, will be able to perceive a reflection of the nose or the chin of the golfer. When the swing is executed with the golf ball thus positioned, the golfer will be permitted to concentrate his attention where it belongs, on the golf ball, while at the same time being able to perceive any head movements inherent in his swing. Even the slightest deviation of head position will be observed from the fact that the initial reflection, for instance the nose or the chin, will disappear from view if there has been any movement or displacement of the head.

The golf swing may be completed and the ball actually struck, permitting the golfer to execute not only a practice swing but and actual golf stroke.

Due to the off-balance nature of the golf ball and the non-aerodynamic or eccentric configuration thereof provided by the planar portion, the flight pattern of the ball will not be comparable to the flight of a normal ball. However, this is an advantage from the instructional standpoint in that the non-aerodynamic or eccentric condition of the ball will overemphasize the effects of any improper spin imparted to the golf ball.

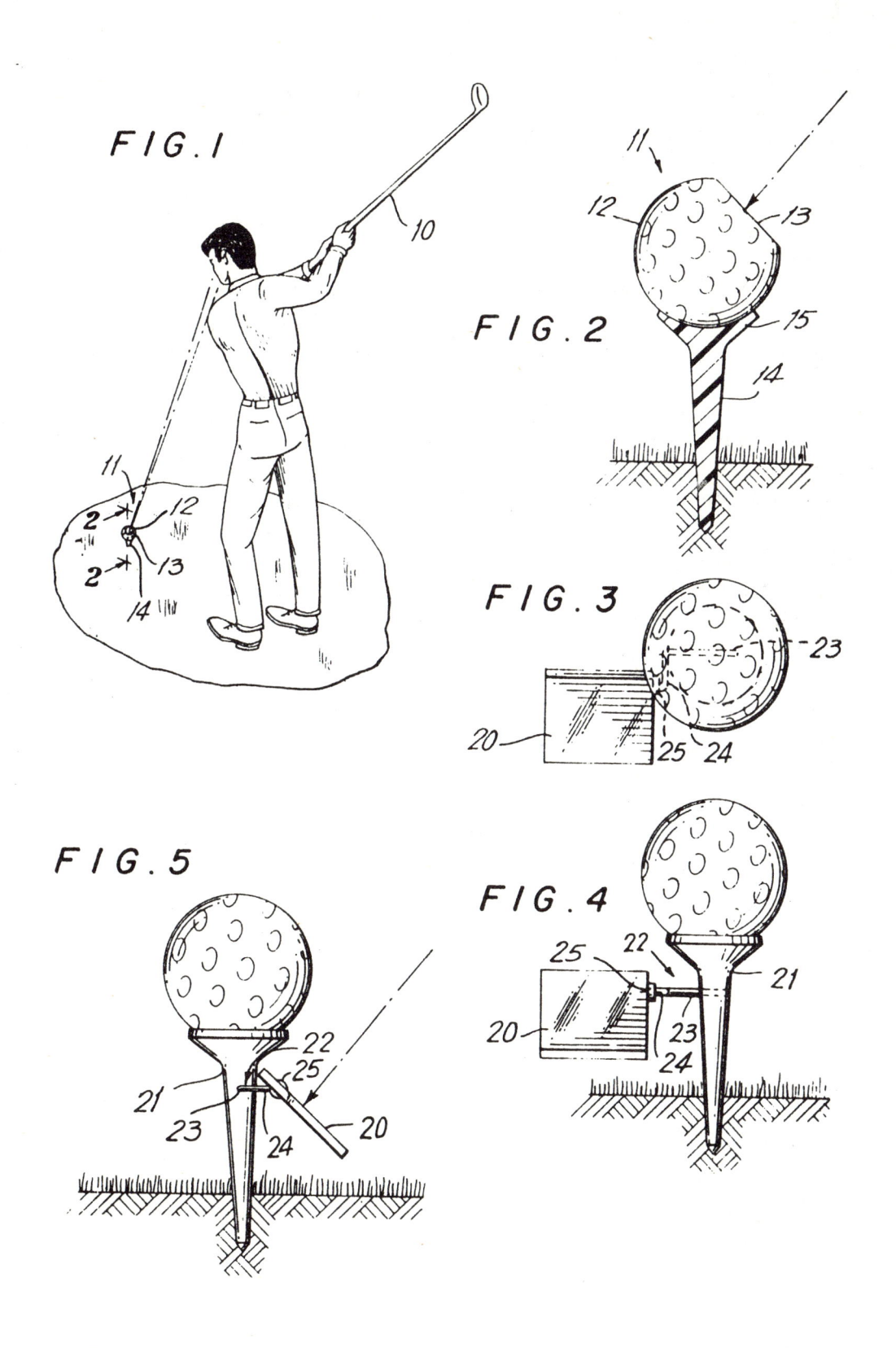

FIG.1

FIG.2

FIG.3

FIG.5

FIG.4

The Patent Duffer 151

Golf Ball
Patent No. 3,782,730 (1974)
Stephen Horchler of Eskbank, Scotland

This invention relates to a golf ball containing an electric oscillator circuit which assists in the recovery of golf balls lost during a game of golf. It is a well known fact that many golf balls are lost due to the fact that during play the golf ball lands in a particularly overgrown area of the golf course. The loss can occur even though the ball may have been visible during its entire flight and the approximate region of the landing of the ball is known. The loss of a golf ball not only entails financial loss to the player it also means that the player is put at a disadvantage as far as that game is concerned. The present invention reduces the occurrence of lost golf balls and players employing golf balls which can be recovered are at an advantage both financially and by not losing unnecessary points over lost balls.

Conveniently the oscillator circuit is tuned to a particular frequency and generates an induction field at that frequency, the oscillatory circuit squegging so that its output comprises bursts of oscillation at the desired frequency interspersed by longer periods of non-oscillation. The bursts of oscillation can be kept stable and the repetition of these bursts appear in a detector unit (which maybe a simple radio receiver tuned to the frequency of the oscillator circuit) as a modulation frequency characteristic of the oscillator circuit employed. By filtering this pulse repetition frequency the detector unit can respond to different frequencies making identification of different golf balls possible.

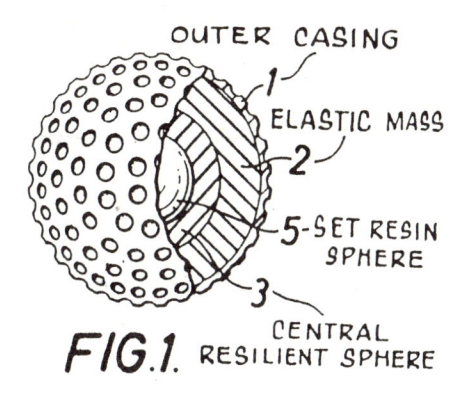

FIG.1.
- 1 OUTER CASING
- 2 ELASTIC MASS
- 5 SET RESIN SPHERE
- 3 CENTRAL RESILIENT SPHERE

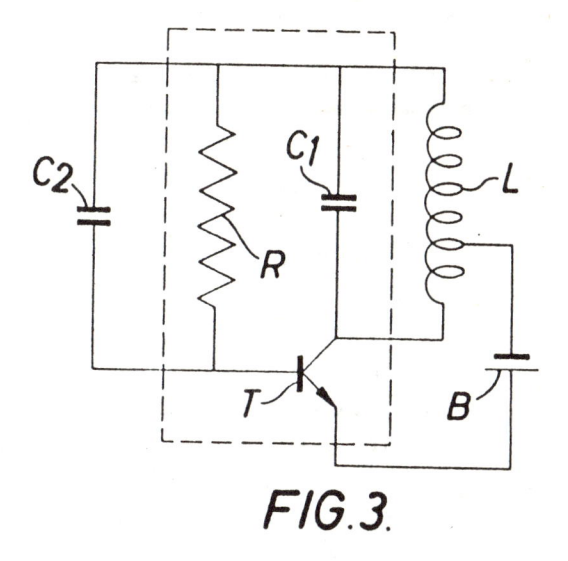

FIG.3.

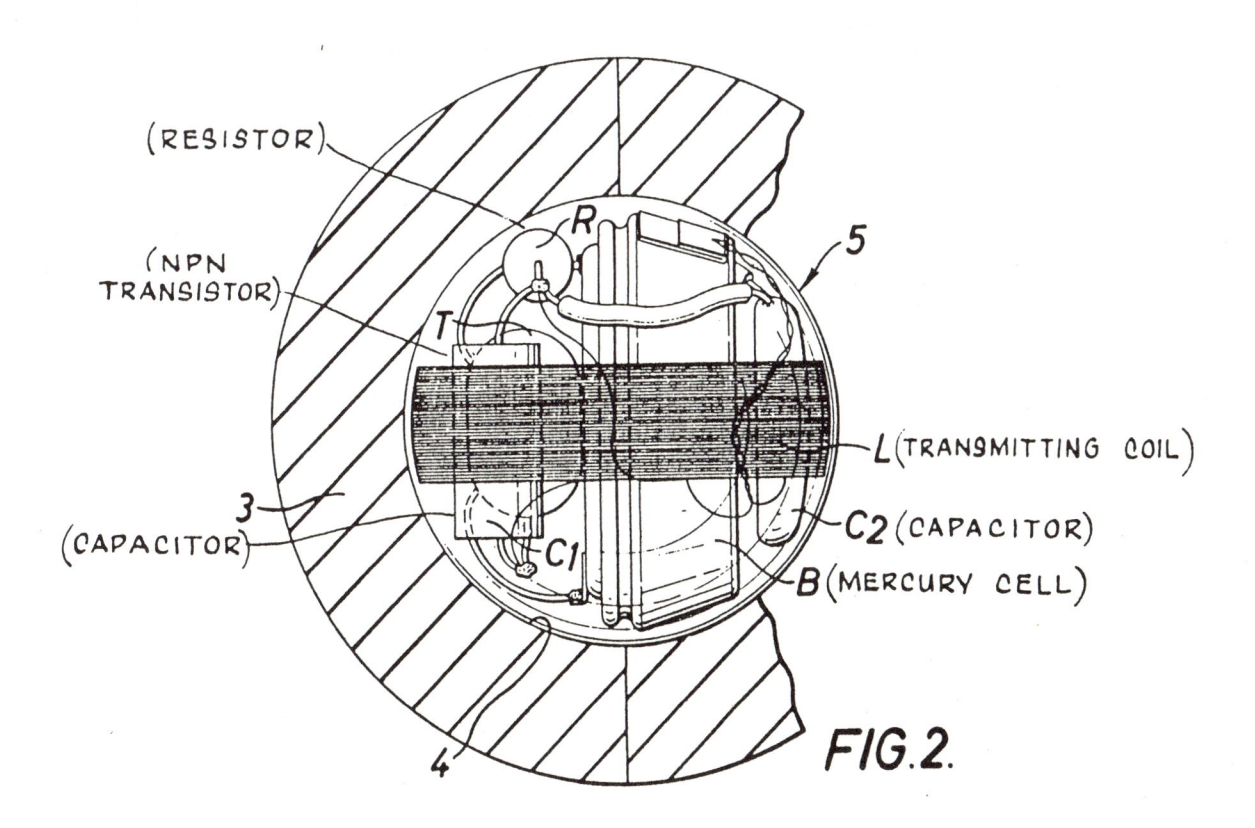

FIG.2.
- (RESISTOR) R
- (NPN TRANSISTOR) T
- (CAPACITOR) C1
- L (TRANSMITTING COIL)
- C2 (CAPACITOR)
- B (MERCURY CELL)

The Patent Duffer

Electroluminescent Game Ball
Patent No. 3,351,347 (1967)
Charles Smith of West Los Angeles, California
Hugh Jamieson of Los Angeles, California

In general, the present invention comprises a ball for use in sporting activities that provides radiating light, which light makes the ball readily visible in darkness and more easily followed in play. The structure of the ball includes an oscillator circuit as incorporating a semiconductor device and a battery to provide electrical oscillations, which circuit is mounted and dynamically balanced in a core of the ball. A ball body is then provided about the core and contiguous the outside cover, electroluminescent means radiates light, energized by the electrical oscillations. Various switching structures may be included in accordance with the invention for activating the oscillator circuit when the ball is ready to be used.

The light is not usually intense at best, but rather is somewhat above a glow level so that the ball can be clearly viewed in good contrast to surrounding darkness or low-level natural night illumination. In this regard, the ball hereof offers a somewhat considerable advantage in use over a conventional ball on an illuminated golf course, because, natural light (or darkness) is substantially uniform over the course and intensely-bright light sources that often temporarily blind players are avoided.

The Patent Duffer 155

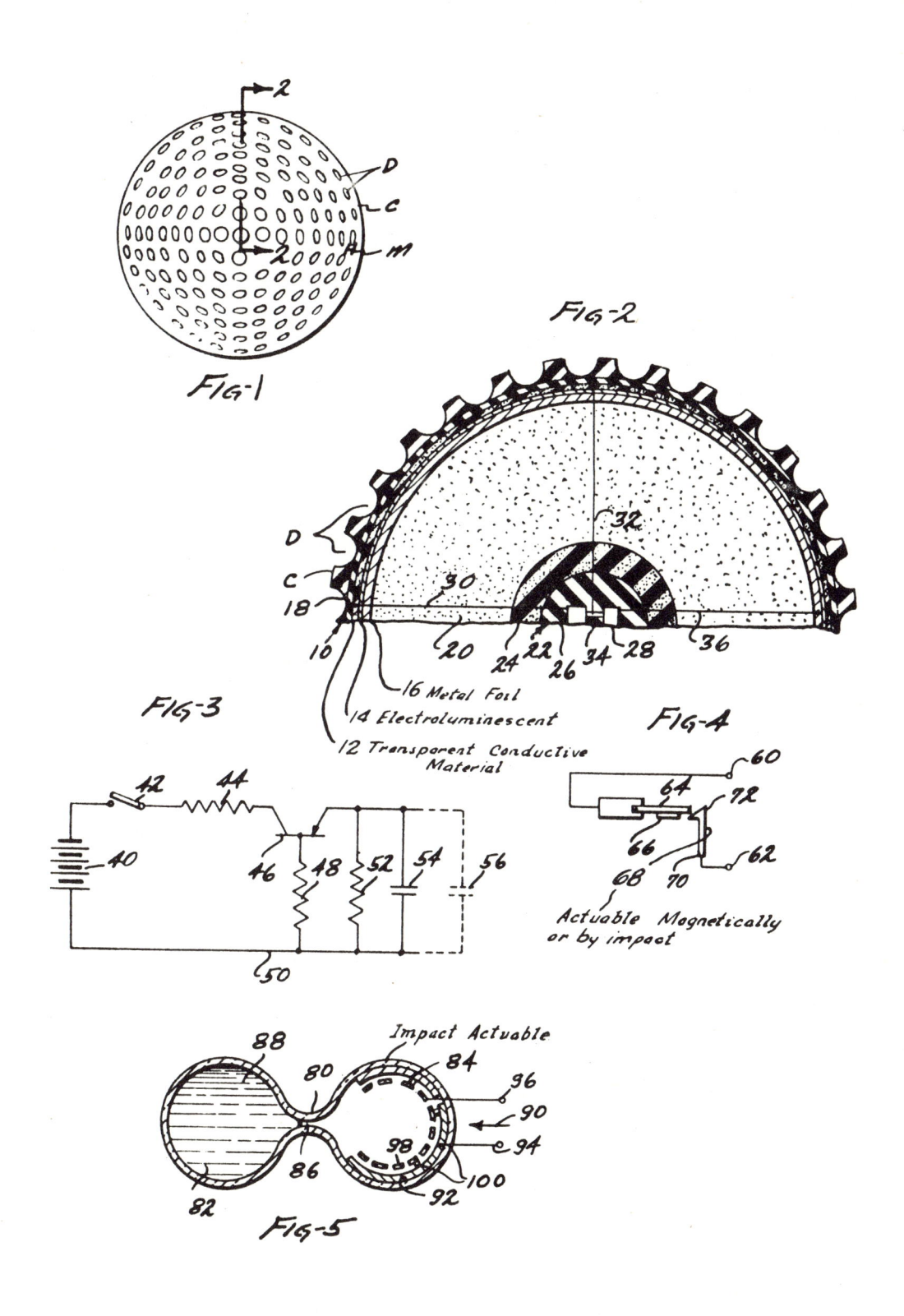

Parachute Golf Ball
Patent No 3,147,979 (1964)
Harmon Wolfe of Dearborn, Michigan

The best practice is considered to be to hit an actual golf ball because this most closely simulates actual golfing and permits the golfer to move from practice to actual play with a minimum of change in the conditions. The present invention offers a solution to this problem by providing a practice golf ball which comprises a real golf ball having a parachute attached thereto to impede the flight of the ball after it is hit.

In use of the practice golf ball assembly, the golfer **58** places the ball on a tee **60** with the painted surface **52** facing away from the line of flight. The canopy **16** is positioned in front of the ball to the end that the ball will have a relatively free flight until it passes over the canopy and travels a distance there beyond approximately equal to the length of the cords **18, 20**. Thus, the golfer gets the same feel that he would get if hitting a ball on the golf links or at a golf driving range.

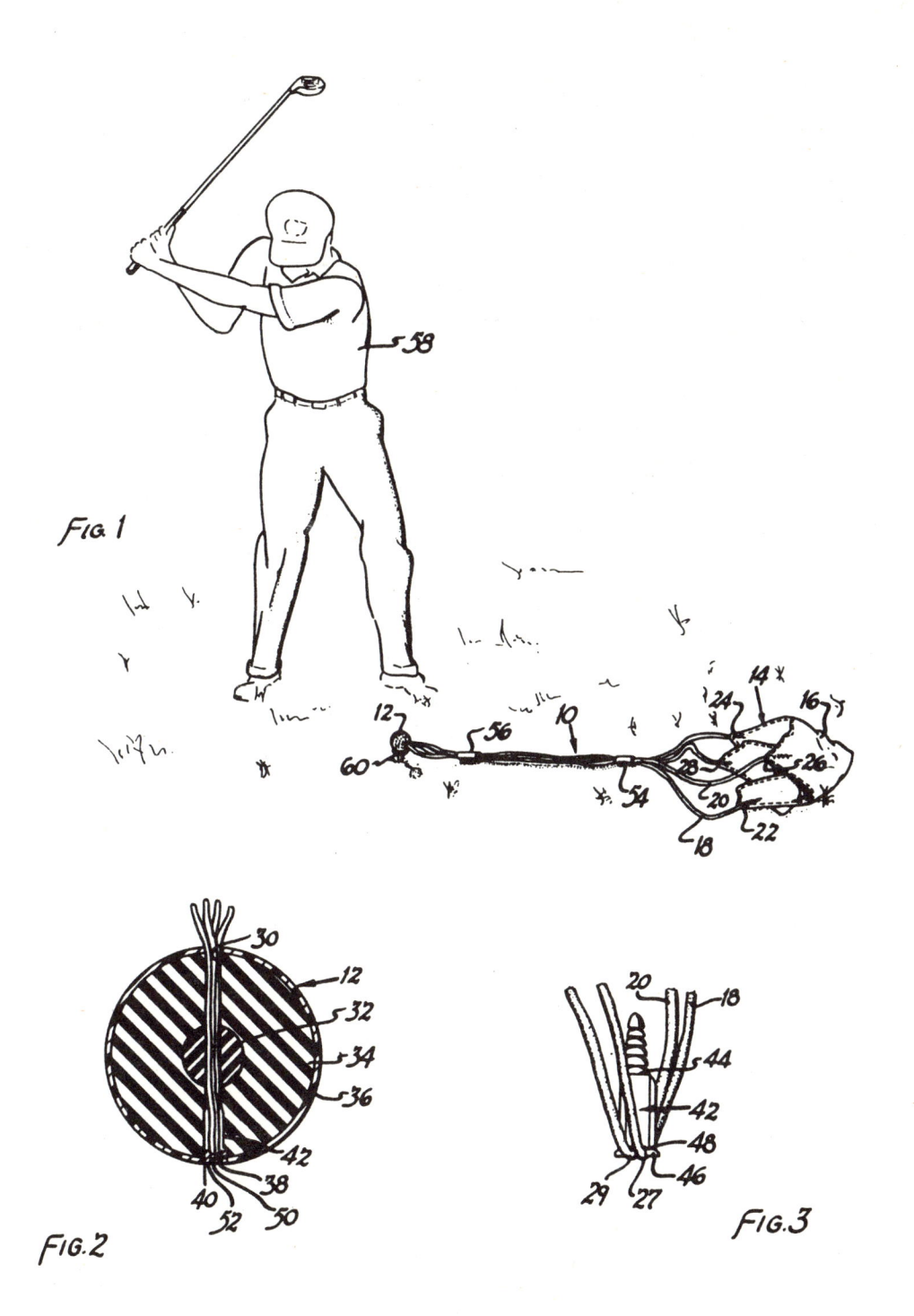

Fig. 1

Fig. 2

Fig. 3

The Patent Duffer

Golf Ball
Patent No. 1,583,721 (1926)
Philip Kane of Kane, Pennsylvania

My present invention has the provision of a golf ball provided with signal means, preferably visible signal means, which will permit the owner and others to tell exactly where to find the ball in tall grass for instance where it would ordinarily be difficult and require time to find.

In Figs. **2,** and **4,** I have shown a squib **17** with a short fuse **18** which is lighted before the ball is driven so that its flight may be more readily traced and the spot where it finally comes to rest may be easily seen. By virtue of the slow burning powder or squib and the emission of smoke for a considerable period no trouble is encountered in locating the ball even in high grass where this is ordinarily a difficult matter.

The Patent Duffer 159

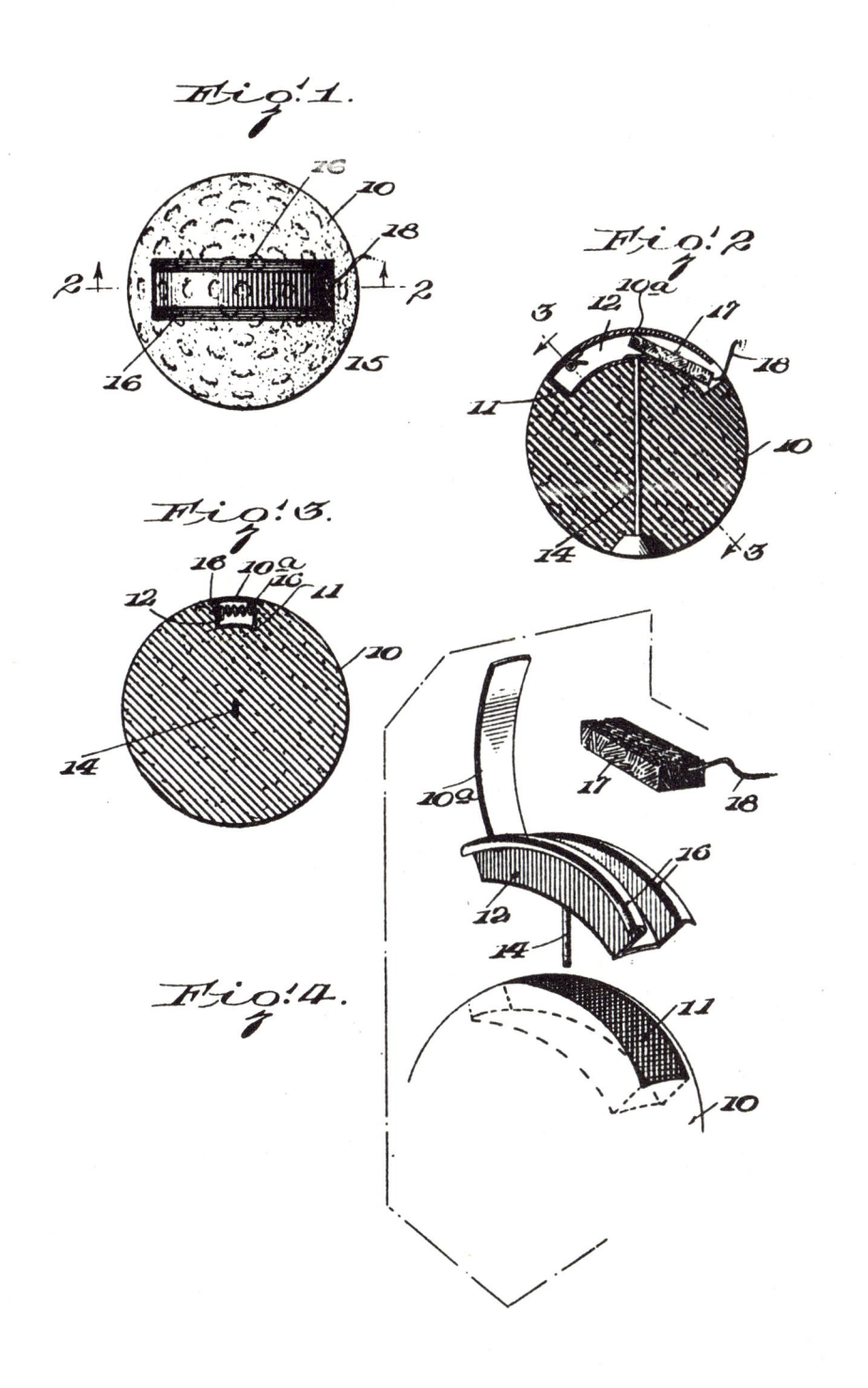

Practice Ball
Patent No. 3,081,091 (1963)
Harlow Grow of Pacific Palisades, California

A principal object of the present invention is to provide a practice ball for exuding a marking medium on the face of the club, by which a golfer may evaluate and perfect his swing for each one of the clubs he may use.

In carrying out the invention, a practice ball is provided of hollow character, to contain a fibrous material impregnated and/or coated with a powdery substance, so that a portion or portions of the powdery substance will be exuded onto the face of the club in such manner that the markings and positions thereof produced on the face of the club will indicate imperfections in the swing of the club that results in a poor contact of the club with the ball.

In order to position the ball for the particular club to be used, the exterior face of the ball is provided with a series of pips or other indications **11**, each identified by an initial or by a number corresponding to the numbers of the golf clubs to be used. For example, the ball illustrated shows pips representing a five iron, a two iron and a brassie. The pips **11** are arranged in a circumference of the ball that includes the orifice **9**, and they are spaced different distances from the orifice **9**, so that when a club is selected, the ball is positioned with the pip **11** designating the club uppermost. This positions the orifice **9** directly in a position so that if the golfer executes a proper swing the face of the club will strike the ball squarely on the orifice **9**. The impact will flatten the ball at the side of the impact, as shown in FIG. **3**, to compress the fibrous material sufficiently to loosen the powdery substance at the site of the orifice.

Fig. 1.   Fig. 4.

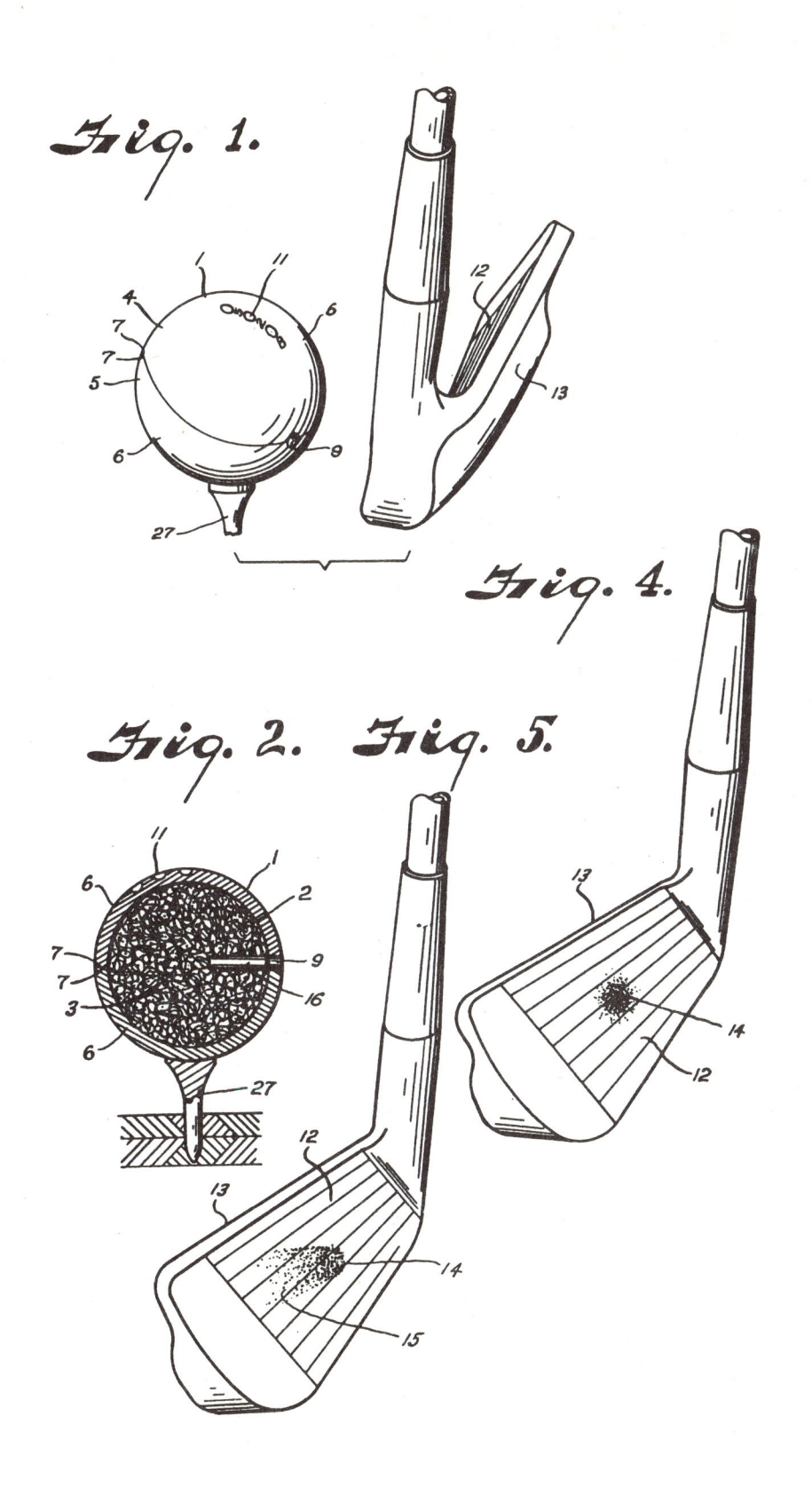

Fig. 2.   Fig. 5.

The Patent Duffer   161

Golf Practice Device
Patent No. 3,721,447 (1973)
Charles Louderback of Milwaukee, Wisconsin

It is a primary purpose of this invention to provide a golf practice device which will include a contact engaging textile material covered ball which will cling to a similar adhesive pad to be secured to the face of the head of the golf club.

Another object of this invention is to provide a golf practice device in accordance with the preceding object wherein the pad will be scored with red lines, a horizontal one, a center line, a heel line and a toe line, thus enabling the golfer or beginner to know when he has struck the ball correctly, the ball clinging to the pad so as to indicate to the golfer whether they would have had a potential slice, hook, or a tendency to top the ball and enabling the beginner to adjust himself and his club to produce a correct swing.

If the ball is hit on the toe or heel, it will indicate a slice or hook. if the ball is hit in the center, it would indicate a good hit. The ball may be placed on a tee or the ground and when the golfer swings at the ball and makes contact, the ball will adhere to the pad on the club thereby making it obvious to the golfer where he has make contact in order that he will make the necessary adjustment to correct his swing.

FIG. 1
FIG. 2
FIG. 3
FIG. 4
FIG. 5
FIG. 6
FIG. 7
FIG. 8

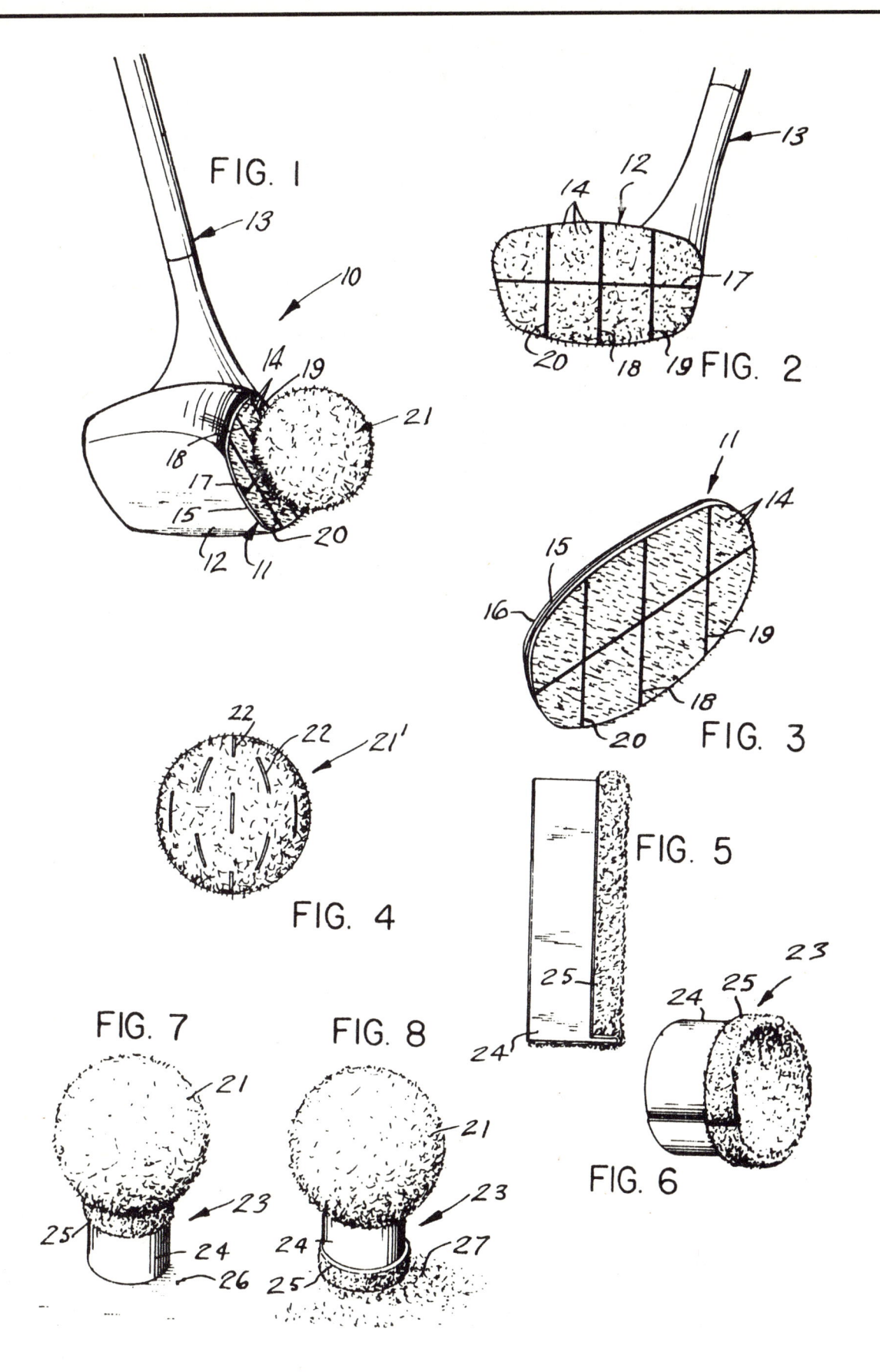

The Patent Duffer 163

Walking Golf Ball
Patent No. 3,572,696 (1971)
Donald Poynter of Cincinnati, Ohio

The walking golf ball comprises a spherical hollow casing containing a motor, and legs activated by the motor to cause the golf ball to advance with a walking motion toward a cup or other target selected by the player. Control of the motor preferably is by means of a small lever or the like projecting from the ball at a location of little prominence, and which may be manipulated more or less casually by the head of a golf club. The mechanism includes means for directing the ball along a generally straight course, with a deliberate side-to-side wobble.

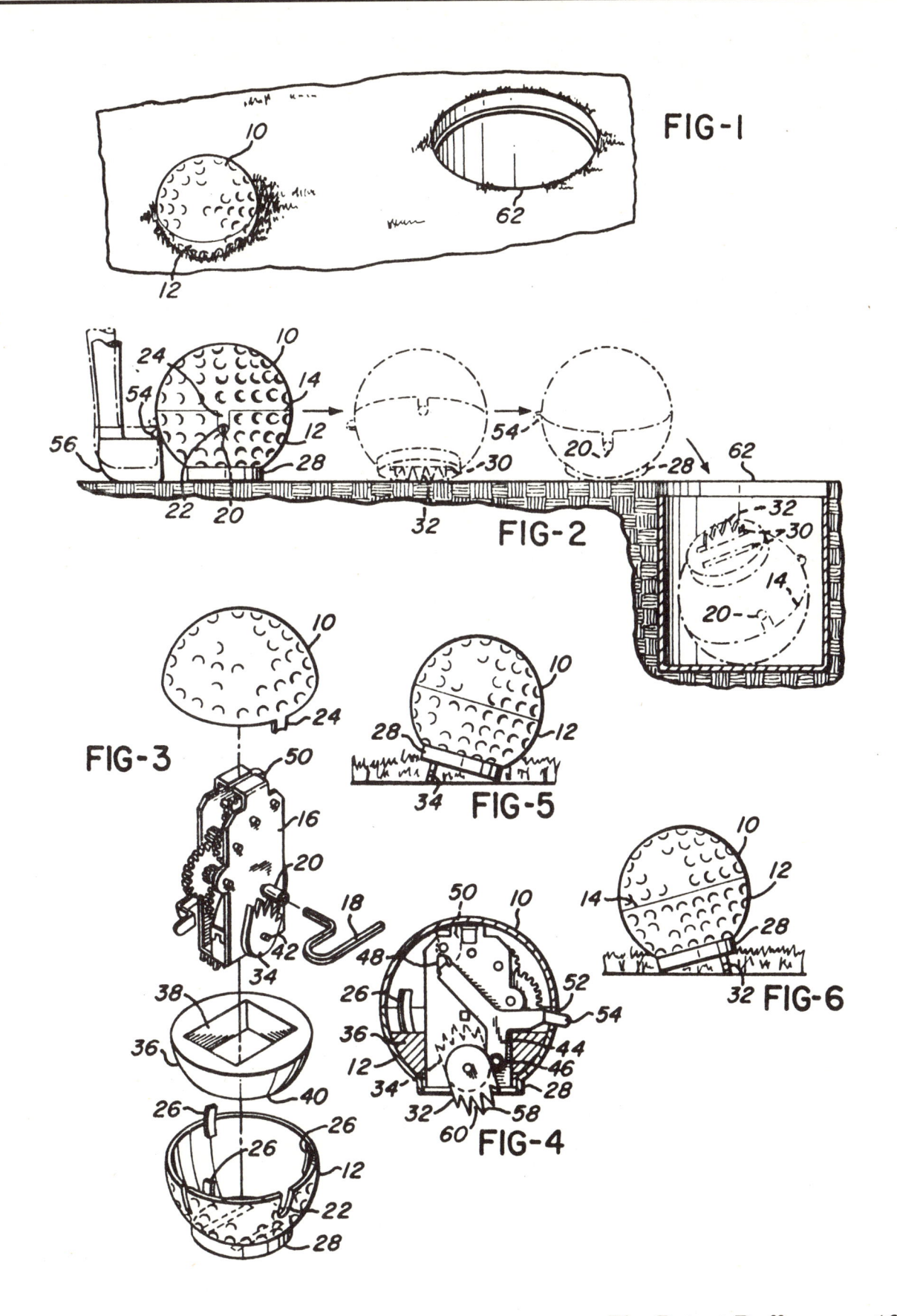

FIG-1

FIG-2

FIG-3

FIG-4

FIG-5

FIG-6

The Patent Duffer 165

Golf Practice Projectile

Patent No. 3,357,705 (1967)

Roger Blanchard of Tucson, Arizona

In general, my golf practice device comprises a pair of spheres **10** held in dumbbell-like spaced relationship by a flexible, normally straight member **11** having a maximum cross sectional dimension less than the diameter of said spheres.

When one end of my device is struck with a golf club, the portion struck starts to move (Fig. **2**) The flexible member bends, thereby absorbing some of the energy imparted by the blow and the entire article is propelled through the air (Fig. **5**). In flight, the flexible member bends first one way and then another, thereby substantially continuously altering the center of rotation of the device. Thus, the practice device flies through the air in an eccentric manner. Apparently, this eccentric flight is a major factor in impeding the travel of my device through the air. When the practice device comes to rest a few feet away, it is ordinarily in its normal dumbbell-like shape with the flexible member substantially straight.

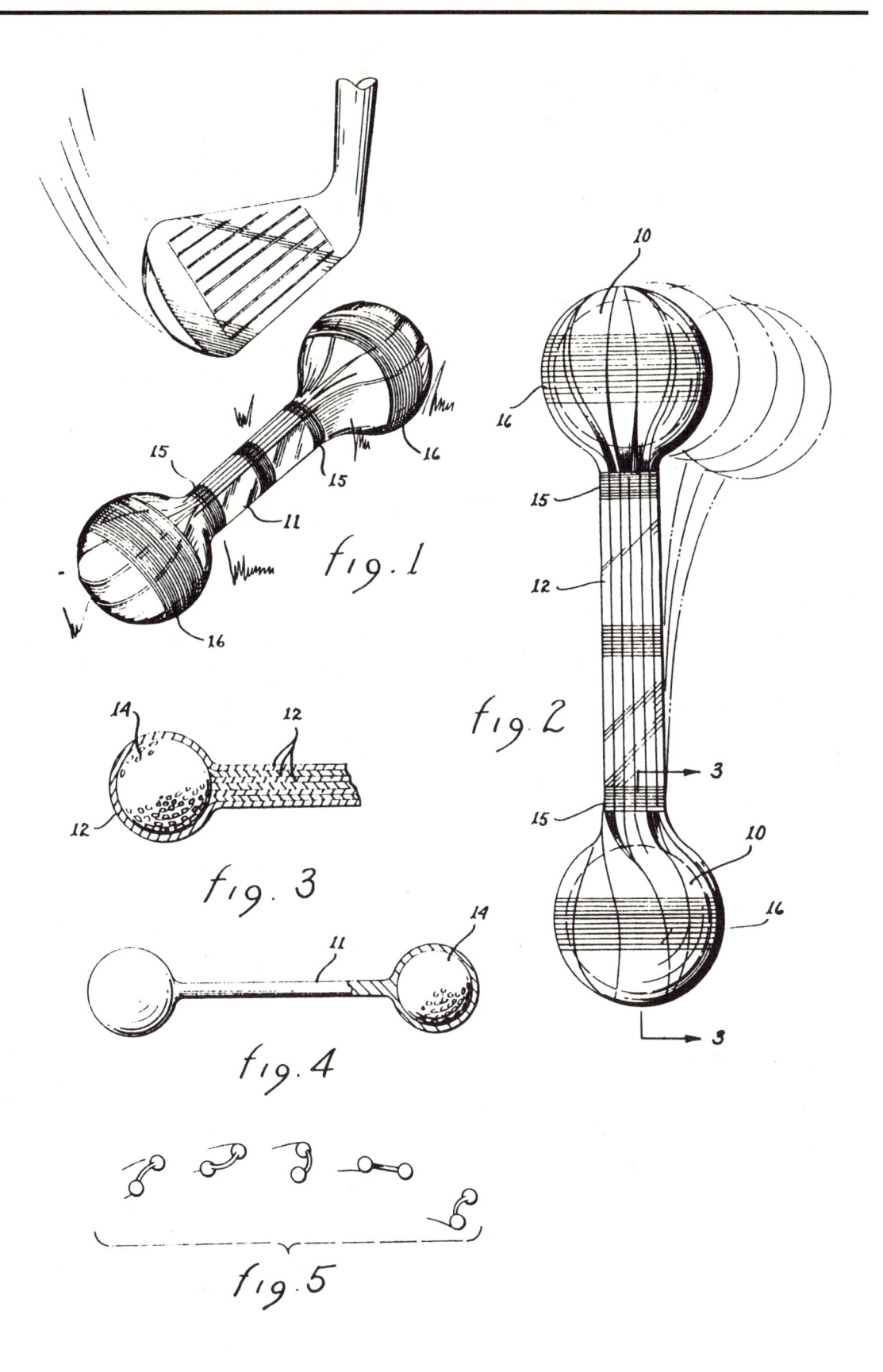

fig. 1

fig. 2

fig. 3

fig. 4

fig. 5

The Patent Duffer 167

Practice Golf Ball

Patent No. 1,43,165 (1924)

Washington Eaton of Holyoke, Massachusetts

This invention relates to practice golf balls, more particularly to a type of ball which may be used either indoors or outdoors. It is especially adapted, however, for use where distances are limited or where one desires to avoid losing the ball or injuring objects such as windows in adjacent buildings, or the furnishings in a building in which it may be used.

The object of the invention is to provide a practice golf ball simulating as far as possible a regulation ball, but so constructed as to travel a limited distance; and at the same time to provide the mental hazard of the regulation gall, in appearance and manner of flight, though falling short in distance.

The wall **5** of the ball is provided with a large number of apertures **7** which so change the properties of the ball that, when it is hit, it does not travel far in response to the blow. In Figs. **1** and **2** the apertures **7** are shown as being square holes. These holes so disturb the air currents about the ball that very high air resistance is brought about, thereby causing the ball to fall short.

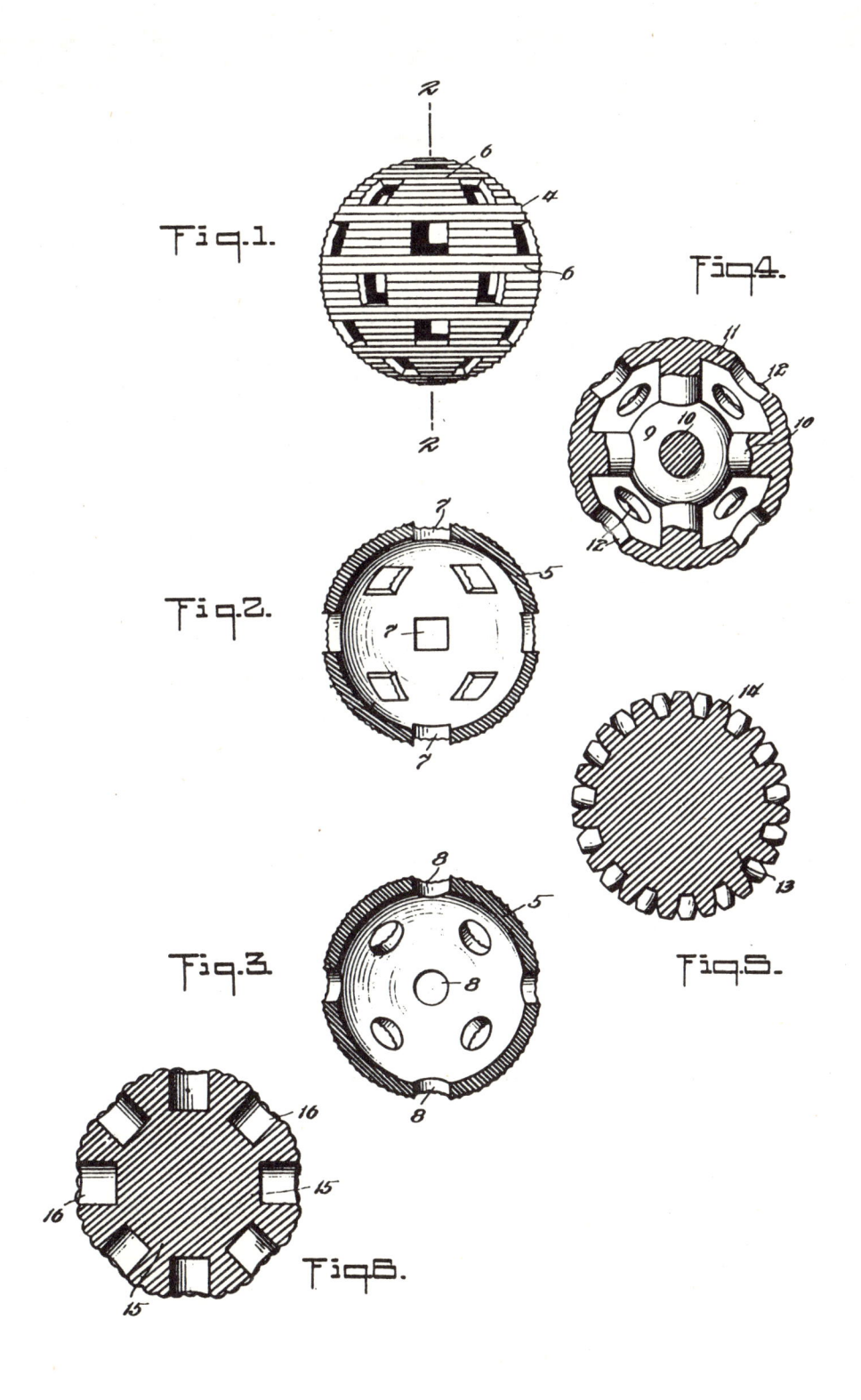

Fig.1.

Fig.2.

Fig.3.

Fig.4.

Fig.5.

Fig.6.

The Patent Duffer 169

TEN

The Art of Putting

Aside from attire, nowhere in the game of golf is individualism more evident than in the art of putting. There are few hard and fast rules which apply to the putting stroke. The width of the stance, the amount of bend at the knees and hips, the position of the ball, whether the ball is struck with a wrist or arm stroke, a smooth follow-through or a smart slap, elbows close to the body or away, all of these inclinations have their supporters, with seemingly equal degrees of success. Jack Nicklaus displays a style in which he has a considerable bend at the waist, with his arms close to his body, and a smooth stroke. Chi Chi Rodriguez is almost upright and takes a kind of quick slap at the ball.

As widely divergent as putting styles are, the putters themselves are equally varied. While its true that some of the short sticks have stood the test of time and are little changed in appearance from a hundred years ago, technology and physics have added a new twist on the dance floor. As with drivers, space age materials and techniques enlarged the arsenal of the putter designer. Graphite and titanium shafts and exotic-metal heads and designs, are now being used in the search for the perfect putter.

Weight distribution in the head of the putter is one of the latest improvements to come under scientific analysis. It has been found that if a greater mass is concentrated towards the head and toe of the putter, the blade will resist twisting when the ball is struck off center. The result will be a putt that stays closer to the intended line.

One of the more famous examples of this theory is Karsten Solheim's original heel and toe weighted Ping Putter. He received a patent for his **Golf Club** (page 172) back in 1962. Besides the special weighting, one of the more resounding features of the club was its ability to "ring with a clear note when the proper spot on the face of the club strikes the ball".

> Putting shouldn't count in golf. My secretary, who weighs 97 pounds and has never swung a club before, has just as good a chance of dropping a 4 footer as I do.
>
> *Jack Marty*

Most of the more imaginative putters are illegal under USGA rules, but that doesn't seem to stop their canny creators. Clarence Fritz of Bay City, Michigan must have missed more than a few putts with a regular putter, as his contribution to the game is the **Billiard Cue Shaped Golf Putter** (page 184). Though it might be highly effective, its use in regulation play is banned. Besides, what self-respecting golfer would ever stoop to such chicanery? On second thought, it's probably a good thing the putter is not legal.

What do you get when you cross shuffleboard, roller skates and golf? You probably get something that looks like a **Golf Putter With Wheel-Supported Head** (page 182). James Fine of Detroit has created this deadly-looking club. Hopefully he repairs the skid-marks after putting.

If you're not quite sure why your putts are heading off line, you need the **Putting Stroke Analyzer** (page 192). Robert Rawson of Anaheim, California has created this clever device that looks like a golf ball on wheels with some arrows and a gauge sticking out the front. The arrows indicate to what degree the blade of the putter cuts across the ball, and what point the blade contacts the back of the ball.

Finally, there is one putt that all golfers have encountered on the green at one time or another for which no piece of equipment can be of any help, one putt that elicits the most anguished groans and oaths from the hapless player, one putt that even the most steely-eyed pro falls prey to. This putt is, of course, the putt that peals the putter blade with a sweet note, takes every break perfectly, looks impeccable in terms of speed, rolls dead on line, and stops one revolution away from dropping. Naturally the putt is immediately serenaded with the familiar refrain of, "Never up, never in", or maybe, "Nice putt Nancy", or even, *"You know, I think I'd have hit that just a little harder"*. Unfortunately, no one seems to have come up with anything to cure this particular affliction.

Golf Club
Patent No 3,042,405 (1962)
Karsten Solheim of Redwood City, California

At no time during his game does a golfer require more accuracy than when putting on the green for at that time the target is a hole only four and one-quarter inches wide. To achieve that order of accuracy, a golfer must use a club so constructed as to enable him not only to see and feel his stroke but also to hear it for then he may concentrate through the maximum use of all his senses. In addition, he must use a club so constructed as to impart a desired over-spin or back-spin to a ball struck by the face of the club.

The principal object of this invention is to provide a golf club for imparting desired over-spin or back-spin to a ball struck by a face of the golf club.

Another object of this invention is to provide a golf club having a head of novel construction which rings with a clear note when the proper spot of the face of the club strikes the ball.

The Patent Duffer 173

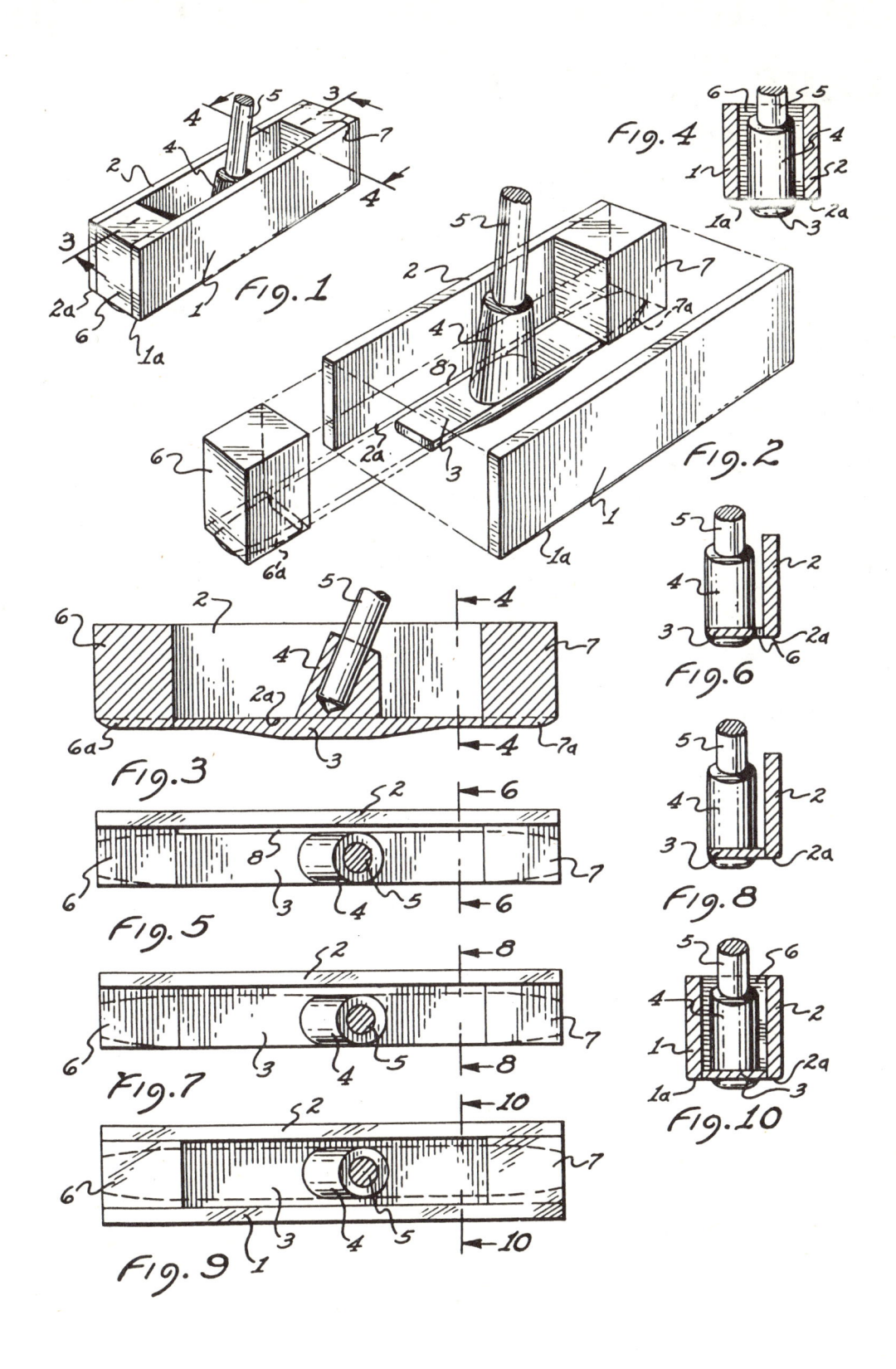

Golf Club With Slope Indicating Means Thereon

Patent No. 3,306,618 (1967)
Jon Liljequist of Chicago, Illinois

The greens on a golf course are designed with numerous compound curves and irregular shapes which deceive the experienced as well as the inexperienced golfer, and therefore, each green is a new and challenging obstacle to a low score. Many devices have been designed to teach a golfer how to putt straight, but putting straight, cannot of itself give an indication to the golfer as to the direction in which he should putt so that his ball, under the influence of the various curves on the green, will properly curve toward the cup. Some golfers are physiologically unable to detect any curvature whatever on a gradually sloping green, and are therefore seriously limited in their ability to get a respectable golf score.

It is a specific object of the present invention to provide a new and improved putter having a level forming a part of the head of the putter operatively associated with the bottom surface of the putter to provide the golfer with information as to the slope of the surface on which the putter rests.

The Patent Duffer 175

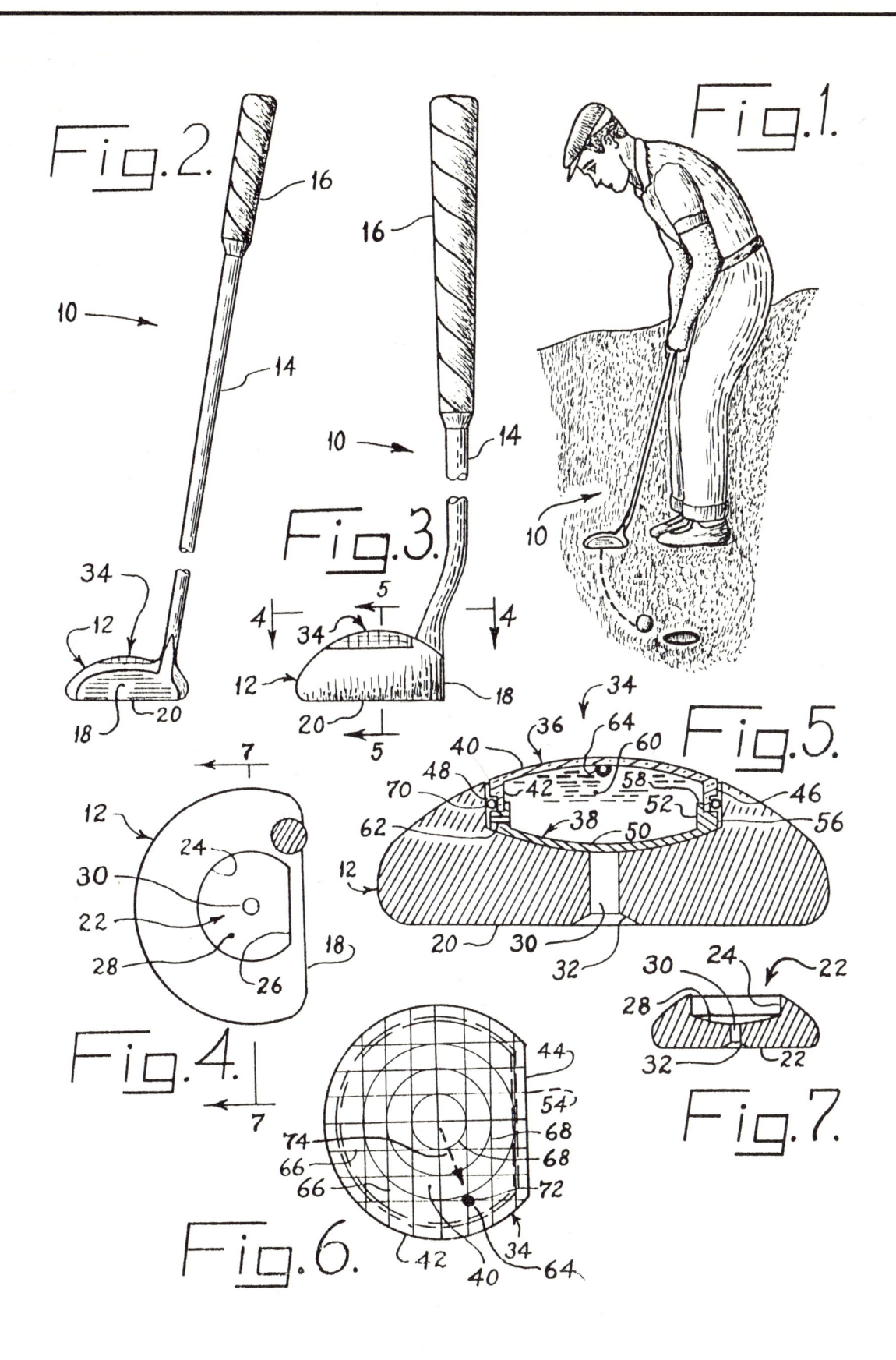

Golf Putter With Aligning Device
Patent No. 3,667,761 (1972)
John Palotsee of Youngstown, Ohio

It is an objective of the invention to provide an aligning device for use with a golf putter which may be used not only to indicate the correct alignment of the putter relative to the ball and hole but also the length of stroke required to drive the ball the distance to the hole.

When the golfer desires to use the putter and aligning device, he positions the telescoping rod **14** in the groove **26** with the sections **34** and **36** projecting outwardly beyond the ball striking face **16**. The magnet **30** pulls the outer-most section **32** tightly into the groove **26**, holding the aligning rod **14** in position and assuring that it is correctly aligned relative to the face **16**. The golfer now positions the putter with the striking face **16** immediately adjacent the golf ball **B**. He then adjusts the position of the putter until the aligning rod **14** passes directly over the midpoint of the ball and points directly toward the midpoint of the cup or hole into which the ball is to be driven. At this time, the putter is correctly aligned so that when the ball is struck it will be driven directly toward the hole. Since the distance that the ball is driven is proportional to the stroke through which the putter head is moved prior to hitting the ball, the aligning rod mat also be used to aid the golfer in determining the correct stroke to drive the ball the full distance to the hole without driving it so hard as to cause to to continue beyond the hole.

FIG. 4
FIG. 2
FIG. 3
FIG. 1

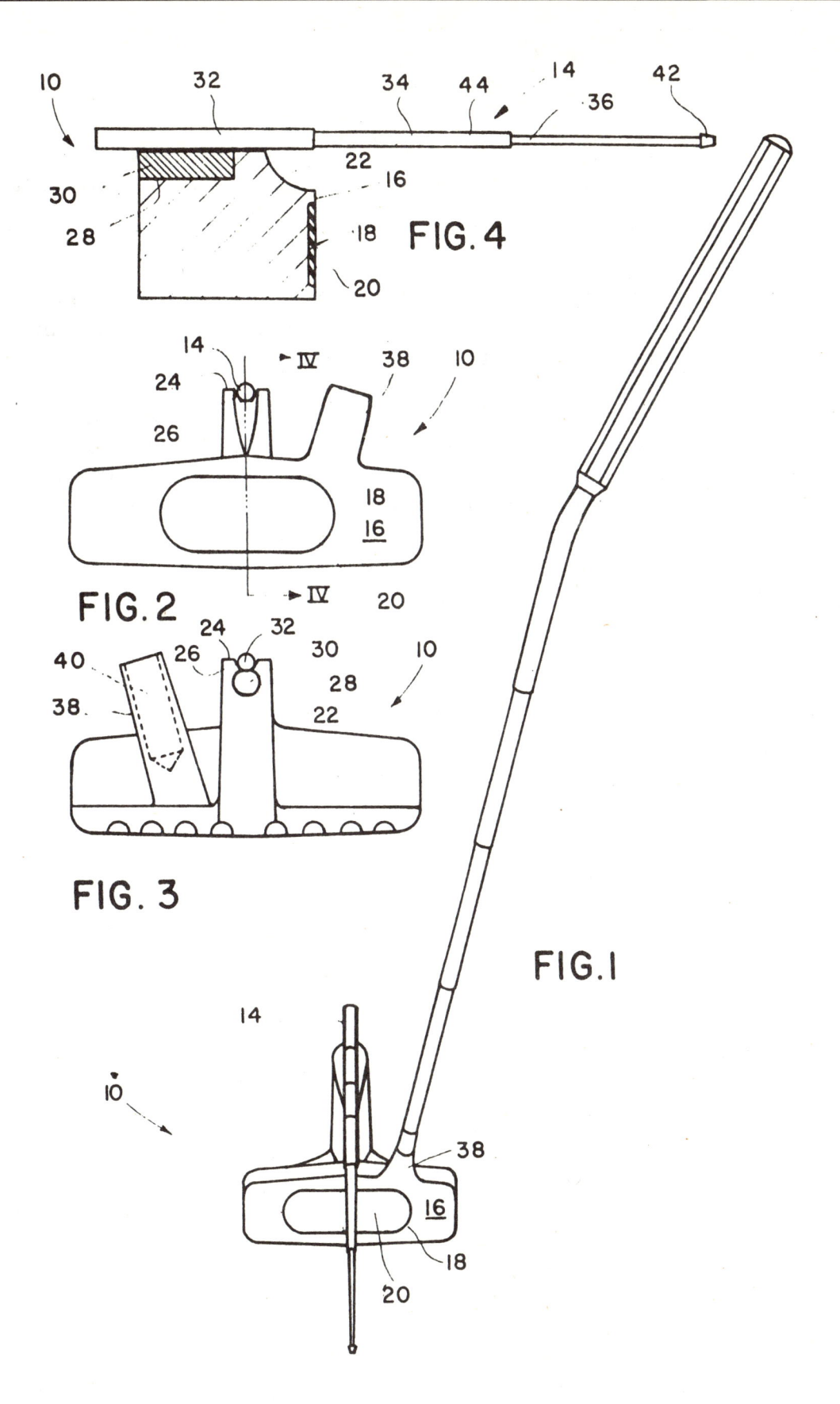

Golf Putter

Patent No. 3,708,172 (1973)

Joseph Rango of San Pedro, California

The head is substantially symmetrical with the hole being located near the center of the head so that the mass is distributed towards the heel portion and toe portion in order to counterbalance and minimize twisting tendencies by the putter head during misaligned contacts between the striking face and the golf ball.

The hole has a fixed diameter equal to or slightly larger than the diameter of a given golf ball permitting the hole to be used as a quick check ball gauge and a ball roundness detector. The hole fixed diameter may be 1.680 inches or the minimum acceptable diameter established from time to time by the United State Golf Association.

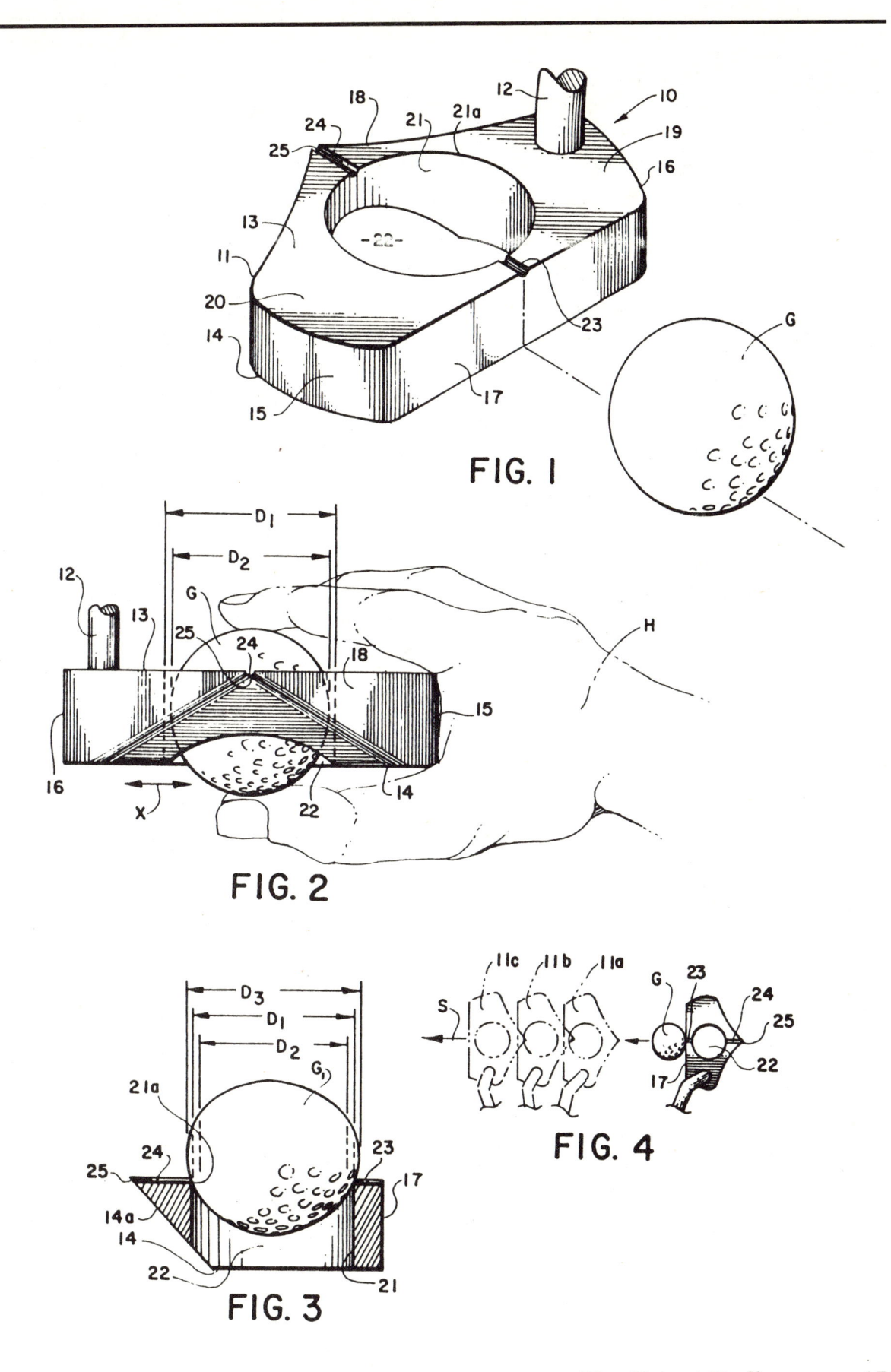

FIG. 1

FIG. 2

FIG. 3

FIG. 4

The Patent Duffer 179

Golf Putter
Patent No. 2,843,384 (1958)
Theodore Schmidt of Greenville, Michigan

An important object of the invention is to design a golf putter in which the grip, stance, and the stroking of the ball by the putter will become more standardized to improve accuracy in the stroking golf the ball.

Another object of the invention is to construct a golf putter for swinging with a pendulum movement from a position with the eyes of the golfer directly above the ball whereby the ball will be aligned with the cup with greater accuracy and the stroke delivered to the ball with less tendency on the part of the golfer to move his head or body to thus increase accuracy in the path followed by the ball.

A still further object of the invention is to construct a golf putter with a relatively short shaft and handle whereby the stoking of the ball may be better controlled.

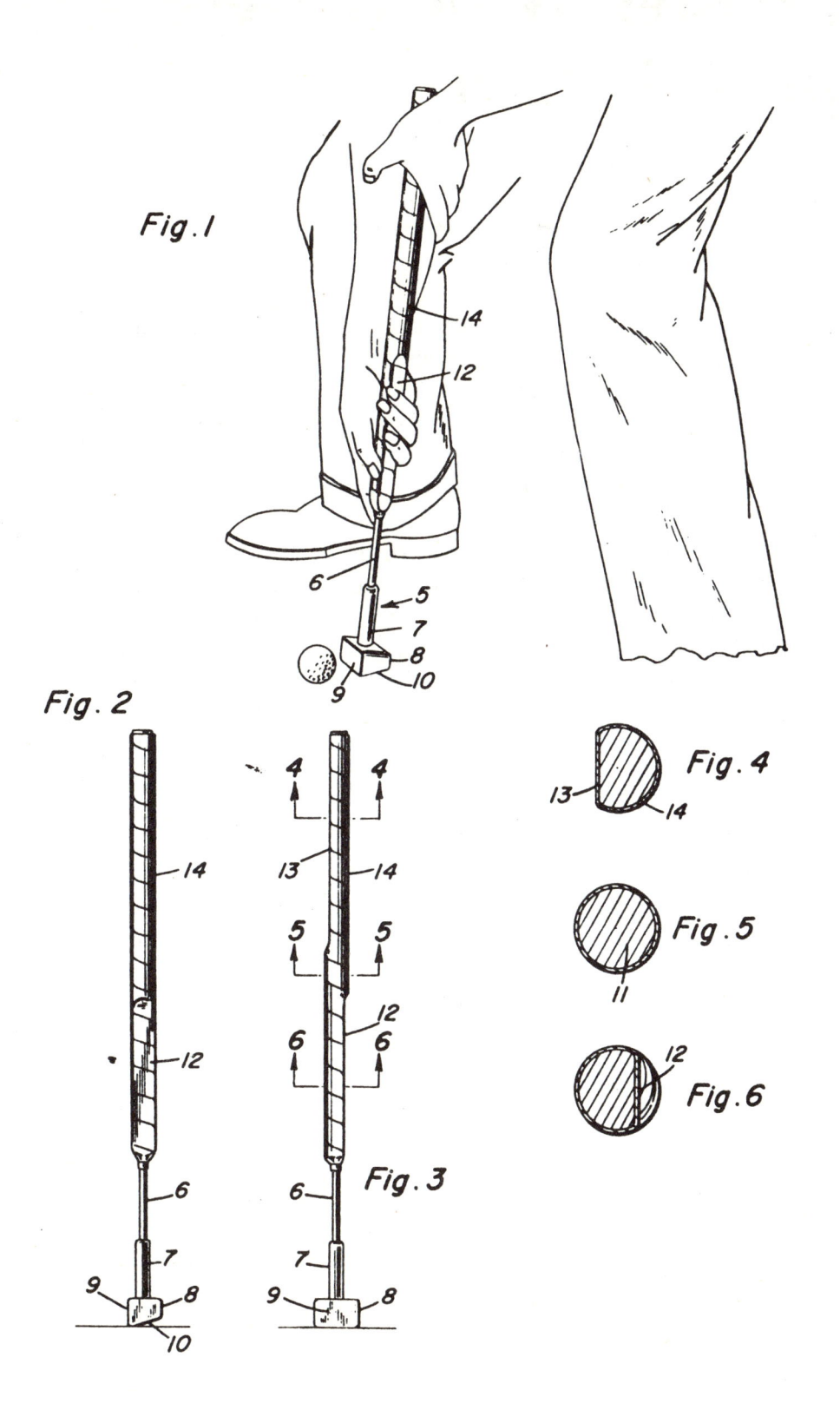

Fig. 1

Fig. 2

Fig. 3

Fig. 4

Fig. 5

Fig. 6

The Patent Duffer 181

Golf Putter With Wheel-Supported Head

Patent No. 3,220,730 (1965)

James Fine of Detroit, Michigan

In operation, the putter **10** may be disposed as illustrated in FIGURE 1 while the golfer addresses the ball **16** from a crouching or kneeling position after making his survey of the green. While so addressing the ball, and due to the fact that a major portion or length of the handle or shaft **26** is substantially parallel to and, most importantly, contained in a vertical plane containing the central longitudinal axis of the putter head or body **12**, the golfer may sight along and align such portion of the handle or shaft through the ball in relation to the preselected or predetermined path of travel necessary for the ball to drop in the cup on the green. Such alignment of the handle or shaft necessarily results in similar alignment of the central longitudinal axis of the head or body **12** with the ball **16** to permit stroking the head or body along its axis and a path corresponding to the preselected path of travel for the ball. Immediately following this aligning process and rather than returning to an upright position as is usual with convention putters, the golfer need merely impart a reciprocal or pushing movement to the handle or shaft **26** at the hand grip **28** and substantially parallel to the ground resulting in the head or body **12** stroking through the ball along the pre-sighted or aligned axis or path aforementioned, the center of the putting surface **14** preferably striking substantially centrally of the ball.

The Patent Duffer 183

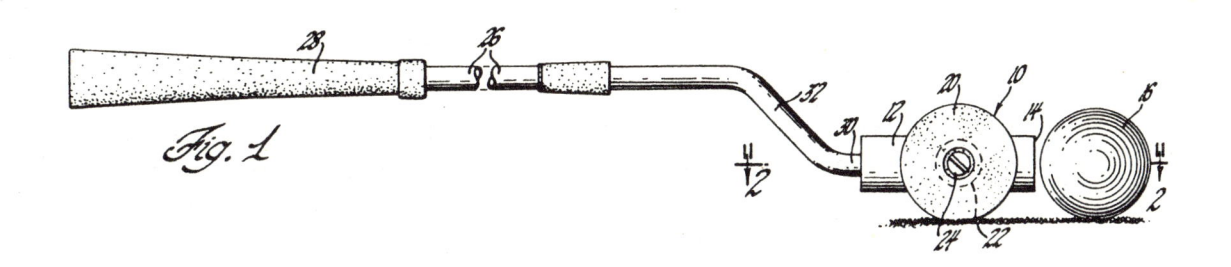

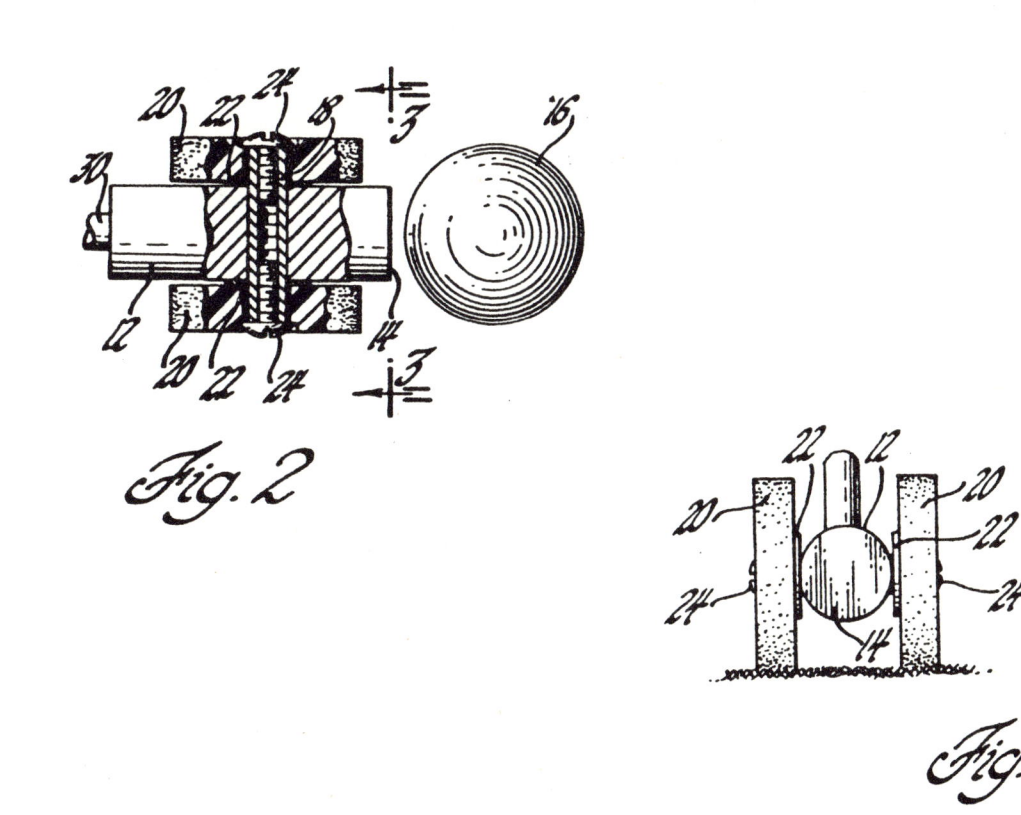

Billiard Cue Shaped Golf Putter
Patent No. 3,445,112 (1969)
Clarence Fritz of Bay City, Michigan

The club is handled and the shot is made in a different manner than with the conventional putter; it is of the end striking type and is a much more accurate club than are the putters presently in general use, and the user can (when making a shot) point the head of the club so that the head, golf ball, and the cup are in a straight line. When making a shot there is no arc-like swinging action of the golfer's body and shoulders, merely the sliding action of the putter in the left-hand support, the club stroke being made by the right hand of the golfer. For left-handed golfers the club will slide in the right hand is actuated by the left hand.

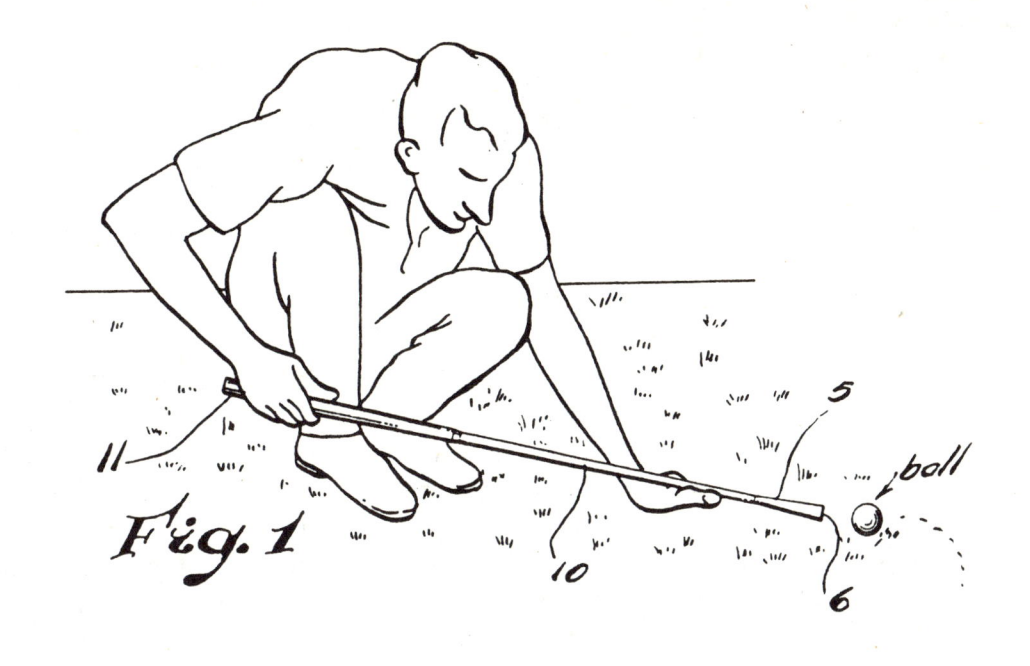

Fig. 1

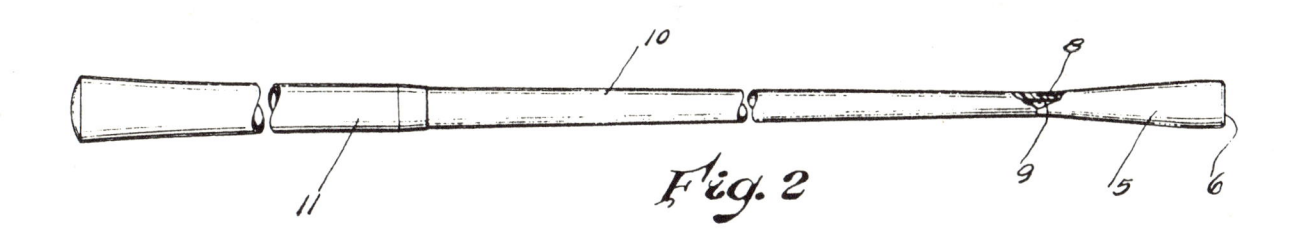

Fig. 2

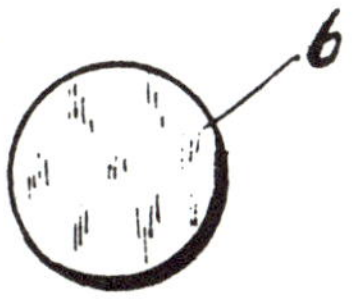

Fig. 3

Fig. 4

The Patent Duffer

Golf Putter
Patent No. 3,430,963 (1969)
John Wozniak of Warren, Michigan
Edward Jacques of Rochester, Michigan

FIGURE 1 illustrates the golf putter 10 being used in a putting stroke. Initially the golfer brings the ball contacting surface 18 of the putter 10 into contact with the ball 44. The golfer then utilized the groove 18 and the straight sharp longitudinal lines of sight 33 to line up the putter head 12 with the ball 44 and the cup or hole 46 on the putting green 48. Thus the golfer sights the ball 44 and orients the putter head 12 at right angles to the line of the putting stroke. Thereafter, with the putter head 12 resting on the putting surface 48, the golfer moves the putter 12 in a linear back stroke away from the ball 44 a relatively short distance and thereafter the golfer completes the forward stroke by moving the putter head 12 across the putting surface 48 to strike the ball 44 towards the cup 46.

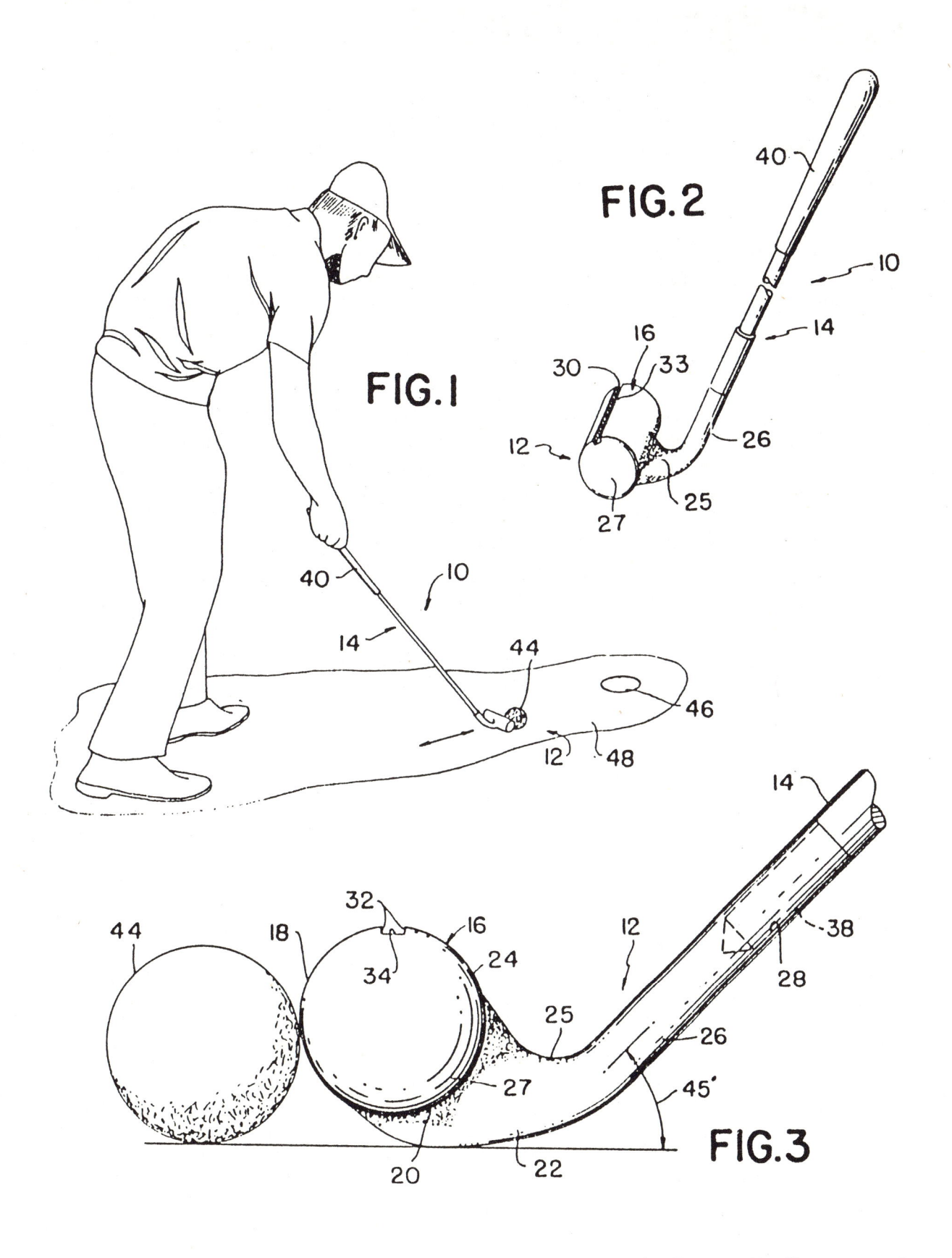

FIG.2

FIG.1

FIG.3

The Patent Duffer   187

Golf Putter Hand Grip
Patent No. 3,459,426 (1969)
Aaron Sherwood of Hyattsville, Maryland

In FIGURES 3 and 4, the technique of using the putter is illustrated. The player stands facing the chosen initial direction of the ball which is the same as the direction of movement of the club head 20. The centerline of the player's feet are parallel to the club head movement. The club head is swung first backward and then forward between the player's legs by rotating the two hands about an axis through the player's wrists. The hands are pressed firmly against the two sides or cheeks 17 and 18 of the handle 10 so they directly oppose each other. The fingers 25 are outstretched in a comfortable position. This position varies from player to player but typically the fingers project downward and forward at a 10 to 15 degree angle to the vertical. The opposing relationship of the hands 24 and the fingers 25 is more clearly shown in FIGURE 4. In the natural position of address, prior to stroking the ball, the shaft 12 of the putter is vertical. In the preferred handle design it is necessary for the golfer to apply a small amount of torque to keep the shaft 12 vertical since in this position the club head 20 is in front of the hands. This is considered advantageous since it encourages a smooth, effortless back swing which is a necessary prelude to the forward or hitting stroke.

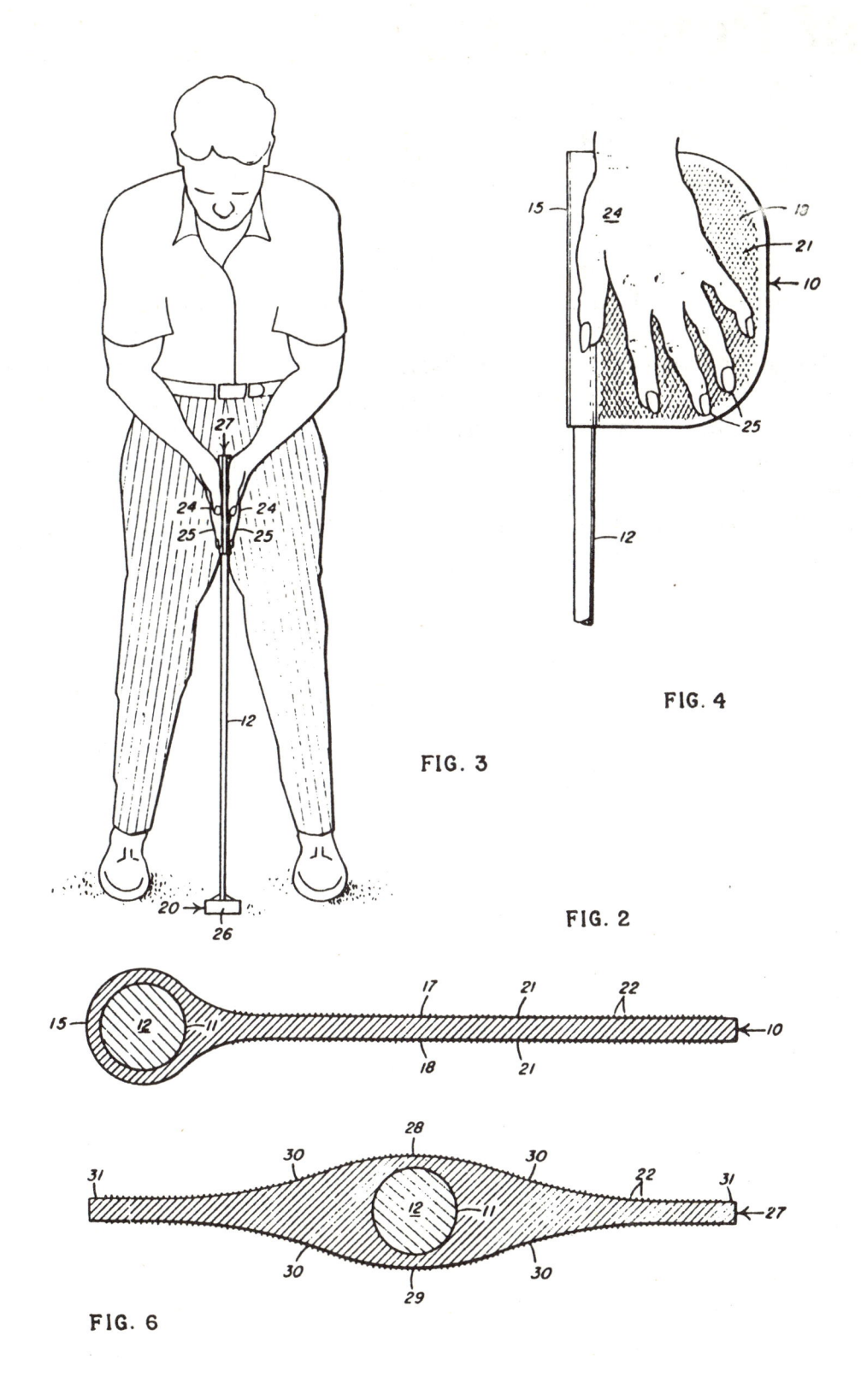

FIG. 3

FIG. 4

FIG. 2

FIG. 6

The Patent Duffer 189

Golf Putter Grip
Patent No. 2,962,288 (1960)
Edwin Lowden of Bridgeton, New Jersey

It has been found that a golf club may conveniently gripped for both a power and guiding stoke by the right hand of a right handed golfer or a left hand of a left handed golfer by placing the shaft of the golf club between the index and forefingers of the appropriate hand and permitting the shaft to ride across the palm and along the heel of the thumb. However, at first this grip will appear unnatural to a golfer and it is desirable that there be provided a convenient grip device which may be grasped in one's hand and which is provided with a recess for receiving the golf club shaft so that the hand becomes accustomed to so gripping the golf club shaft.

Fig. 1 Fig. 2 Fig. 3

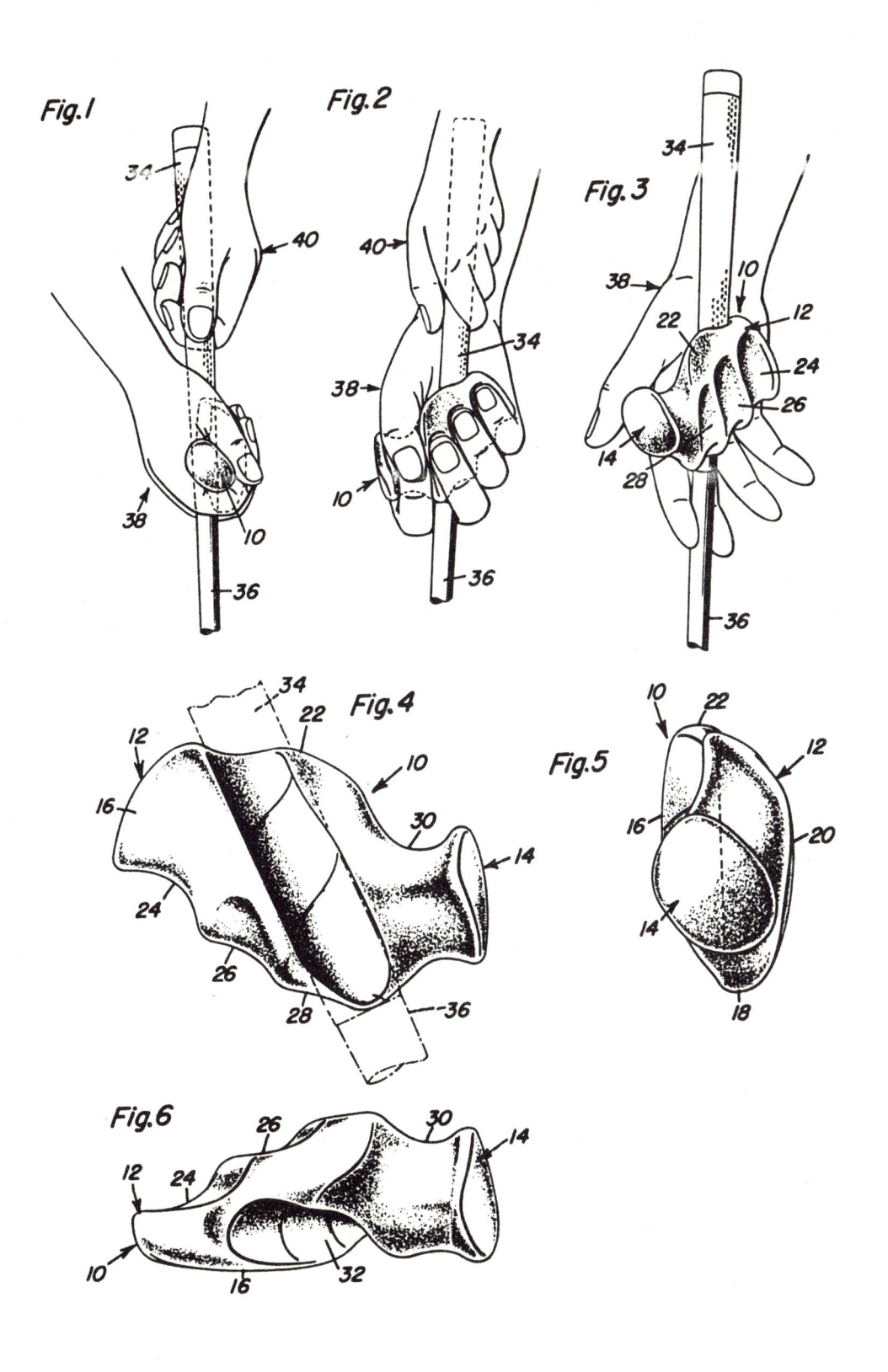

Fig. 4 Fig. 5

Fig. 6

The Patent Duffer 191

Putting Stroke Analyzer
Patent No. 3,788,646 (1974)
Robert Rawson of Anaheim, California

The invention comprises a 2 to 3 ounce assembly including a carriage bearing a simulated golf ball to be addressed and struck with a putter, sensors resposive to the address and to the stroke which actuate corresponding indicators, which in turn magnify and display errors in the putter-face position and in the putter-stroke-direction. The carriage is designed to move in response to the stroke when suffiecient force is exerted, thus limiting excess force on the analyser and affording a follow throufh as in striking a ball.

The upper indicator and scale show putter face angular position. As shown in FIG. **4**, prior to putting, the putter face **P** is squared with the intended line of putt as represented by the line of indicator **2** along the axis of the invention. Any departure from perpendicularity of the putter face with the intended line of putt registers through sensor rods **12, 12'**, and shows as a displacement of indicator **2** on upper scale **23**.

Both direction and amount of angular error are indicated. When error is indicated, after correcting his stance, his grip, or whatever combination appears to him to cause the error, the golfer again addresses the putter face to the invention. Assuming that the putter face angle error now registers at zero, as it will when the sensor rods **12, 12'**, are depressed equally, the golfer now soles his club and prepares to stroke the simulated ball.

Following the stroke, the last angle of contact of the putter face with the device during the stroke will remain registered on upper scale **23**.

The lower indicator and scale show putting stroke angular direction with respect to the intended line of putt.

As the golfer putts, his club face first contacts and depresses the sensor rods **12, 12'** and continuing through the stroke strikes the rear of the simulated golf ball **22**. If the putting stroke deviates from the intended line of putt as represented by the line of indicator **10** along the fore-and-aft axis of the invention, the simulated golf ball swings to one side or the other.

As a result of the sideways swing of the simulated golf ball under putter impact, the lower indicator, indicator **10**, deflects to one side or the other, showing direction and degree of putting stroke misalignment.

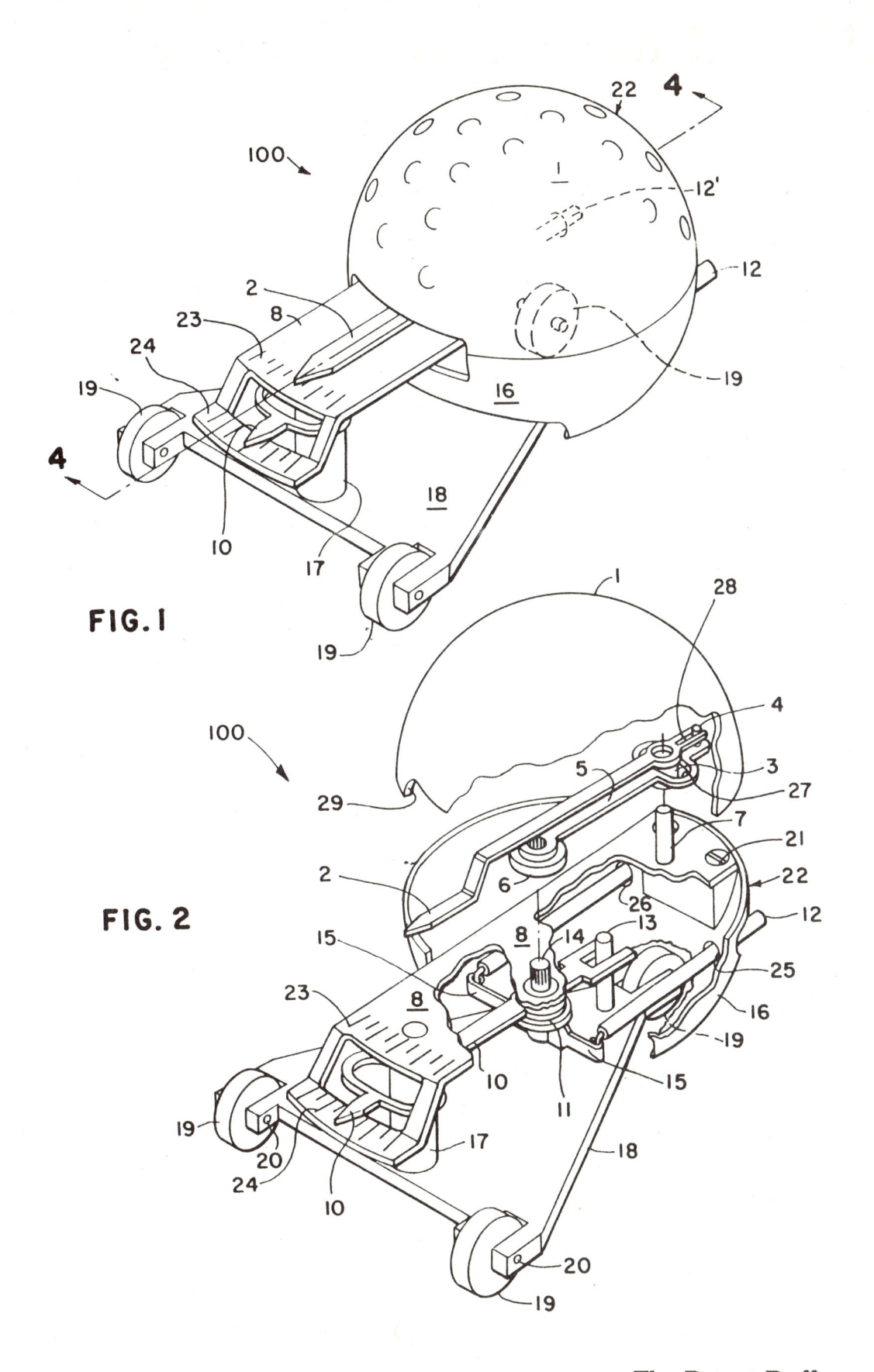

FIG. 1

FIG. 2

The Patent Duffer   193

Golf Putting Practice Device
Patent No. 3,796,435 (1974)
James Dale of Rancho Mirage, California

It is an object of this invention to provide a device which will enable a golfer to determine the accuracy of the striking attitude of the golf club against a surface which simulates a golf ball surface.

In FIG. 4, the putter club **7** is shown with surface **8** inclined at an angle from the perpendicular path of FIG. 3. For purposes of illustration, the angle is much exaggerated. It has been found that even a 1° inclination of the striking face of the putter causes a substantial deviation in the direction traveled by the putting device. The concentration of mass at the center of the putting device increases the effect of any errors in striking the surface of the putting device. High speed photographs show that for several feet after the putter device has been struck at even a very slight angle, the device oscillates about a vertical axis, then the rotation is stabilized and the device continues rolling without oscillation, in a direction away from the intended path.

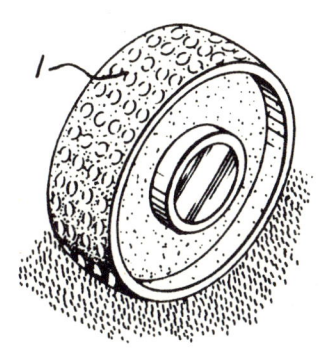

FIG. 1

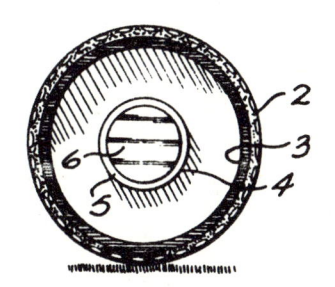

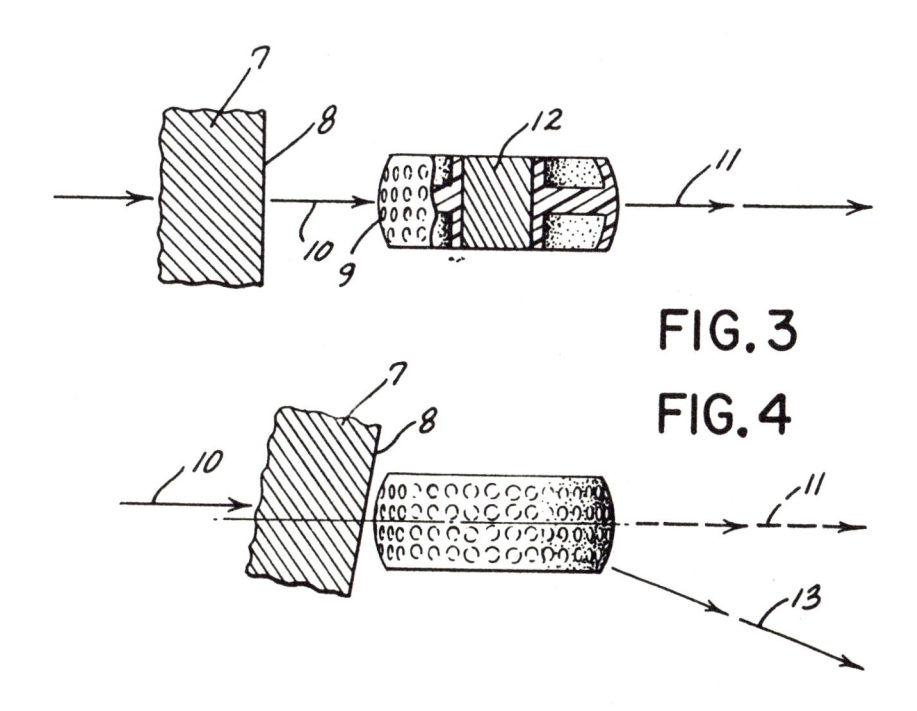

FIG. 2

FIG. 3

FIG. 4

The Patent Duffer   195

Golf Club Head

Patent No. 3,019,022 (1962)

Murray Ehmke of Escondido, California

The general object of this invention is to provide a putter having a reflector to provide an image of a part of the putting green, cup and/or flag pin, to reflect the image upwardly directly to the player's eyes and to establish simultaneously a satisfactory arbitrary reference sight line which is fixed in relation to the putter head, all with a view to enabling the player to accomplish the putting stroke with greater directional precision, it being obvious that this results in increased confidence and lessened nerve strain with generally heightened playing efficiency and pleasure.

The problem solved by this invention arises from the necessity for a golfer in putting to determine what he believes to be the optimum path for the ball to follow on it trip to cup and, while retaining this mental concept of direction, remove his eyes from the flag pin or cup and usually concentrate on the rear side of the ball. In sighting the pin, the lie of the green is very seldom completely level and the ball must be stroked in a direction other than straight toward the hole. Consequently the club should be positioned at a small angle to a line normal to the line joining the ball and hole. This small angle is difficult to guess but with the present invention, the user can quickly learn to gauge the angle more accurately. In the rare case when the ball is to be stroked directly toward the pin, the ball will hide the pin but will provide the effect of bracketing the reflection of the pin so that the player can ascertain when the striking face is normal to the line from ball to cup.

The Patent Duffer 197

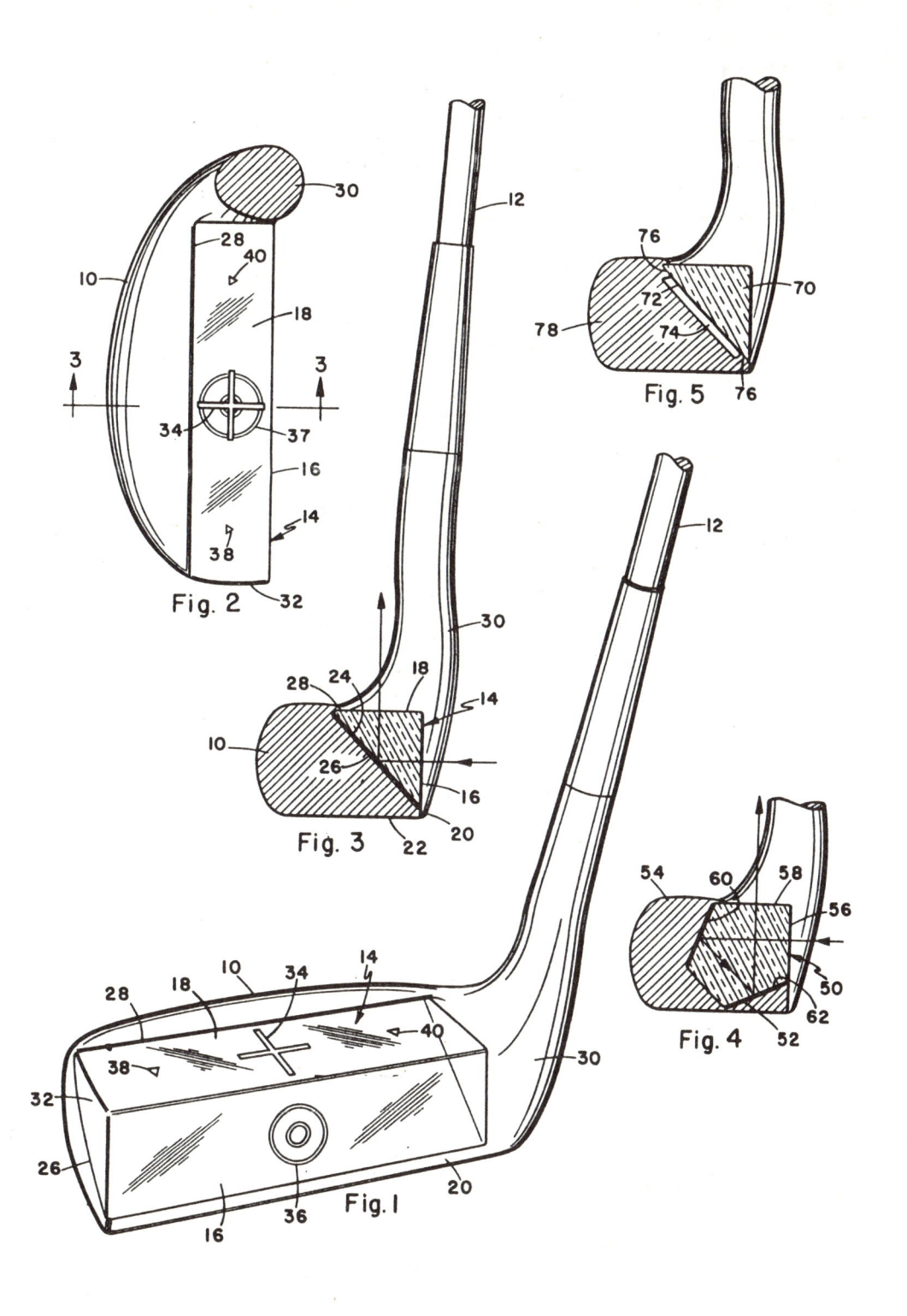

Optical Device For Reading Golf Greens

Patent No. 3,186,092 (1965)

Charles Bertas of Covina, California

The device is clipped or snapped on the golf club shaft below the grip portion of the club, with the vertical index line **26** parallel to the shaft, as shown. With the club held vertically in the manner of a pendulum, as indicated in FIGURES **1** and **2**, the reference line **28** is horizontal. Holding the club in this manner behind the golf ball, the golfer sites along the path between the hole or cup **10** and the golf ball. The golfer establishes an imaginary line between the ball and the cup.

By observation of the green with reference to the horizontal reference line and the imaginary line between the ball and the cup, he is able to estimate or determine any slope or undulation of the green along the line between the ball and the cup. With such observations, the golfer is able to determine the amount of deflection or deflection angle required in putting the ball, in order to cause the ball to take an appropriate curved path to the cup. He is also able to estimate with relative accuracy the amount of force with which the ball must be stroked.

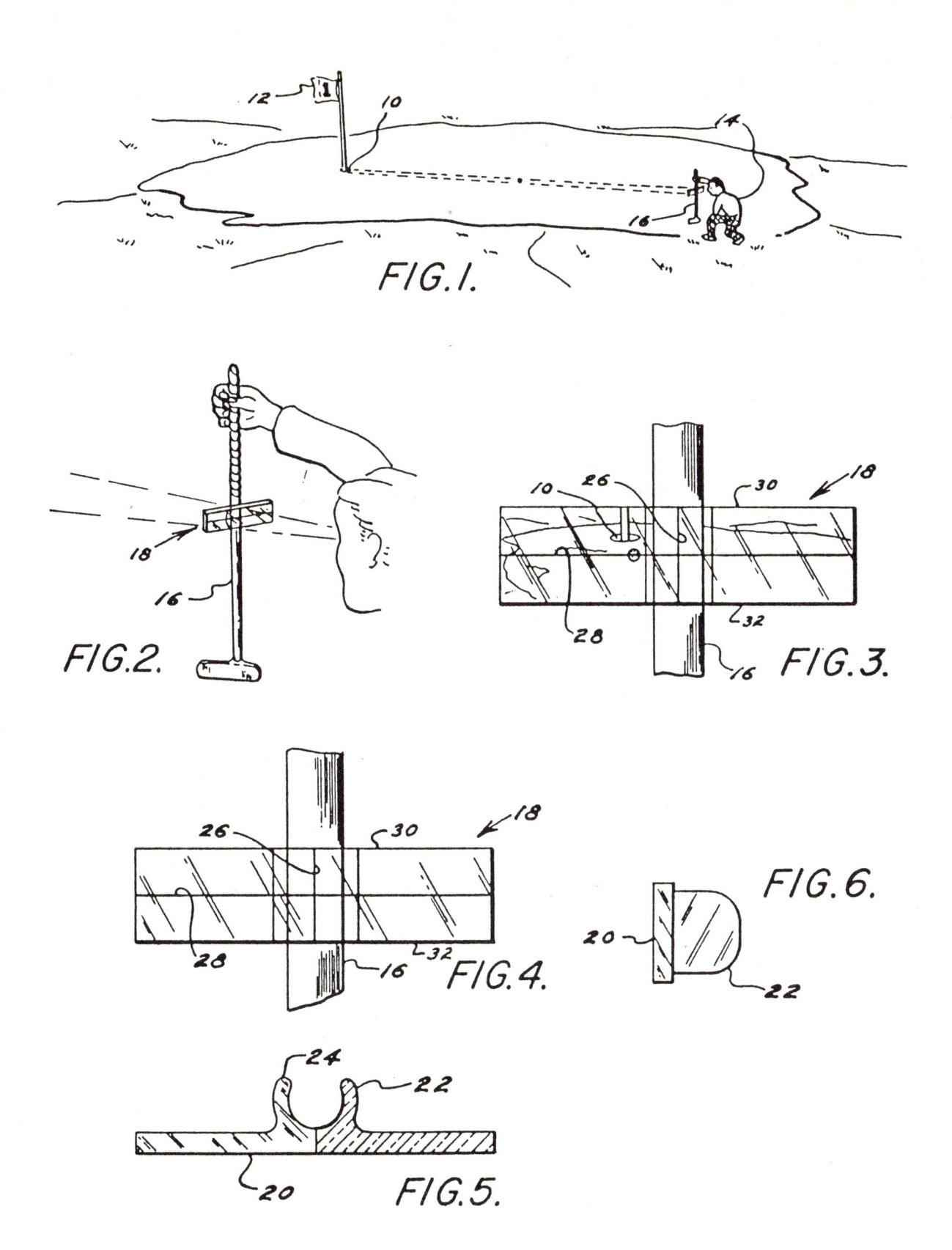

FIG.1.

FIG.2.

FIG.3.

FIG.4.

FIG.5.

FIG.6.

The Patent Duffer 199

Mechanical Putter
Patent No. 3,466,046 (1969)
Hugh McTeigue of Hollywood, Florida

As a practice device, the invention permits a golf player to repeat a selected arc of the club as many times as is necessary for him to learn the effect of the club-head on the ball for that arc of motion. The practicing player may then select a new position at which the golf club is released for its forward swing motion. The practicing player may then select a new position at which the golf club is released for its forward swing motion, and can continue the process until he has learned the effect of golf-head stroke and speed from a number of positions. With concentrated practice, therefore, the golfer learns just how far the back-swing of the putter should be in order to effect a desired striking force on the ball consistent with a particular distance through which the ball should be propelled.

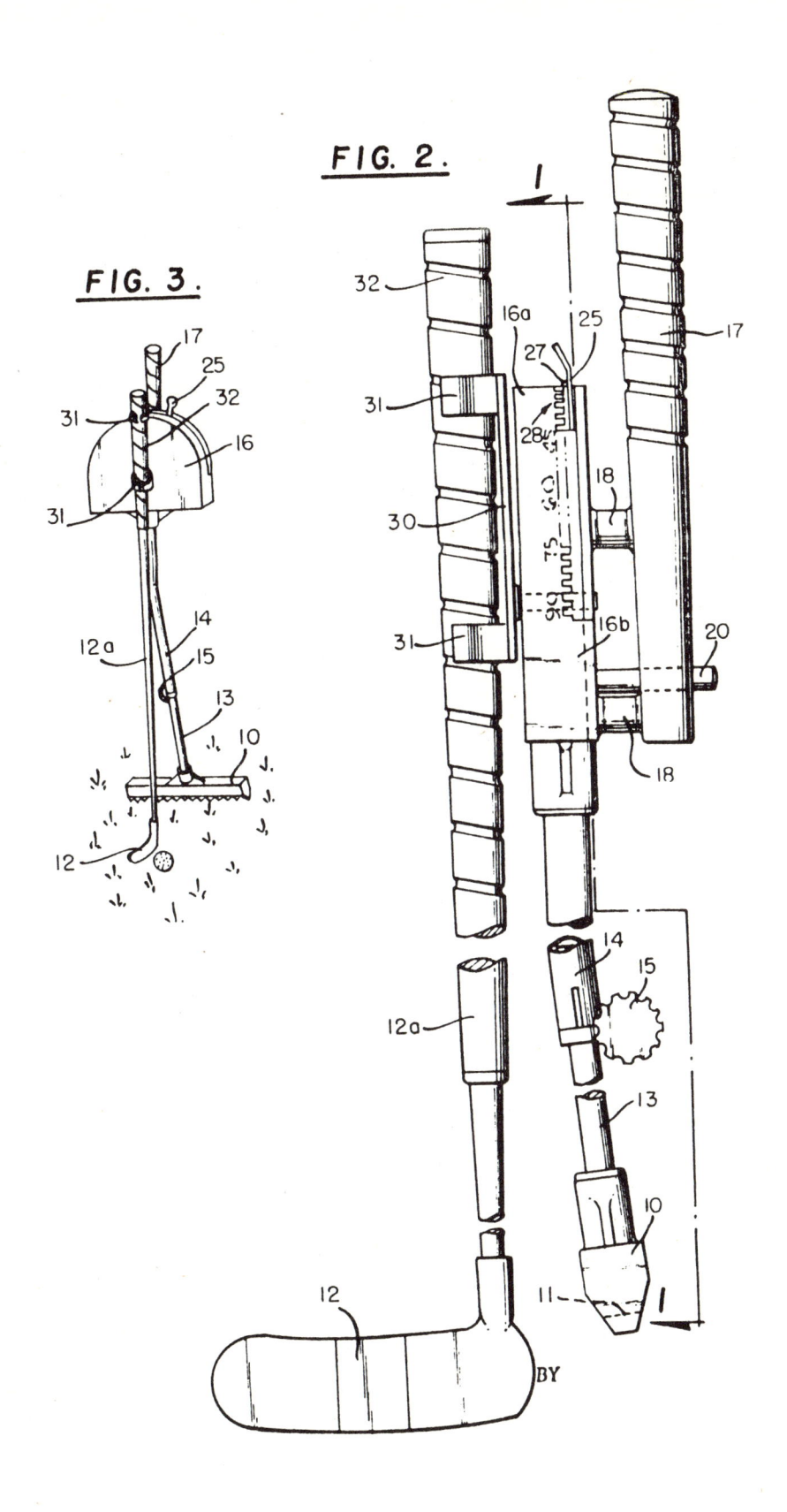

FIG. 3.

FIG. 2.

The Patent Duffer

ELEVEN

Tees

Consider the lowly tee for a moment. If you have been playing within the last 60 years or so, chances are the tee you use is made out of wood and looks a lot like the tee on page 204. The main reason this is the tee you use is because it's next to impossible to find a tee that looks any different. The design is simple and elegant, they are cheap to produce, and, no matter how bad a golfer you are, you can use them successfully every time. In fact, it's hard to imagine that tees ever looked any different.

One can almost picture a hardy band of Scotsmen out on the heather-laden links, teeing up their "featheries" on the simple wooden peg. Reality, though, isn't this romantic. It's safe to say a "feathery" never was teed up on anything which resembled our wooden tee. For 400 years, tees were nothing more than a bit of wet sand which was shaped by hand into a small mound, on which the ball was perched before the drive.

400 hundred years worth of tradition came to a screeching halt because of one dentist who didn't like to get his hands dirty and didn't even take up the game until he was in his late 50's. This tradition wrecker was one Dr. William Lowell of Maplewood, New Jersey. The good doctor started out by shaping his **Golfing Tee** (page 204) out of the same material he used to make false teeth, namely, gutta-percha. The design was good, but the material couldn't stand the punishment. Wood from an unfortunate flagpole in his front yard was used to whittle a new batch of tees shaped like the original ones molded out of gutta. These proved durable enough, and soon a batch of 5,000 was produced and painted green. The color was later changed to red, and because the tees were always ready (as opposed to tees which had to be molded out of wet sand), they were named "Reddy Tees".

It was Walter Hagen and Joe Kirkwood, though, that really popularized the tees. They were persuaded by Dr. Lowell to use them in their cross-country exhibitions.

> Golf is like a love affair: if you don't take it
> seriously, it's no fun: if you do take it
> seriously, it breaks your heart.
>
> *Arnold Daly*

The pros would saunter around he course with the tees stuck behind their ears and leave them on the ground after their drives. Hordes of golf urchins swarmed over the tee box in an attempt to pocket these new tees. The stampede got so bad at the Shinnecossett Club in Groton, Connecticut, that the club had to rope off the tees. This is reportedly the first instance of gallery-control ropes being used.

Unfortunately for Dr. Lowell, his patent was worded so loosely, enforcement of his rights was impossible. In a few short years, hundreds of competitors were making and selling his design. Of course, in the great American spirit of innovation and invention, they weren't content with leaving his tee as just a simple little peg.

Harley Clarke of Evanston, Illinois, for example, added a kind of inclined ramp to the basic design with his **Golf Tee** (page 218). This tee makes those "grounders" a thing of the past, as the ball is launched up a ramp which is an integral part of the tee.

Having trouble with a hook or a slice? What you need is the **Rubber Shield Tee** (page 210). Charlie Williams of Seattle, Washington designed a tee with a rubber cup which covers the back of the ball. As an errant driver cuts across the ball, the rubber absorbs the slicing action of the club and the ball is driven in a straight trajectory.

The next time you really want to burn one down the fairway, try Charles Cowan's **Golf Tee Match Book** (page 224). With conventional tees you can only tee up the ball, or clean the mud off your spikes, or scrape the grooves of your clubs. Now, not only can you tee up the ball, you can also conviently set fire to your scorecard after a particularly disastrous round.

For some reason or another, most of the tees in this chapter don't seem to be around anymore, but at least we have Dr. Lowell to thank for coming up with the mother of all tees.

The Patent Duffer

Golfing Tee
Patent No. 1,493,687 (1924)
William Lowell of South Orange, New Jersey

This invention relates, generally, to improvements in that class of devices, known as tees for use upon the green of a golf course, and for the placing thereon of a golf-ball, the device being very simple in its construction and being easily forced into its proper position upon the green, so as to be of immediate use, and to enable the player to dispense with the building up with wet sand of the usual tee.

The golfing tee being formed of a single piece of material comprising a cone-shaped shank having a pointed end so as to be readily forced in the ground, and having a disc-shaped member connected with and carried by said shank, said member being dished or concave in its upper surface to conform to the surface of the golf-ball and being surrounded by a marginal ball-retaining and supporting rim, and said shank being centrally disposed with relation to the said ball-supporting member.

The principal purposes of the present invention is to provide a neat and cheap teeing device, which can be carried in the pockets of the player, the cost of production of the device being so slight, that the loss of an individual teeing device may be considered nil, and the device, if struck by the player may be readily replaced by another; or, if not struck may be left in the green, another teeing device being used by the player upon the next green.

The device, which is usually made of wood, may also be made of matter, which will disintegrate and will act in the manner of a fertilizer, if left in the green.

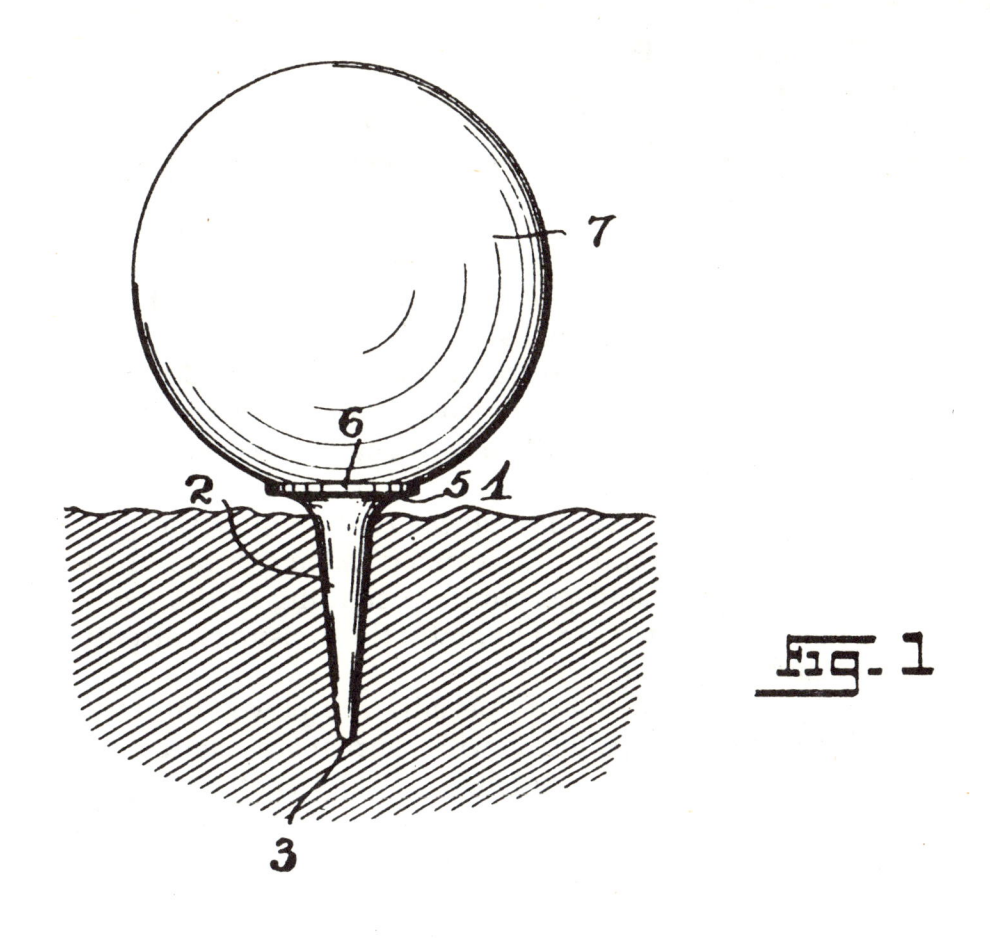

Fig. 1

Fig. 2

Fig. 3

The Patent Duffer

Golf Tee
Patent No. 2,119,044 (1938)
Thaddeus Davids of Rochester, New York

The object of this invention is to provide a tee from which a golf ball can be driven, which tee also furnishes a sight for the intended direction of the flight of the ball.

The beam and the diverging members 3 and 4 furnish a sight to the golf player for the purpose of indicating the direction of the flight of the ball, the flight of the ball being along the axis of the rod 6, but the members 3 and 4, having diverging lines and converging planes, constitute an optical focusing device that enables the player to more accurately drive the ball in the given direction. The rod 6 can be used as a sight member, and permits the sighting of the ball to be made separately, and this in turn eliminates the division of attention between the ball and the green.

The location of the rod permits the player to place himself in parallel relation thereto, which will insure more accurate driving of the ball. The presence of the members 3 and 4 enable the player to more accurately sight, so that in driving, the desired contact between the head of the club and the ball is achieved.

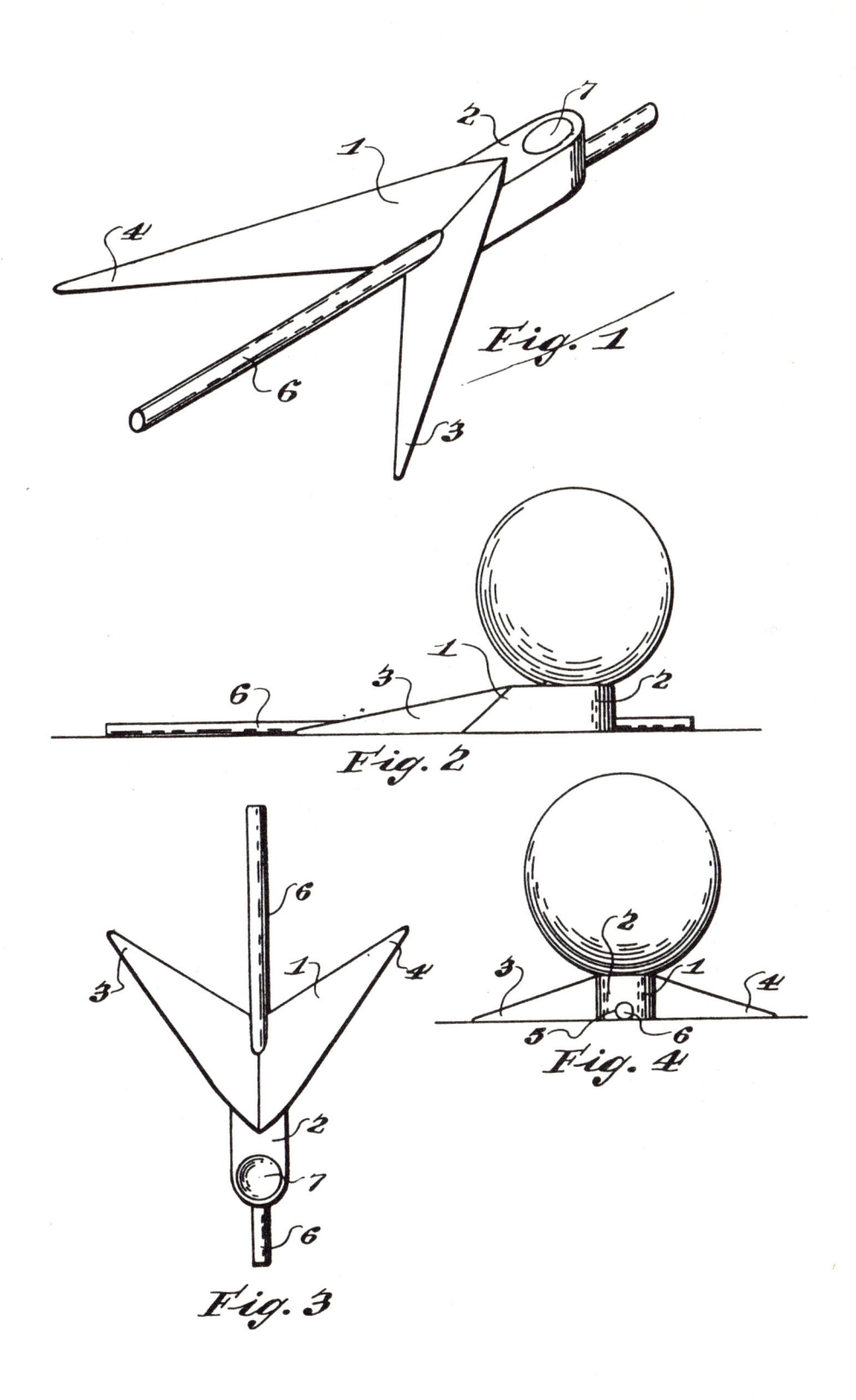

Fig. 1

Fig. 2

Fig. 3

Fig. 4

The Patent Duffer   207

Golf Tee
Patent No. 1,850,560 (1932)
Karl Midendorf of Kansas City, Missouri

The present invention relates to golf tees, and has for its object to provide a golf tee of novel form and substance, which, by reason of its peculiar form, is particularly adapted for teeing a golf ball, and, furthermore, because of its substance, is edible.

The form of tee disclosed is, because of the novel shape, a very satisfactory form of tee, both for use in playing golf, and, furthermore, it lends itself readily to manufacture. Because of its symmetrical shape and the duplication of contour on the opposite sides, it may be readily struck or molded from any suitable material at small expense, but I propose to use, as one material of which it may be made, an edible substance, such, for example, as a confection or candy of proper strength and consistency, so that, when molded, it will have the necessary rigidity to serve as a golf tee, and will yet be useful as a candy. Such candy can, of course, be suitably flavored and colored, as may be desired.

Fig. 1.

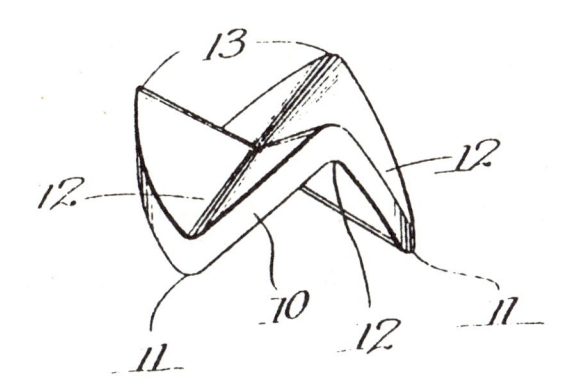

Fig. 2.

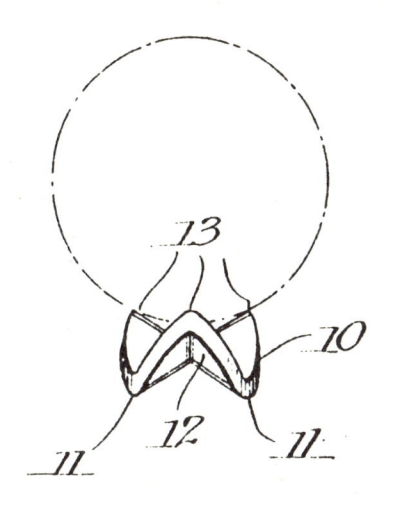

Fig. 3.

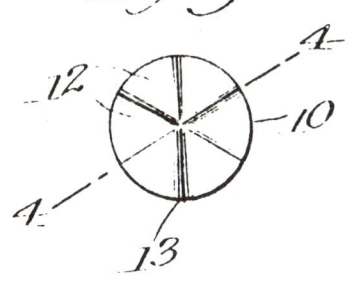

Fig. 5.

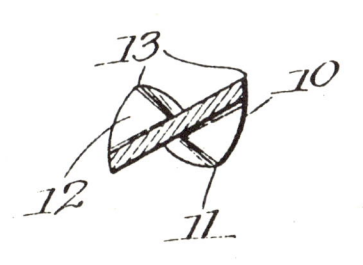

Fig. 4.

The Patent Duffer

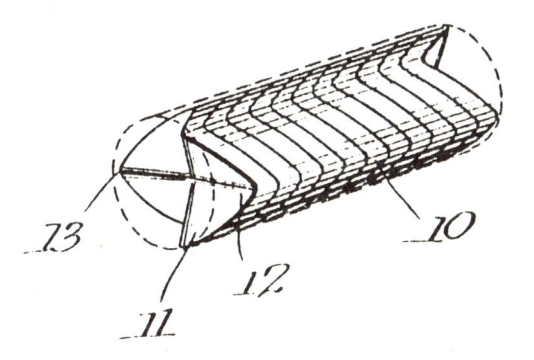

Rubber Shield Tee
Patent No. 2,033,269 (1936)
Charlie Williams of Seattle, Washington

My invention relates to rubber shield tees and certain objects of the invention are to provide an indestructible tee, preferably made of rubber and having an upstanding cup-like shield which partly covers a golf ball and against which the head of a golf club strikes in making a shot thus protecting the ball from cuts, protecting wooden clubs from checks and bruises, preventing slices and hooks, and absorbing the shock and eliminating the sting of the club handle when making forceful drives. Further objects are to provide a tee comprising an upstanding shield joined to a base portion and which base portion is secured to the found or may by the ordinary wooden peg whereby the device may be tilted backward at different angles for the purpose of regulating the height of the ball in its flight. Still further objects are to make the base in the form of a pointer projecting outwardly in a direction that is concentric with and opposite to the concavity of the shield portion which pointer assists in driving a golf ball in the desired direction.

Fig. 1.   Fig. 2.

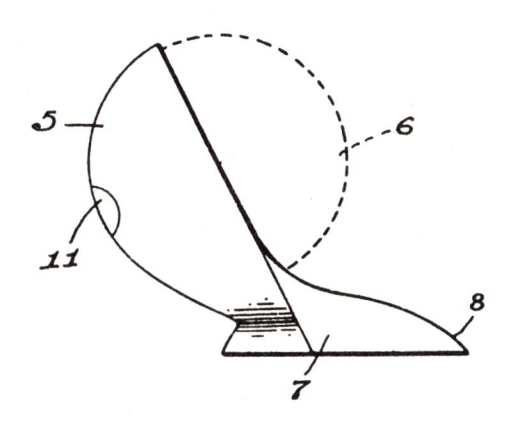

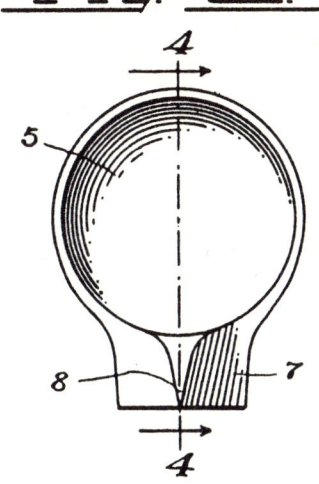

Fig. 3. 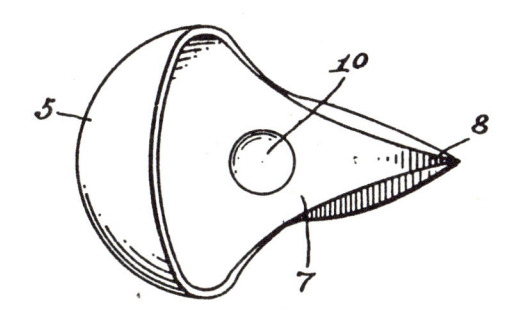   Fig. 4.

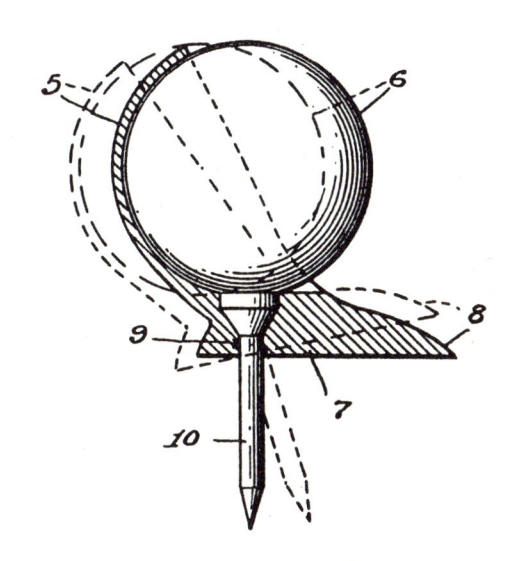

Fig. 5.

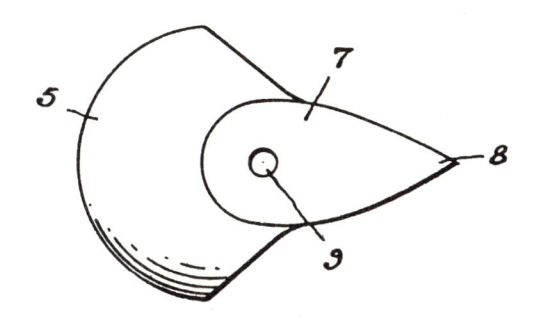

The Patent Duffer   211

Golf Tee

Patent No. 2,074,519 (1937)

Edward Shephard of Oakland, California

It will be obvious that any one of the cups is capable of engaging a golf ball and that a selected one of the pointed stems **10** and **12** may be made to engage the ground and to support its related cup, and the ball therein, in position to be struck by the club. After the shot has been made it is not necessary for the golfer to stoop to retrieve the tee, since this may be accomplished by pressing a flat face of the club, which is usually moistened with dew from the grass, against the top of one of the cups and pushing downwardly on the club so as to expel the air from the cup whereupon the tee will be securely affixed to the club head and may be lifted from the ground. It may then either be removed from the club head, or if the golfer sees need of the tee at the position of the next shot, it may be left attached to the club and placed in the ground at the above mentioned point by merely again pushing downwardly on the club with sufficient pressure to cause the tip to enter the soil. The contact between the tee and the club head may be then easily broken by twisting the club so as to cause distortion of the cup and permit air leakage under the edge thereof.

FIG.1

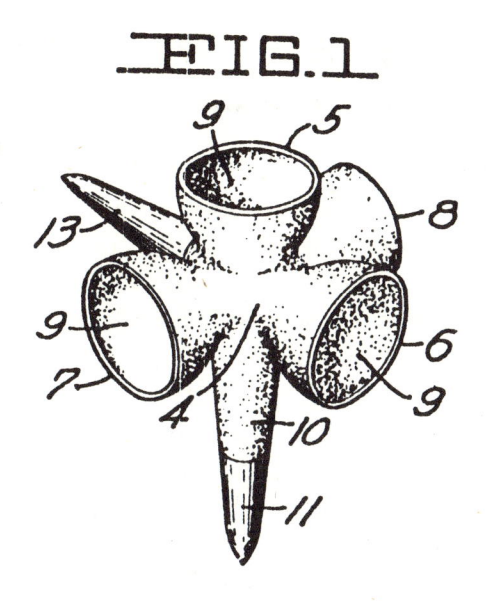

FIG.2

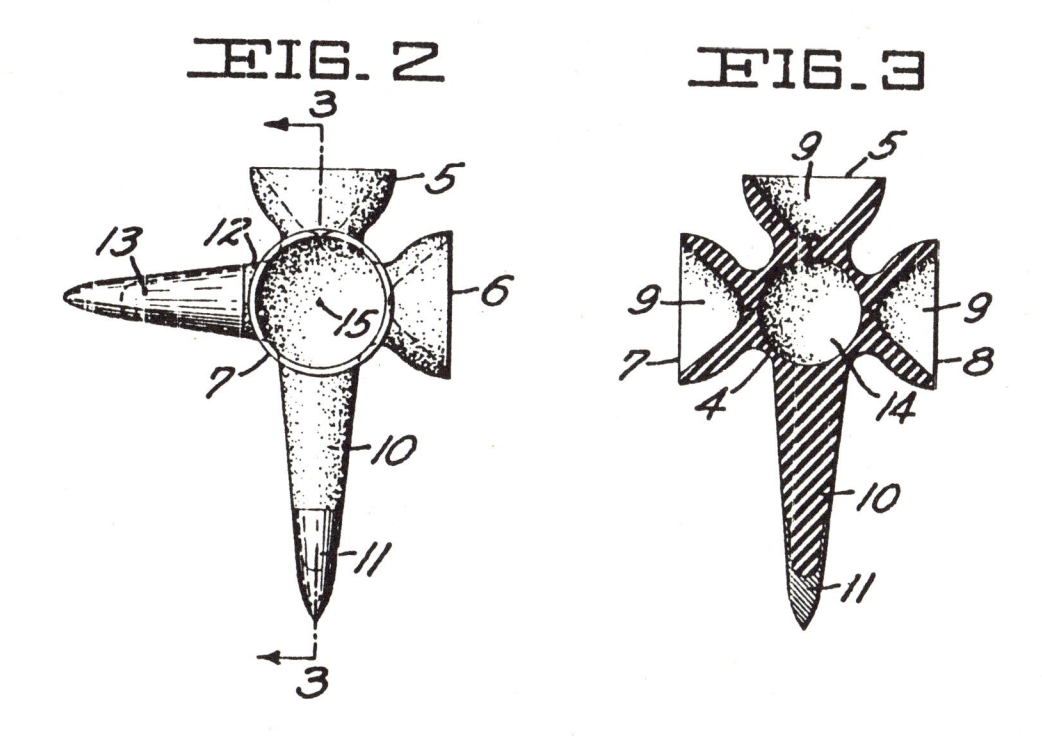

FIG.3

The Patent Duffer   213

Golf Tee
Patent No. 1,924,473 (1933)
William Walsh of Omaha, Nebraska

In using my device, the pin **10** may be put in place when driving off the tee at any desired spot within the limits provided. When used on fairways, however, as is quite common in certain golf courses, during those periods when the course is soft from rain or frost, the loop **24** is placed over the center of the ball and the pin **10** is then located. This provides that the position of the ball itself will not be materially affected. Assuming the tee in place with the ball **B** located on loop **24** will carry member **23** around to the position indicated in Figure **1** by the dotted line position, or often much beyond this. In this way member **23** is not actually struck by the club at all, is thus not subject to damage and in no way interferes with the follow-through of the club. I have found it desirable to make member **23** preferably of spring wire. In this way it will not be easily deformed, even though accidently hit, as might occur when a player does not strike the ball fairly.

I have further provided a bend in member **23** at **28**. It is intended that this will form a point of adjustment so that the user may bend member **23** at the point **28** so as to provide the most desired height for the ball. Some players prefer to have the ball but slightly raised from the ground, while others, given to raising up slightly during their drive, may wish to have the ball held at considerable height. By providing a point as indicated the user will naturally make the adjustment at this point and will thus not interfere with the workings of the device.

The Patent Duffer 215

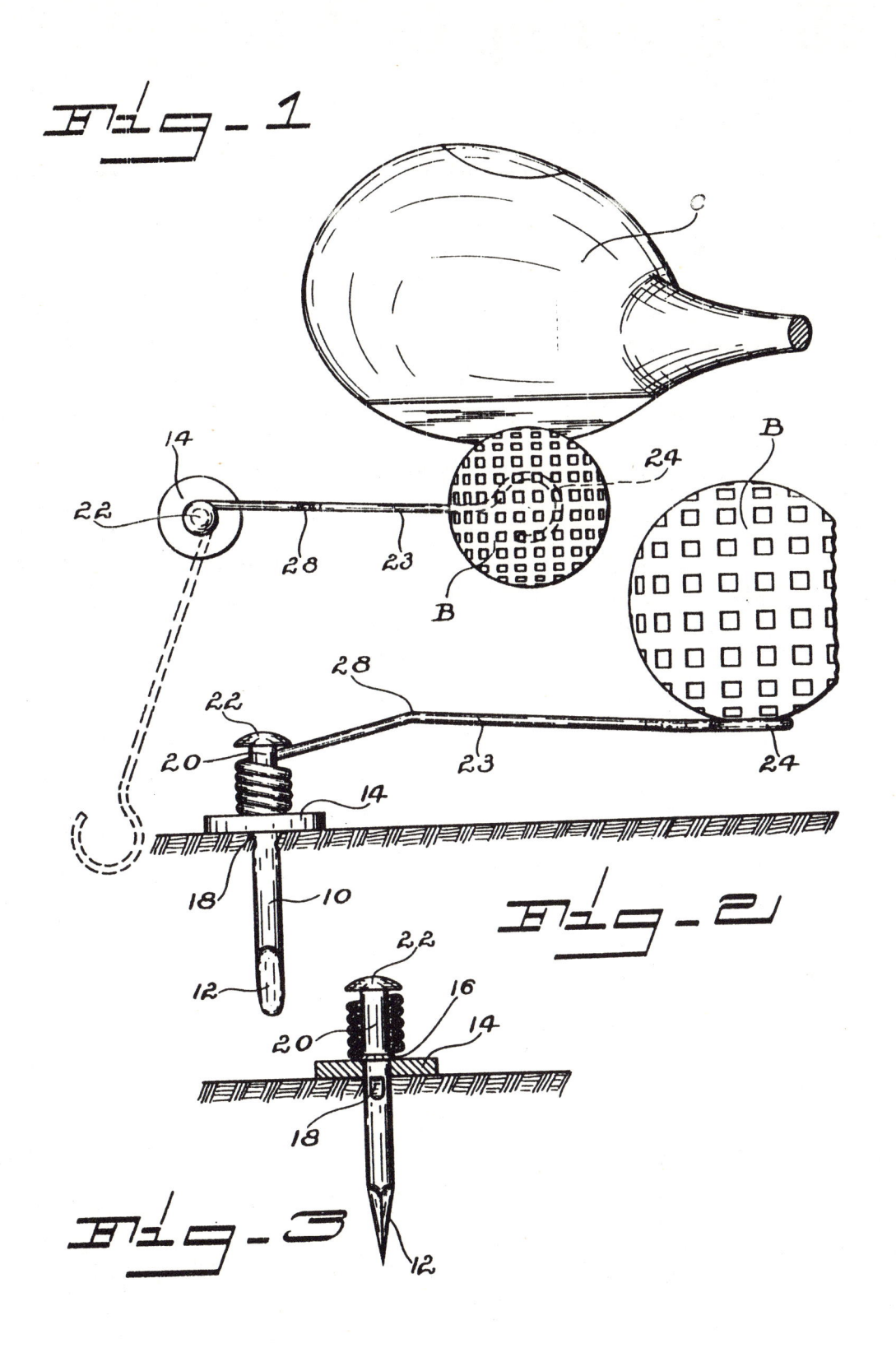

Disappearing Golf Tee
Patent No. 1,479,689 (1924)
Jacob Zeller of Los Angeles, California

My invention relates to a golf tee, the principal objects of my invention being to provide a tee or supporting element for golf balls that may be readily adjusted so as to support a golf ball at different elevations relative to the surface of the ground adjacent to the tee, and further to provide a device of the character referred to that will eliminate the time and labor involved in building up or forming the usual tee of sand.

Further objects of my invention are to provide a readily adjustable golf tee that may be easily and cheaply produced, and further to construct a ball receiving member of relatively soft rubber or the like, and to mount the same so that it will yield readily in the direction of travel of the club utilized in striking or driving the supported ball.

In the use of the device, after the pivot arm has been adjusted so that the upper end of member **20** occupies the desired horizontal plane, the ball is positioned on the upper end of said tubular member, and said ball is then struck or driven in the usual manner.

After the ball leaves the upper end of tubular member **20**, the counter-balancing weight **19** restores the arm **17** and member **20** to their normal positions, and should the upper end of the member **20** be engaged by the club when the ball is struck, said member **20** will yield readily at the narrow neck **20b** without offering appreciable resistance to the force of the club.

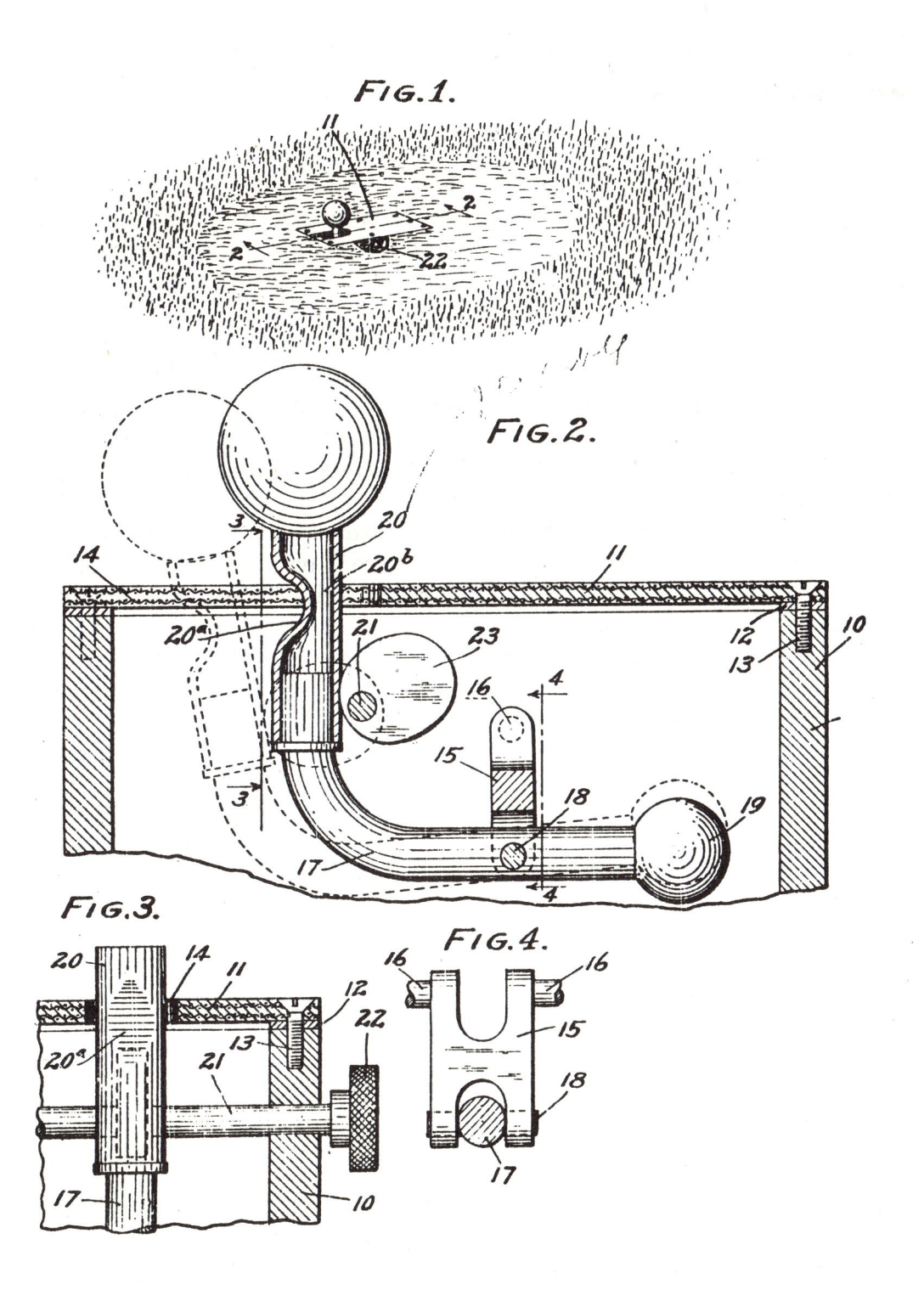

FIG.1.

FIG.2.

FIG.3.

FIG.4.

The Patent Duffer 217

Golf Tee

Patent No. 1,671,813 (1928)

Harley Clarke of Evanston, Illinois

My improved tee provides means for overcoming to a notable extent the effects of poor strokes resulting in "grounders," or balls leaving the tee with a low, or practically no, trajectory, the ball traveling or bouncing along close to or upon the surface of the ground. The tee is designed also to provide some lateral directional effects.

In the device of Figs. **1** and **2** the track elements **11** are substantially at right angles to the axis of the spike **15**. At the time of use the spike as **15** will usually be forced into the ground at a substantial angle to the vertical, as shown in Fig. **1**, whereby the track elements **11** are directed upward at a corresponding angle. Should the driving blow be such, for example, as to drive the ball forward horizontally, it would at once encounter resistance to that horizontal movement in the upwardly inclining track elements of the runway, and this resistance is communicated to the spike **15** firmly imbedded in the ground. I have demonstrated that in such case the ball is diverted upward by the track elements and that instead of the "grounder" which otherwise would have ensued the shot produces a ball well clearing the ground.

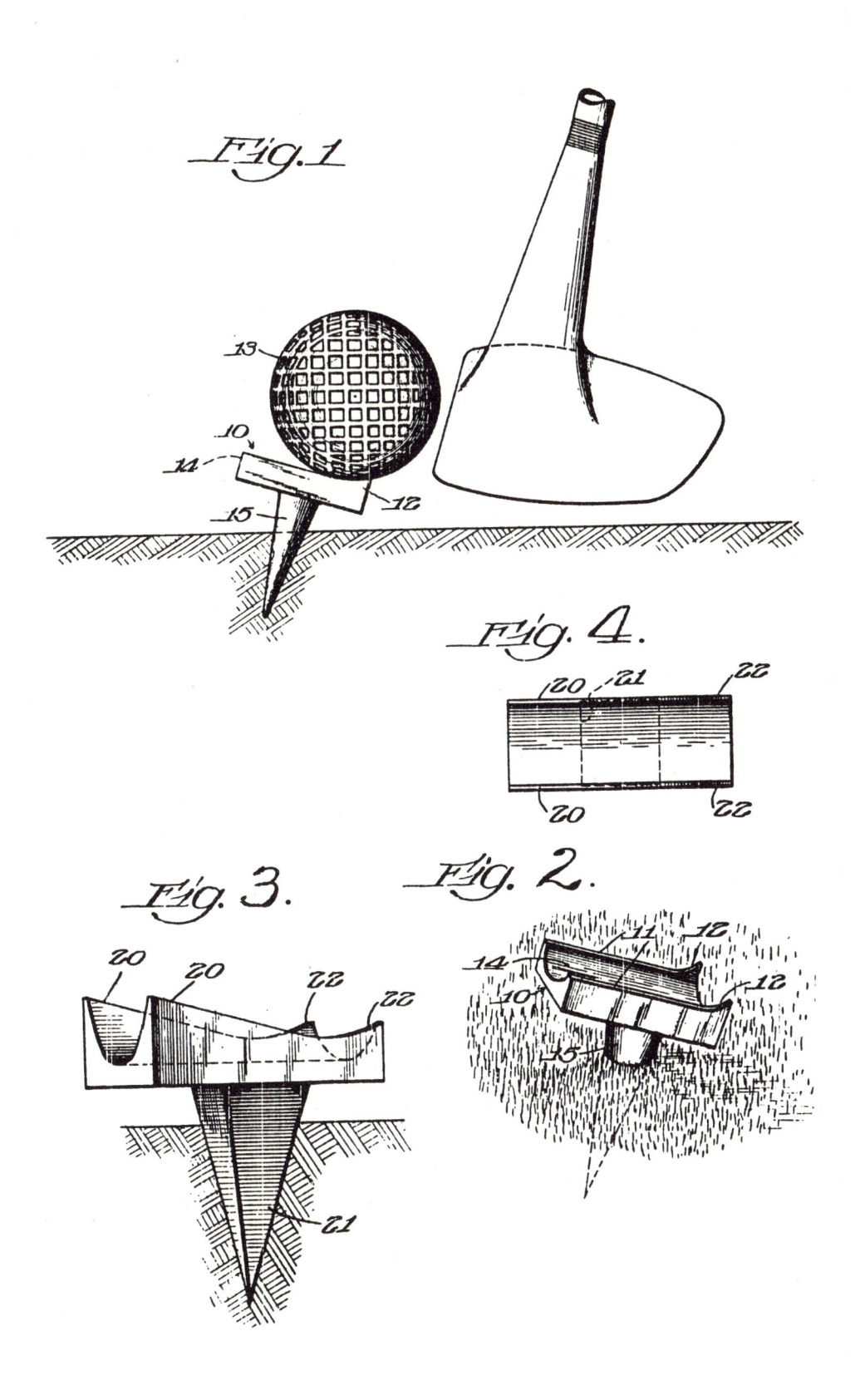

Fig. 1

Fig. 4

Fig. 3

Fig. 2

The Patent Duffer

Golf Tee
Patent No. 2,160,122 (1939)
James Bundy of Chicago, Illinois

By my invention I provide a tee which will maintain the ball at a uniform height above the ground and which is in no way dependent upon the penetration of the ground by any portion of the tee.

When ball **15** is hit by a club, golf tee **10** will be pushed over as shown in Fig. 2 so that it initially falls upon front arm **13**. By suitably shaping arms **11**, **12**, and **13** it is possible to prevent any reaction of the golf tee on the ball when the tee is turned over.

The Patent Duffer 221

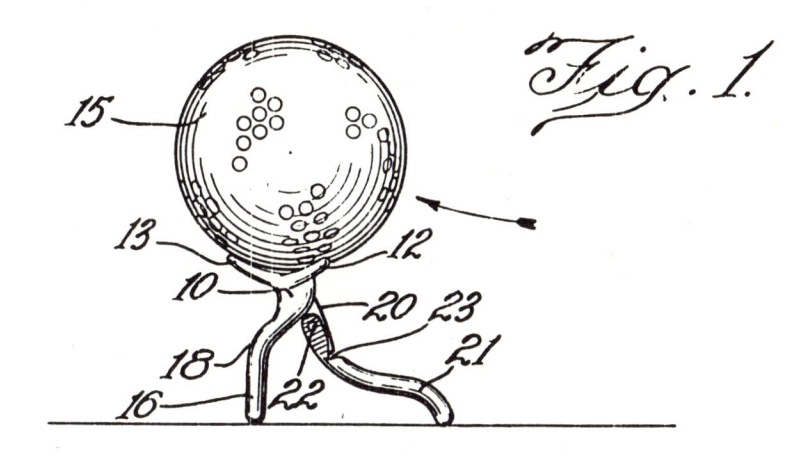

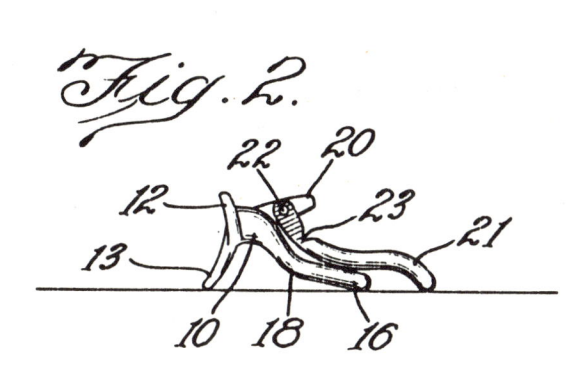

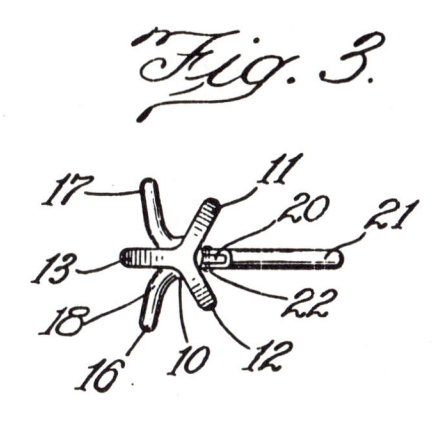

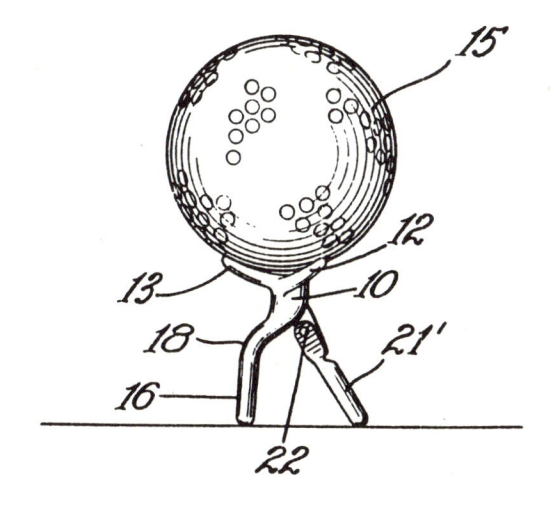

Writing Implement
Patent No. 1,730,046 (1926)
William Stow of Mountain Lakes, New Jersey

One of the objects of my invention is to form golf tees so that they will nest or stack and be temporarily supported one upon the other by friction or otherwise, to form a composite unit, each tee of the stack however, being separable from the group, so that it may be used as a golf tee or support for a golf ball as intended. By releasably aggregating a series of golf tees in the manner described, renders the tees convenient for packing, handling and carriage and especially convenient when carried in the pocket of the player, since they are not apt to be severally lost or mislaid.

A further object of my invention is to cooperatively associate the stub of a pencil with a stack of tees of the character referred to in such manner that the tees from a substantial hand grip, thus producing a writing implement in which the nested golf tees form the handle portion. The golf player is thus provided with a convenient writing implement, for score keeping purposes and at the same time he has available and convenient for use as golf tees the separable units of which the handle is formed.

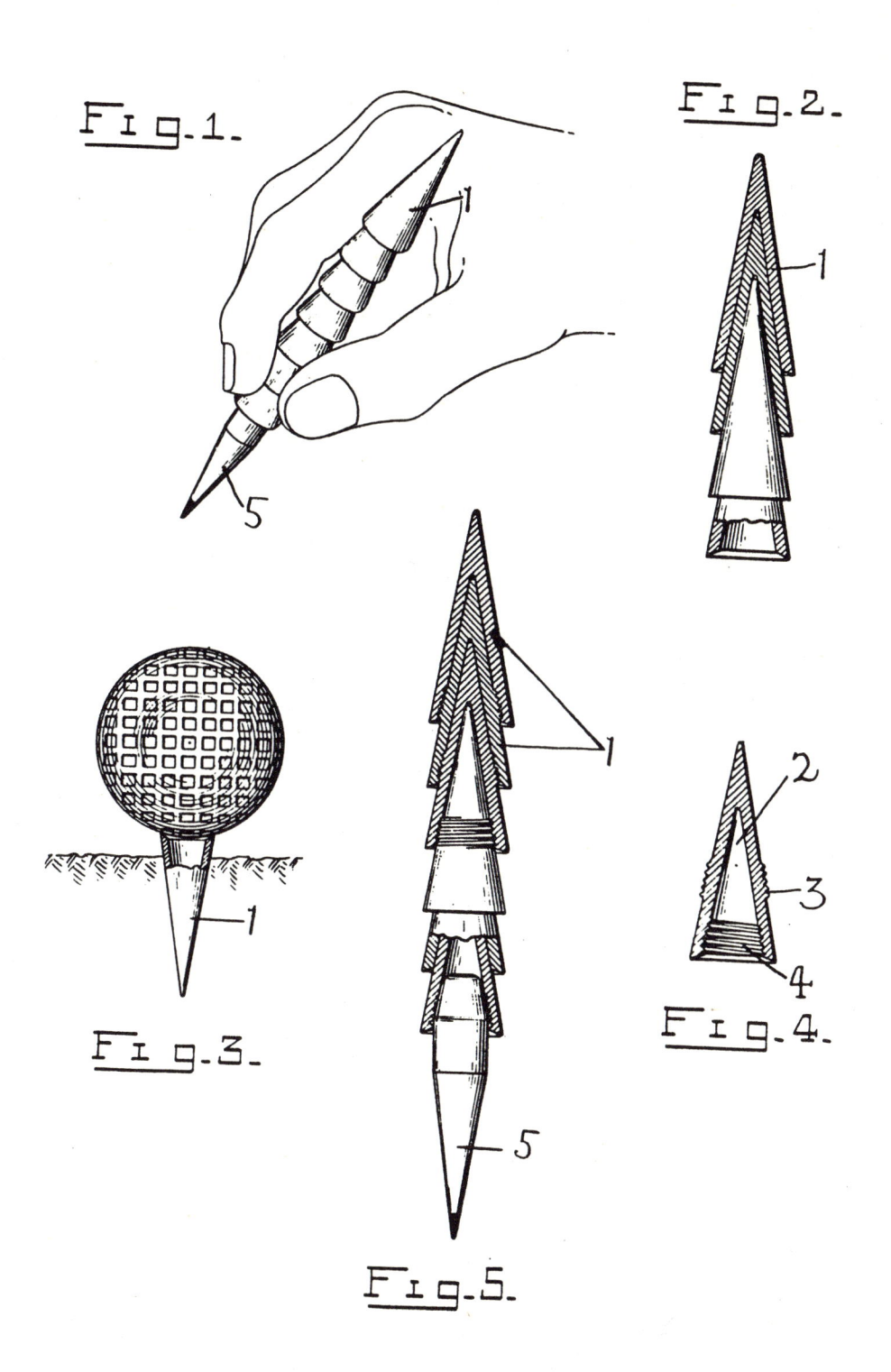

Fig.1.

Fig.2.

Fig.3.

Fig.4.

Fig.5.

The Patent Duffer 223

Golf Tee Match Book
Patent No. 2,930,615 (1960)
Charles Cowan of Albuquerque, New Mexico

By making new and novel improvements in the conventional match book I have provided a match book which, when opened, will support a golf ball in position for teeing off. If by chance the golf club should strike the match book, the fact that the match book is not connected to the ground allows it to be driven a short distance through the air without injury to itself. The match book will offer considerable resistance to flight through the air so that the distance traveled will be substantially shorter that traveled by a conventional golf tee driven under like circumstances. The larger size of the golf tee match book as compared to a conventional golf tee makes it easier to find after it has been driven by the golfer. Inasmuch as a match book is a common means of advertising, it usually is provided free to the golfer and is therefore expendable. It should be noted that there is no danger of fire from ignition of the matches if the conventional safety matches are provided in the match book.

Fig. 1

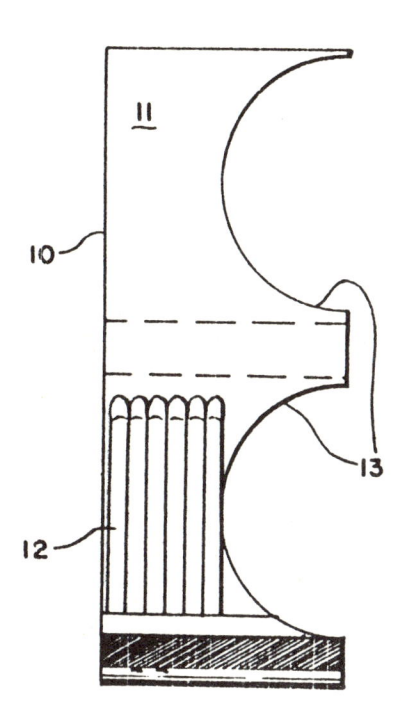

Fig. 2

Fig. 3

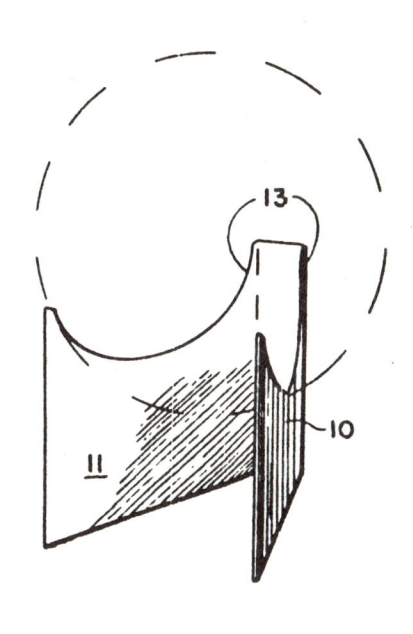

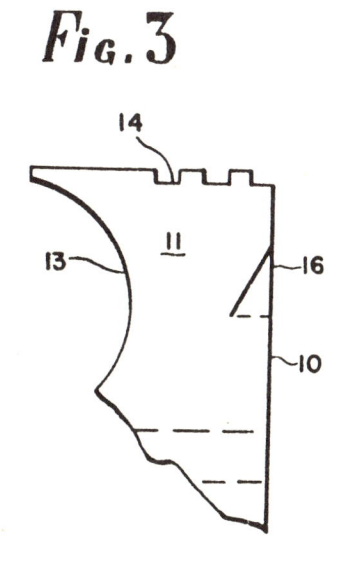

Fig. 4

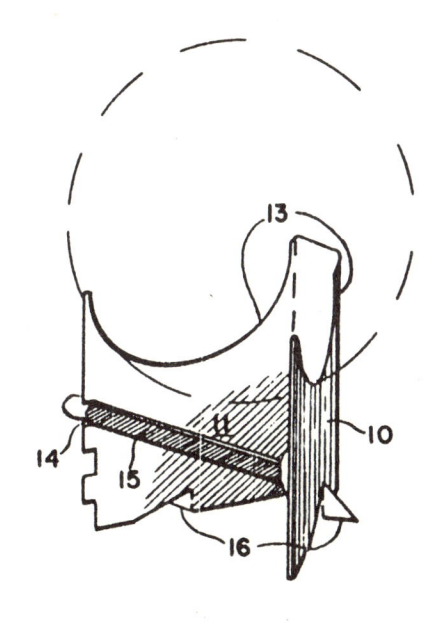

The Patent Duffer 225

APPENDIX

Patented Jan. 20, 1953

2,626,151

UNITED STATES PATENT OFFICE

2,626,151

GOLF PRACTICING APPARATUS

George M. Troutman Jenks, St. Petersburg, Fla.
Application January 28, 1949, Serial No. 73,264
16 Claims (CL273–35)

This invention relates to a golf practice apparatus and more particularly concerns a golf practice apparatus adapted to coordinate the movement of different parts of a golfer's body during the course of numerous practice swings for ultimate attainment of an ideal golf swing.

The broad idea of controlling the movement of a single member of a golfer's body during the course of a practice swing has been for several years an accepted method of teaching and perfecting a golf swing. Among others, numerous devices have been proposed to date for restraining a golfer's head to prevent him from looking up before the club head has contacted the ball. There are also devices on the market for preventing excessive sliding motion of the hips; while other devices have been devised to hold the right elbow in an elevated position during the swing of the club. Other harnesses and straps for restraining the shoulders have been marketed from time to time, but the foregoing devices do not appear to have met with any great success because they correct the motion of only one part of the body while permitting other parts of the body to repeat old mistakes or even to develop new incorrect motions as a result of the restriction of the corrected member. In order to teach an ideal golf swing by restricting the movements of a golfer's body. I have found that it is necessary to treat the entire body as a unit and coordinate the individual motions of the several pertinent parts of a golfer's body in such a way that the movement of any single part of the body is dependent upon the movements of other parts. To my knowledge the various devices of the prior art have failed to do this and have consequently failed to accomplish their broad purpose.

It is accordingly an object of this invention to provide a golf practice device which coordinates the individual motions of the principal parts of a golfer's body and thereby teaches an ideal golf swing.

A further object is to provide a mechanism for correlating the motions of the golfer's hands, wrists. arms, head, shoulders, hips, knees, and feet into one integrated motion.

A still further object of this invention is to provide a golf practice apparatus for holding various parts of a golfer's body in definitely spaced relationship during successive stages of the golf swing.

A further object is to provide a means for controlling the respective motions of different parts of a golfer's body so that the motion of a single body member is actuated by movements of other parts of the body. Another object of this invention is to provide a mechanism adapted to be attached to the body of the golfer that receives an initial force from the hands. arms and shoulders of the golfer and transmits said force to other parts of the golfer's body to create an integrated coordinated motion through the entire course of a golf swing.

The Patent Duffer 229

Other objects and means for attaining them will appear from the accompanying drawings wherein:

Fig. 1 is a view in side elevation of a golf practice apparatus conveniently embodying the present improvements. with portions thereof broken out to expose important details which would otherwise be hidden, and showing a practice golfer in the act of executing a golf swing.

Fig. 2 is a fragmentary view in longitudinal section of a portion of the mechanism for controlling the arm and wrist movements of the practice golfer.

Fig. 3 is a fragmentary view in top plan looking as indicated by the angled arrows III–III in Fig. 2.

Fig. 4 is a fragmentary view in section taken as indicated by the angled arrows IV–IV in Fig. 2.

Fig. 5 is a view partly in elevation and partly in vertical section taken as indicated by the angled arrows V–V in Figs. 2 and 1.

Fig. 6 is a view in longitudinal section of another portion of the arm and wrist motion control mechanism.

Fig. 7 is a fragmentary view in top plan looking as indicated by the angled arrows VII–VII in Fig. 1.

Fig. 8 is a view in side elevation looking toward the bottom of Fig. 7.

Figs. 9 and 10 are horizontal sectional views taken as indicated respectively by the angled arrows IX–IX and X–X in Fig. 1.

Fig. 11 is a fragmentary view in top plan showing foot plates on which the practiced golfer is adapted to stand, and the parts by which said plates are directly actuated during the execution of a golf swing.

Fig. 12 is a fragmentary view in vertical section taken as indicated by the angled arrows XII–XII in Fig. 11.

Fig. 13 is a fragmentary view in longitudinal section of the means provided for controlling the head movements of the golfer incident to swinging the golf club; and

Fig. 14 is a horizontal sectional view taken as indicated by the angled arrows XIV–XIV in Fig. 13.

Figs. 15 and 16 are diagrams showing the circuits for various electrical devices employed in the apparatus.

Fig. 17 is an axial sectional view of a rotary control switch shown in Fig. 16, the section being taken as indicated by the angled arrows XVII–XVII in the latter illustration.

Figs. 18, 19, 20 and 21 are views respectively like Figs. 1, 2, 11 and 12 showing the various mechanisms of the apparatus arranged for producing record graphs or generating templates for use in cutting different cams instrumental in bringing about the desired arm, hand, hip and foot movements necessary to an ideal golf swing.

Fig. 22 is a perspective view of a portion of the linkage illustrated in Figs. 2 and 3.

I have discovered from studying the golf swings of leading golfers both during actual play and from photographs, that although there are individual differences of minor nature in their strokes, there is a substantial similarity in the basic patterns of motion of the different parts of the body and a definite relationship of the timing of these motions with respect to each other. A detailed analysis of the arm motions discloses that the arms travel in substantially a single plane in the swing of most experts and that the hands describe a nearly circular arc about a center in the neighborhood of the left shoulder. During the swing of the arms, the wrists are cocked and uncocked in definite relationship with the rest of the golf swing. The hips move in a definite relationship to the movements of the hands and wrists and describe a combined rotary and sliding motion. Similarly the feet and knees move in relation with the other members of the body.

With more detailed reference first more particularly to figs. 1 and 9 of these illustrations, it will be seen that my improved golf practice apparatus comprises a base 1 which serves as a platform and which has divergently arranged inset foot plates 2 and 3 adjacent one end thereof whereon the golf player is adapted to stand. Rising from the base 1 at the opposite end to the front of the player's station is a hollow post 4 with a telescopic extension 5 which is vertically adjustable and securable in adjusted positions by a hand screw 6. Supported by the post 4 is a mechanism 7 by which the arm, hand and wrist movements essential to the execution of an ideal swing of a golf club C grasped in the hands of the player, are controlled. The mechanism 7 includes an L-shaped bracket 8 which is pivotally adjustable about the axis of a manually operable clamp screw 9 at the top of post 4, the upstanding portion of said bracket being hollow and terminating in spherical head 10 (see Fig. 2). In preparation for the use of the apparatus, the adjustments at 7 and 8 are so made that the axis of an inclined shaft 11 journalled in the head 10, would if extended, pass approximately through the left shoulder of the player standing on the platform 1. Slidably mounted on a tubular radial projection 12 of the head 10 through which the shaft 11 passes, is a cylindric housing 13 whereof the central hub 14 fits slidingly over said projection. The shaft 11 is not only rotatable in the head 10, but axially shiftable as well against the force of a compression spring 15 for a purpose later explained. Through engagement of a fixed collar 16 on the shaft 11 with the outer end of the hub 14 of the housing 13, the housing 13 together with the parts contained therein and the elements yet to be described connected to them are caused to move axially with said shaft. Anchored in a lug 17 at the top of head 10 is a pin 18 with which an eccentrically disposed boss 19 at the back of housing 13 is slidingly engaged to prevent rotation of the latter as it is axially shifted. To the front end of shaft 11 is affixed a fork 20 whereof the extremities 41 are pivoted at 21 to the extremities of an oppositely arranged fork 22 at the contiguous end of a tubular shaft 23 extending at an obtuse angle to said shaft 11 toward the player's station. Secured to shaft 23, at its distal end, is a hollow arm 24. Rotatable in an angularly disposed bearing 25, which is fixed to the outer end of arm 24, is a sleeve 26, see Fig. 6, through which the handle end of the golf club C is passed and in which said club is removably secured by a clutch collar indicated at 27. Axially within the tubular shaft 23 is an independently rotative shaft 28 composed of telescoping sections from which motion is transmitted, through a pair of bevel gears 29, 30, to a shaft 31 within the hollow arm 24, and from the latter shaft through another pair of bevel gears 32, 33, to the sleeve 26 in which the golf club C is held to induce the desired wrist movements of the practice golfer. The shaft 28 (Figs. 2 and 3) protrudes from the upper end of tube 23 where, through a universal joint 34 it is coupled with a short shaft 35 which is rotative in a bearing 36 on a carriage 37 disposed within the frontal upper part of the housing 13. As shown, the carriage 37 has outward arms 38 pivoted at the top which. through similarly pivoted links 39, are pivotally coupled with arms 40 upstanding from the extremities 41 of the fork 20. The carriage 37 also has pendent arms 42 pivotally connected to arms 43 independently of shaft 11 and hub 14 and extending from the yoke 22 beyond the pivots 21. The pivotally connected arms 39, 40, 42, 43 constitute a pair of spaced-apart, collapsible parallelogram linkages. Affixed to the inner end of shaft 35 is a spur pinion 45 that meshes with a spur gear 46 on a parallel shaft 47 rotatably supported in another bearing on the carriage 37. The gear 46 is axially slidable on the shaft 47 and has an eccentrically disposed axis stud 49 for mounting a roller 50 arranged to ride within the differently shaped inner peripheries of ring cams 51 and 52 each fixed in the rear of the housing 13. Pivoted at 55 on the bearing 36 of carriage 37 is an arm 56 with roller 57 which is adapted to travel within the differently shaped cams 58, 59 secured in juxtaposed relation within the housing 13 at the front. As shown the roller arm 56 has a lateral hook projection 60 engaging a circumferential groove in the hub of the gear 46 whereby said gear will be shifted longitudinally on the shaft 47 as said arm 56 moves about its pivot 55. The means for shifting the roller arm 56 comprises a push-pull solenoid 61 whereof the armature 62 bears against one side of said arm. The spring shown at 63 serves to normally maintain the roller 56 in the position in which it is shown in Fig. 2. while springs 64 in tension between the arms 40 of fork 20 and a collar 64a free on shaft 28, urge collar 64a against the upper end of tube 23 and accordingly urge the carriage 37 upwardly within the housing 13, and roller 57 against cams 58, 59.

Affixed to the end of shaft 11 protruding from the back of the head 10 is an arm 65 whereto is pivotally connected a smaller arm 66 with a roller 67 thereon arranged to be shifted at different times during the execution of a golf swing, as liter on explained, from one to the other of two concentric cam rings 68, 69 rigidly secured to said head 10. For the purpose of shifting the roller 67

The Patent Duffer   231

between these cams 68, 69 there is provided a pill solenoid 70 on arm 65 whereof the armature 71 is coupled with lever projection 72 on the arm 60. Cam rings 68, 69 have specifically shaped surfaces contacting roller 67. serving to move roller 67 bodily toward and away from the lug 17. thus causing controlled axial movement of shaft 11. during the course of the golf swing.

The foot plates 2 and 3 (Figs. 1, 9 and 11) are disposed within openings in the top of platform 1, and connected to said platform by hinges 80 for capacity to rock independently up and down within said openings. The means for actuating the foot plates 2 and 3 includes a pair of rotary cams 81 and 82 affixed side by side on a horizontal shaft 83 beneath the platform 1. As shown in Figs. 11 and 12 the cams 81 and 82 are engaged by rollers 84, 85 on bell cranks 86, 87 which are rockably supported by fixed bearings and connected by links 88 and 89 to the respective foot plates 2 and 3. The spring indicated at 86a acts upon the bell cranks 86, 87 to keep the rollers 84, 85 in engagement with cams 81, 82.

The means relied upon to induce the desired back hip, and knee movements during the club swing includes a belt 90 which is attached about the waist of the player. At opposite sides and at the back, the belt 90 has pivotal connections with the upper ends of upright link rods 91, 92 and 93. As shown in Fig. 9, the rods 91, 92 extend down through arcuate clearance slots 95 in the top of platform 1, and at their lower ends are connected to the tops of upright arms 96, 97, medially pivoted on the outer ends of horizontal arms 100, 101, fulcrumed for independent up and down movement, to a fixed collar 102 on a vertical shaft 103 which extends down through the platform 1 in the axis center of the arcuate slots 95. Rollers 105, 106 it the outer ends of arms 100, 101 run on the bottom edge of an arcuate cam 107 affixed to platform 1 in concentric relation to shaft 103, while rollers 108, 109 at the lower ends of the arms 96, run against the outer circumferential face or an arcuate cam 110. The bottom end of rod 93 is similarly connected to the upper end of a vertical arm 111 which is rockably supported at the end or a third radial arm 112 capable of up and down movement about a pivotal connection with a collar 113, on vertical shaft 103 above the platform 1. Likewise as shown. the arm 111 is provided with a roller 114 to run against the outer circumferential face of an arcuate cam 115 on the platform 1, and the radial arm 112 with a roller 116 to run on the top edge of arcuate cam 117 above platform 1. Springs 118, 119 and 120, influential upon the arms 96 and 111, serve to hold the rollers 105, 106 and 114 to the cams 107 and 115, respectively.

Rotary motion is imparted to vertical shaft 103, through gears 120a, 121, from the horizontal shaft 83 which is imparted to be actuated in turn through bevel gears 122, 123 by a "Vickers" hydraulic transmission unit 125 (Figs. 1, 7 and 8), located together with in electric motor 126, beneath the platform 1. Associated with the motor 126 is a speed reducer 127 to one end of the output shaft 128 of which is secured a cam disk 129. This cam disk 129 is engaged by a roller 130 on a rocker arm 131 connected by a link rod 132 to the lever 133 of the control 135 on the transmission unit 125. Alongside the unit 125 and operatively connected thereto by a belt 136, is a second hydraulic transmission unit 137 with a control 136 whereof the actuating arm 139 is coupled, through a link rod 140, with a rocker arm 141 having a roller 142 bearing upon the periphery of a rotary cam 143 at the other end of the shaft 128 of speed reducer 127. By means of bevel gears 145, 146 the unit 137 is connected to one end of another horizontal shaft 147, the distal end of which is in turn connected by bevel gears, 148, 149 (Fig. 1) to a short vertical shaft 150 rotatively supported in a suitable bearing on top of platform immediately forward of the post 4. Through a universal joint 151, shaft 150 is connected to the lower end of extensible link 152 whereof the component sections are telescopically interengaged, and whereof the upper section 153 is connected by universal joint 155 to the bottom end of a shaft 155a (Fig. 2) rotatably supported in the hollow upright portion of angular bracket 8. A bevel gear 156, (Fig. 2) at the top end of shaft 155a meshes with a bevel gear 157 splined to shaft 11 within the spherical head 10. As a consequence of the interposed connections just described, it will be seen that the back, hip, knee and ankle movements of the golfer are all controlled by the mechanism of

Fig. 7 in properly timed relation with the arm and hand movements during the execution of a golf swing.

The means provided for controlling the head movements of the practice golfer as he swings the club C, includes a cap 160, see Figs. 1, 13 and 14. This cap 160 is secured by a jaw strap 161, and extending over the top thereof from opposite sides of a crown band 162 is an arch piece 163 with a central upstanding stud 165. As shown, the stud 165 has an enlargement 166 at its upward end which fits, with capacity for rotation. Into a fixed spherical socket member 167 at the end of a tubular support 168. Independently pivoted on the enlargement 166 of stud 165 are arcuate shoes 169 which are normally maintained in frictional engagement with the inner surface of the socket 167 by springs 170 to prevent rotation of the cap 160 and hence of the golfer's head until after the ball is contacted by the club C as later on explained, and which are arranged to be withdrawn upon energization of an electrical magnet 171 fixed upon said enlargement. The support 168 is in the form of a diametrically reduced flexible prolongation of the upper vertically adjustable section 172 of a tubular post 173 immediately to the rear of the golfer's station on the platform 1. The prolongation 172 is fixable in adjusted positions by the clamp screw indicated at 175.

As diagrammatically shown in Fig. 15. current flow to the coils of the roller aim shifting solenoids 61 and 70 is controlled by a switch 176, which, see Figs. 2 and 4, is mounted on the back of head 10 with its actuating lever 177 in the path of a stud 178 extending outward through an arcuate slot 179 from a disk 180 within said head. The disk 180 is tree on a spacing sleeve 181 surrounding the shaft 11 within the head 10 and frictionally engaged by the flanged end of a slide sleeve 182 which fits over the hub of bevel gear 157. The sleeve 182 is subject to the action of compression spring 183 and obliged to rotate with gear 157 through engagement of diametral slots therein with pin projections 185 on the gear hub. This arrangement is such that the stud 178 is moved away from the switch lever 177 during the drive swing of the golf club. and moved toward said lever to operate the switch 176 for simultaneous closing of the circuit through the solenoids 61 and 70.

The coil of the magnet 171 of the brake means for the cap 160 is connected in a current supply circuit 187, 188 (Fig. 16) with a rotary switch 190. Projecting from the shaft 191 of this switch are three equally spaced spring contact arms 192, 192a and 192b adapted to be successively moved into engagement with the fixed contact at 193; and secured to said shaft is a ratchet wheel 194 with six teeth adapted to be picked one at a time by a pawl 195. Freely oscillatable about the shaft 191 is a spring pulled arm 196 which carries the pawl 195, and which, through a rod 197, is coupled to the armature 198 of a pull solenoid 199 interposed in a current supply line 200, 201. Current flow through the coil of solenoid 199 is controlled by a rotary switch 202 which, see figs. 1 and 17, is supported by an upwardly reaching arm 203 on bracket 8 (Fig. 1) that carries the mechanism 7. The diametrically reduced rear end of shaft 11 extends axially through the casing 204 of switch 202, and splined to it is a disk 205 which is confined to rotation in said casing, see Fig. 17. Projecting from the disk 205 is an eccentrically disposed stud 206 which is yieldingly engaged by the radial arm 207a of a coiled contact spring 207 affixed to an axial bearing boss 208 of casing 204. The contact stud at 209 projects from a holder piece 210 of insulation secured to the switch casing 204 with capacity for adjustment circumferentially thereabout, and extends into the path of the radial arm of contact spring 207. The terminals of current supply line 200, 201 in which the solenoid coil 199 is interposed are connected respectively to the shaft 11 and the contact 209. By closing of a push button switch 211 in a branch circuit 212, 213 it is possible to operate the solenoid 199 for a purpose also later explained. Likewise, the ratchet wheel 194 and the parts associated therewith may be placed in any convenient location, for example, an arm 203 (Fig. 1) which supports the switch 202. The wiring from the switch 202 to the magnet 171 for holding the cap against rotation is in practice run beneath the platform 1 and threaded up through the hollow post 173 and its hollow prolongations 172 and 168.

Operation

Let it be assumed that the player has taken his position on the platform with his feet engaged in the straps 2a and 3a of the foot plates 2 and 3, that the posts 4 and 173 have been adjusted to set the mechanism 7 and the cap 160 at the proper height, that the cap has been strapped to his head, and that the belt 90 has been secured about his waist, all as shown in Fig. 1. With his head now facing forwardly, the player or an attendant then pushes the button 211 with the result that the solenoid 199 is energized and the ratchet wheel 194 racked by one tooth to move the arm 192 on shaft 191 to the broken line position in Fig. 16 off the fixed contact 193. The circuit 187, 188 is thereby opened. the magnet 171 de-energized. and the brake shoes 169 (Fig. 14) released to the action of the springs 170 to temporarily prevent the player from moving his head. The motor 126 is finally started in readiness for the player to execute a swing with the club C grasped in his hands. During the swing, the player's arms will be constrained to move through a non-circular are having its axis substantially in the line of shaft 11, his hands being incidentally raised and lowered by swinging movement of the tubular shaft 23 about its pivotal connection at 21 in response to the action of cams 58, 59 (which move roller 57 toward and away from shaft 11 driving the swing). with corresponding change in the relationship of the parts constituting the parallelogram 37, 39, 40 and 43 by which the shaft 23 and the club holder are sustained from the mechanism 7. The movement of the golfer's hands relative to his own body is governed through concurrent axial shifting of shaft 11 by action of cam 68, 69 upon roller 67. The golfer's hands are thus adjusted in position toward and away from his body during the course of the swing. Also at the same time, a twisting movement is concurrently imparted to the player's wrists by rotation of the shaft 28 inside tubular shaft 23. This motion is transmitted to the shaft 28 from shaft 35 (Fig. 2) by the gears 45, 46 as the roller 50 travels in the groove of cam 51, and from said shaft 28 to the club holder sleeve 27 (Fig. 6) through the shaft 31 and bevel gears 29, 30, 32 and 33. At the moment of contact of the club with the ball, the various parts of the control mechanism occupy the positions in which they are shown in Figs. 3 and 5.

At about the time that the ball is struck with the club C, the spring contact 207a (Fig. 16) encounters the fixed contact 209 to close the circuit 200, 201 through the solenoid 199 which is thereby energized and the ratchet wheel 194 racked another tooth to move the arm 192a into engagement with fixed contact 193. The circuit 177, 178 is accordingly closed and the magnet 171 energized to withdraw the brake shoes 169 so that the player may now move his head to follow the flight of toe ball as he completes the drive swing. Upon initiation of the reverse or back swing, the stud 178 (Figs. 2 and 4) moves into engagement with the arm 177 of switch 176 to close the circuit (fig. 15) through the solenoids 61 and 70 which will thereby be energized to cause shifting of the rollers 50 and 57 from the cams 51 and 58 to the cams 52 and 59 as shown in broken lines in Fig. 2, and shifting of the roller 67 at the same time from cam 66 to cam 69. Thus during the back swing, the roller 57 will be acted upon by the cam 59, the roller 50 by cam 52, and the roller 67 by cam 69. Accordingly, the movements then imparted to the arms, hands and wrists of the golfer will be different from those imparted during the drive swing as prescribed by the different shaping of cams 52, 59 and 69. As the shaft 11 (Fig. 2) turns as above explained. motion is transmitted by the gears 156, 157 to vertical shaft 155 and from the latter, through bevel gears 143, 149 (Fig. 1) to shaft 147. which through bevel gears 145 and 146, is coupled with transmission unit 137 (Fig. 7) driven together with transmission unit 125 by electric motor 126. The cams 129 and 143 on the shaft of speed reducer 137 associated with motor 126 so govern the operation of the units 137 and 125 that the shaft 83, connected to the latter unit by the bevel gears 122 and 123, is turned at the proper speeds and in the proper directions for communication to the vertical shaft 103, through bevel gears 120, 121, of the required motions for actuation of the means by which the player's hip, back and ankle movements are forced. Thus in practice with my improved apparatus, all of the body movements of the golfer are coordinated in timed relation, so that by persistence, he will ultimately acquire an ideal swing. By employing the relay power devices 125, 126, 137 in the way described, no restraint is imposed upon the player to interfere with the ready and easy swing of the club.

In initially setting up the apparatus, it is theoretically possible to make geometric calculations beard upon detailed analysis of photographs of an expert golfer's swing and so arrive at adequate curves for the various cams embodied in the interconnected mechanisms of the apparatus. However, the results obtained by this method are at best only approximate, and I accordingly prefer to determine the shape of the several cams experimentally by having a golf expert. preferably one noted as a golf stylist, swing the club C in the apparatus. To prepare the apparatus for this purpose, the solenoid 61 is removed from the link 39, and the arm 66 with its roller 67 removed from the arm 65 at the rear end of shaft 11. After removal of these parts, a relatively stiff disk 220 (Fig. 18) with a paper chart facing 221 is placed. with interposition of a resilient cushioning gasket 222, into the back of housing 13. An annular retaining element 223 is thereupon inserted into the housing 13 and temporarily secured by screws 224, and another chart sheet 225 applied to the recessed frontal face of said element. Another annular retaining element 226 is next temporarily secured by screws 227 to the back of the head 10 and a chart band 228 applied to the interior thereof. For marking the chart sheet 221, a stylus 230 with a backing spring 231 is inserted into the axial bore of the stud 49 by which the roller 50 is ordinarily supported on gear 46. For marking the chart sheet 225, a second stylus 232 with a backing spring 233 is provided, the same being inserted into the socket of a holder 234 temporarily secured to the carriage 37, so that the axis thereof corresponds in position to the axis of the roller 57 which it replaces. For marking the chart band 228, a third spring pressed stylus 235 is used in a projection 236 detachably secured temporarily to arm 65 by a screw 237, the point of said stylus bring positioned to correspond with the tangent point of the roller 67 which it replaces. With this preparation, an expert player is called upon to execute several swings during each of which the styli 230, 232, and 235 trace several different curves on the respective charts 221, 225, and 228 respectively during drive and back swings of the club. A geometrically mean path is taken in each instance which will give the optimum shape for the corresponding cam necessary to the execution of an ideal swing by the practice player. The mean curves thus obtained may be kept for record purposes or used as guides or templates in cutting the cams.

Graphs of the hip and foot movements of a golf player are obtained in a generally similar way as shown in Figs. 19, 20 and 21. by the following procedure: The segmental cams 107, 110, 115 and 117 (Fig.1) are removed and respectively replaced by segmental supports 240, 241, 242 and 243, for marking sheets 244, 245, 248 and 247. The cam rollers 106, 108, 114 and 116 are also removed and replaced respectively by styli 248, 249, 250 and 251 to mark the respective sheets. The rotary cams 81 and 82. (Figs. 11 and 12) are in turn removed from the shift 83 and replaced by plain disks 252, 253 (Figs. 20 and 21) for the support of marking sheets 254, 255, and the rollers 84 and 85 replaced by styli 256 and 257 respectively. With the apparatus as now prepared, the golf player executes a free club swing incident to which the attendant hip and foot movements are transmitted through the rods 92, 93 and foot plates and intermediate parts to the several arms 96, 101, 111, 112, and recorded by the styli 248–251 and 256, 257 upon the marking sheets or charts 244–247 and 254, 255 in a manner which will be readily understood.

An advantage attained in the use of the particular mechanisms described herein is that the cams that control the exact courses of movement are removable and replaceable. This means that the golf swing to be taught to a small person need not a the same as the one studied by a tall player, since changes of the cams can be made in a reasonably short time. The replaceability feature has the additional advantage that the swings of expert golf players having widely varied physical statures can be permanently recorded and reproduced.

The remarkable adaptability of the machine is further demonstrated by the ease with which it can be connected to accommodate a left-handed golfer. An appropriate left-handed golf club is inserted in the holder clamp 27 and the various cams of desired shape are inserted in their respective places and the golf practice device is ready for use. Moreover, reverse cams may be made using curves developed by right handed experts thereby affording an opportunity for left-handed golfers to achieve the usual accuracy attributed to several right-handed golf experts.

Upon reflection it will be apparent that the apparatus I have shown in the drawings and described in the specification herein is only a highly perfected embodiment of my basic invention and numerous other mechanical means for coordinating the motion of respective parts of a golfer's body during his swing will readily occur to persons familiar with the mechanical arts upon reading this disclosure. Accordingly I do not limit my claims to the precise details of the mechanisms illustrated in the drawings but intend them to cover my invention in its entirety.

Having thus described my invention, I claim:

1. A speed-synchronized golf practice device comprising a club holder, a support therefor, connecting means between said holder and support for controlling the movement of the hands and arms of a golf player, motion restrictive mechanism responsive to the motion of the golf player's swing and adapted to control the movement of a remote, participating portion of the golf player's body in three dimensions in interdependent relation with the motion of said swing, an external source of rotary power. a pair of hydraulic speed changers both connected to and driven by said source of rotary power, a pair of cams driven by said power source, means controlled by the surface shape of one of said cams for controlling the output speed of one of said hydraulic speed changers, connecting means for transmitting the driving force of said hydraulic speed changer to the mechanism for controlling the motion of the golf player's hands and arms, means controlled by the surface shape of the other of said cams for controlling the output speed of the other of said hydraulic speed changers, and connecting means for transmitting the driving force of said other hydraulic speed changer to the mechanism for controlling the motion of said other portion of the golf player's body.

2. Golf practice apparatus comprising a platform with a station at one end for a practice golfer, mechanism supported by the platform with a shaft extending therefrom toward the golfer's station having a support at its distal end for a golf club to be swung by the golfer, a post on the platform to the rear of the golfer's station rotatably supporting a cap adapted to be non-rotatably affixed to the head of the golfer, brake means for normally restraining rotation of the cap to prevent the golfer from turning his head, and control means controlled from the mechanism and effective upon said brake means to release the restraining means in predetermined relation to the operation of said mechanism at a definite time during the golf swing.

3. A golf practice apparatus for coordinating the motions of the hands and arms of a golf player and forcing them to execute a preselected swing of a golf club, which comprises a club holder, a support therefor, and a restrictive mechanism connecting said club holder and support and adapted to control the path of said golf club in three dimensions in its swing, another restrictive mechanism including a cam mounted on said support, a cam follower in contact with said cam, and a golf club turning device attached to said cam follower and actuated by said cam, said turning device being driven by the force of said swing in interdependent relation to the action of the first mentioned restrictive mechanism and including an eccentric cam follower constructed and arranged to turn the golf club about the axis of its shaft at varying rates of speed in predetermined relation to the position of the golf club in the swing.

4. A golf practice apparatus for coordinating the motions of the hands and arms of a golf player and forcing them to execute the combined motions of a preselected golf swing, comprising a golf club holder, a support therefor, and a restrictive mechanism connecting said club holder and support comprising a first cam supported on said support and a first cam follower attached to said club holder and in contact with said first cam to control the motion of the player's arms from side to side, a second cam also supported on said support and operative in a plane substantially at right angles to said first cam, a second cam follower attached to said club holder and in contact with said second cam to

control the motion of the player's arms forwardly and rearwardly toward and away from the front of the player's body in dependent relation to the movement of the arms from side to side, golf club turning means; a third cam, a follower eccentrically mounted in contact with said third cam and attached to said golf club turning means to turn the golf club around its axis at varying rates of speed in predetermined relation to the positions of the cam followers in the swing.

5. A golf practice apparatus for coordinating the motions of the hands and arms of a golf player and forcing them to execute the combined motions of a preselected golf swing, comprising a support, golf club holding means, a tube connected to said holding means, a first cam follower attached to said tube, a first cam supported by said support and contacting said cam first follower, said first cam having an irregularly shaped cam surface constructed and arranged to regulate the motion of the golf player's arms from side to side, a second cam follower attached to said tube, a second cam supported by said support and contacting said second cam follower said second cam having an irregularly shaped cam surface constructed and arranged to regulate the motion of the golf player's arms inwardly and outwardly toward and away from the front of the player's body, a third cam mounted on said support, a third cam follower in contact with said third cam, a drive shaft disposed in said hollow tube and connected to said third cam follower and to said golf club, the drive shaft being constructed and arranged to receive and transmit impulses from the cam follower to turn the club about its axis at different rotation rates during the swing of the club in definite relation to the aforementioned movements of the golfer's arm.

6. Apparatus as defined in claim 5 wherein one cam surface consists of two interconnected parts respectively controlling the movement of the club during the backswing and the downswing, and switching means are positioned on said support to switch the corresponding cam follower from one part of said cam surface to the other, said switching means being actuated at predetermined points by the swing of the club.

7. A speed-synchronized golf practice device comprising a club holder, a support therefor, mechanism disposed between said holder and support for controlling the movement of the hands and arms of a golf player, a second mechanism adapted to control the movement of a remote, participating portion of the golf player's body in three dimensions, a pair of variable speed actuators each connected to one of said mechanisms, an external prime mover drivingly connected to both of said variable speed actuators, and differentially variable speed control apparatus on said variable speed actuators, and cam means movable in response to the revolution of said prime mover and effective upon said speed control apparatus to vary the relative speeds of said variable speed actuators at preselected points during each swing of the club.

8. Apparatus as defined in claim 7 wherein the interconnected interdependent means for controlling and varying the relative speeds of said speed varying devices are also adapted to change the relative directions of movement of said speed varying devices.

9. Golf practice apparatus comprising a club holder, a support therefor and restrictive means including a shaft connecting said club holder to said support, said restrictive means also including a first control means fixed on said support and operative as the club is swung by the golfer to determine movement of his arms through a prescribed arc, second control means also fixed on said support in fixed position relative to said first control means, and thereby interconnected with and dependent upon said first means and adapted to determine concurrent endwise movement of the shaft to determine cocked movements of the golfer's wrists, and third control means also fixed on said support in fixed position relative to said first and second control means and thereby interconnected with and dependent upon said first and second means, said third means including a cam and a cam follower rotatable at varying speeds about its axis under the influence of said cam, and thereby being constructed and arranged to determine turning movement of the club about its axis in the holder for impartation of prescribed twist movements to the wrists in predetermined relationship to the movements of the hands and arms.

10. Golf practice apparatus comprising a club holder, a support therefor, and restric-

The Patent Duffer 237

tive mechanism connecting said support and club holder, said restrictive mechanism including a fixed shaft having a fixed axis but slidably and rotatably mounted on said support, a cam surrounding said fixed shaft and a cam follower affixed to said shaft and held in contact with said cam to shift the shaft axially under the influence of the cam, a second cam surrounding said fixed shaft in definite fixed position relative to the first cam, a second shaft pivotally attached to and supported from the fixed shaft, and also attached to said club holder, and a cam follower attached to said second shaft and held in contact with the second cam to control the angle of inclination of the second shaft relative to the fixed shaft in definite relation to the axial shift of said fixed shaft during the swing of the club holder.

11. Golf practice apparatus for controlling the arc of a golf player's swing comprising a club holder, a support therefor, first control means supported by said support, connecting means responsive to said control means and attached to said club holder to move it in a controlled path toward and away from the center of said arc, second control means mounted on said support in definite predetermined fixed position relative to said first control means and also effective upon said connecting means to move said club holder toward and away from the golfer's body in predetermined relation to its movement toward and away from the center of the arc during the course of said swing.

12. Golf practice apparatus comprising a support, a rock shaft axially slidable on said support, first cam means for sliding said rock shaft axially in response to its rocking movement, a club holder arm pivotally supported on a pivot transverse to the axis of said rock shaft, second cam means for swinging said club holder arm about said pivot also in response to the rocking movement of said rock shaft, and in definite predetermined relation to said axial movement, and means for attaching a golf club to said club holder arm.

13. Golf practice apparatus comprising a support, a rock shaft axially slidable on said support, first cam means for sliding said rock shaft axially in response to its rocking movement, a hollow club holder arm pivotally supported on a pivot transverse to the axis of said rock shaft, second cam means for swinging said club holder arm about said pivot also in response to the rocking movement of said rock shaft, an independently rotative shaft disposed within said hollow shaft, third cam means for rotating said independently rotative shaft also in response to the rocking movement of said rock shaft, means for attaching a golf club to said club holder arm, and connecting means for transmitting the rotary movement of said independently rotative shaft to rotate said golf club about its axis.

14. Golf practice apparatus comprising a support, a rock shaft axially slidable on said support, first cam means for sliding said rock shaft axially in response to its rocking movement, a club holder arm pivotally supported on a pivot transverse to the axis of said rock shaft, second cam means for swinging said club holder arm about said pivot also in response to the rocking movement of said rock shaft, and in definite predetermined relation to said axial movement, means for attaching a golf club to said club holder arm, restrictive means for attachment to a remote portion of the golf player's body, remote cam means and follower means effective upon said restrictive means, and connecting shaft means coupled to said rock shaft and to said remote cam means to control the movement of said remote part of the golfer's body in three dimensions in response to the rocking movement of said rock shaft.

15. Golf practice apparatus comprising a support, a rock shaft axially slidable on said support, first cam means for sliding said rock shaft axially in response to its rocking movement, a club holder arm pivotally supported on a pivot supported by the rock shaft transverse to the axis of said rock shaft, second cam means for swinging said club holder arm about said pivot also in response to the rocking movement of said rock shaft, and in definite predetermined relation to said axial movement, means for attaching a golf club to said club holder arm, harness means for attachment in fixed position to the golfer's head, brake means including a first element attached to said harness means and a brake element effective upon said first element to lock said harness in fixed position, magnetic means for moving said brake element relative to said first element, and switch means mounted in predetermined position relative

to said rock shaft and connected to said magnetic means, whereby the harness means is locked and released in predetermined relation to the movement of said rock shaft.

16. A golf practice apparatus comprising a club holder, a support therefor, connecting means including a cam and follower between said holder and support for controlling in three dimensions the movements of the hands and arms of a golf player, a hip controlling device connected to said connecting means and responsive to she motion of the connecting means, and adapted to control the movement of the golf player's hips in three dimensions in interdependent relation with the movements of the golf player's hands and arms, a constant speed source of rotary power, a pair of hydraulic speed changers both connected to and driven at substantially equal speeds by said source of rotary power, a pair of cams driven at substantially equal speeds by said power source, means responsive to the surface shape of one of said cams for controlling the output speed of one of said hydraulic speed changers, connecting means for transmitting the driving force of said hydraulic speed changer to the mechanism for controlling the motion of the golfer's hips and feet, means responsive to the surface shape of the other of said cams for controlling the output speed of the other of said hydraulic speed changers, and connecting means for transmitting the driving force of said other hydraulic speed changer to the mechanism for controlling the motion of the golf player's hands and wrists.

GEORGE M. TROUTMAN JENKS.

REFERENCES CITED

The following references are of record in the file of this patent:

UNITED STATES PATENTS

Number	Name	Date
1,604,118	Glancey	Oct. 26, 1926
1,936,143	Shea	Nov. 21, 1933
2,179,663	Link	Nov. 14, 1939
2,189,613	Paulsen	Feb. 6, 1940
2,299,781	Adams	Oct. 27, 1942
2,328,408	Beil et al.	Aug. 31, 1943
2,458,932	Cottingham	Jan. 11, 1949
2,468,033	Byers et al.	Apr. 26, 1949